Molly Parkin was born in Pontycymmer, South Wales, in 1932. After studying art at Goldsmith's and Brighton, she became a teacher and painter. She started work as a journalist when her first marriage ended and was fashion editor on *Nova*, *Harpers* and the *Sunday Times*, winning the Fashion Journalist of the Year Award in 1972. She moved to Cornwall shortly afterwards, where she started writing full time. The first of her ten bestselling novels, *Love All*, was published in 1974. She has also published poetry and a selection of her journalism, *Good Golly Ms Molly*, and toured a one-woman show around the country. She is now an agony aunt, writes for newspapers and magazines, and appears regularly on TV and radio. Her recent exhibition of paintings at a London art gallery was highly praised, and she is at work on the screenplay of her memoirs. Molly Parkin lives in London.

THE MAKING OF
MOLLY PARKIN

An autobiography

VICTOR GOLLANCZ
LONDON

First published in Great Britain 1993
by Victor Gollancz

First Gollancz Paperback edition published 1994
by Victor Gollancz
A Cassell imprint
Villiers House, 41/47 Strand, London WC2N 5JE

© Molly Parkin 1993

The right of Molly Parkin to be identified
as author of this work has been asserted
by her in accordance with the Copyright,
Designs and Patents Act, 1988.

A catalogue record for this book is
available from the British Library

ISBN 0 575 05751 3

Typeset by CentraCet, Cambridge

Printed and bound in Great Britain
by Cox & Wyman Ltd, Reading

I dedicate this book to the memory of my granny, hoping that I may give to my own much-loved grandchildren – Paris, Jessie and Carson – what she gave to me

CONTENTS

ACKNOWLEDGEMENTS

I should like to thank the following for their support and inspiration on my journey, and not least in the often painful writing of this book: Sarah, Sophie and Michael Parkin, Sally and Granville Gough and their family, Patrick Hughes, Sandy Lieberson and Alastair Fairley, Sylvia Scaffardi, John and Belinda Timbers, Mary Holland, Martha Hill, Wendy and David Phillips, Ivy Roberts, Irene Josephy, Jacqui Evans, Lisa Eveleigh, Liz Knights, Ian Craig, Viv Redman, Joanna Goldsworthy, Lionel Rogosin, Sara Sugarman, Gillian Greenwood, Penny Tompkins, Daisy Rankin, Father Jack, Bob Kingdom, Jack Jones, Barry Humphries, Peter Docherty, Dudley Sutton, Victor Spinetti, Martin Thornton, Karl Francis, David O'Brien Twohig, Sir Anthony Hopkins, Brian Patten, Andrew Peacock, Tony Arden, Dev Basra, Shaun de Warren and Gilly, Barbara Hulanicki, Fitz and Vitold, Andrew Logan and Michael Davis, Ian Spring, Martin Walton, Bruce Lloyd. And, of course, Judy.

M.P.

Page 275: excerpt from article 'Molly in Manhattan' is reproduced by permission of *Men Only*; page 310: review of Molly's one-woman show by Maria Lexton first appeared in *Time Out* magazine; page 338: extract from *Finding My Way* by Sylvia Scaffardi is reproduced by permission of the author.

PART ONE

*'All things bright and
beautiful . . .'*

My cousin Barbara was born with no neck. As she entered this world, the doctor said to his friend, the headmaster, my Uncle Tom, 'If this were my child, Tom, I would allow it to die.'

My Uncle Tom replied, 'If it were your child, I would agree. But she is mine, and as such shall be allowed to live.'

This story, the tale of the fifteen long years that my Auntie May and Uncle Tom had waited for a baby, how she only survived because all the family rallied round, day and night, taking turns to drip-feed her from a fountain-pen, like a new-born lamb, always enthralled me. Though I was dying to ask, but never dared, why they fed her on ink instead of milk. My mother would tell it often, but never often enough for me. When she'd finished, her gaze would sweep over the everything-in-its-place and all-in-working-order bodies of my sister Sally and myself. She'd sigh and place her hands together as if in prayer and, with palpable feeling, gazing above, would murmur, 'Yes, we have much to be thankful for.'

Sickness was always a big thing at home. Sickness and death, lotions, potions, pills, medicine. The accoutrements of high drama accompanying the domestic triumph of having the doctor 'call at the house'. My own birth was a major event, taking three days as it did. An early indication of indecision, a chronic inability to leave anywhere without a fuss, clearly dates from that first terror of leaving the womb.

The family had a tragic track record when it came to infant mortality. My own mother was the only baby to survive from twelve. She'd stare into the fire and put on her chapel voice, recounting how our granny had lost three children in one month alone, all under the age of five. Hilarious stuff to inveterate gigglers like Sally and me, who only needed the word coffin to set us off. Worse if Barbara happened to be present.

'Lost? How do you mean lost, Auntie Ronnie? Lost like sheep up the mountain?' Her shiny green eyes glinting with mischief, her sharp elbows a nudging invitation to complicity.

I would excuse myself, braving the torrential elements of the night, to relieve my small bladder and the build-up of laughter in the back-yard lavvy, hurrying in the knowledge that the flashing torches of Sally and Barbara would shortly arrive for them to do the same.

No one dared to make fun of my mother and that darkness in her, which would deepen over the years from passing melancholia into mental breakdown and manic despair. Only Barbara, whose own grotesque deformity gave her the insouciance to question solemnity, her head jauntily jutting above her nipples, each ear resting saucily on either shoulder. Until the celebrated event of her teenage dentures, which provided her smiling mouth with a palate, it was even impossible to understand what Barbara was saying. And yet we, who knew and loved her so well, certainly managed a fine communication. It was only strangers and those who may have regarded her as a freak who never benefited from her astringent wit and wisdom. Perhaps she intended it to be so. Everything was a joke to Barbara, especially her own existence. Why waste time in mourning, in boring oneself or others? Life, every moment, was meant to be celebrated. Squeezed, like a lemon, to the very last drop.

When her father, my Uncle Tom, died prematurely a

decade after her tortured birth, all our aunties were aghast that Barbara came over to play happily in our house on the day of the funeral. Only my granny spoke up for her, she who had suffered so cruelly at the loss of her brood, but who also believed that life was for the living.

'Undue mourning,' my grave and lovely granny claimed, 'is an indulgence of self, a negation of God's gift of spirit, and displays a lack of acceptance for His will.' When she spoke everyone listened.

It was always the three of us, Barbara, Sally and me. We were born in that order, each divided by several years. I was the youngest, born in 1932. Barbara's house was just a few streets away from our street, the street where my mother and three of her cousins were born. The street where what would have been all my other aunties and uncles, my granny's dead babies, came into the world and went out in their small coffins. The street where my granny's house was, the one Sally and I were born in, and where we spent our holidays and lived for much of the war, when we weren't living in London with our mother and father. My granny's house with its outside lavvy, its indoor plumbing complete with new bath and running hot water, its coal fires in every room, summer and winter. My granny's house in the minuscule mining village, Pontycymmer, in the Garw Valley of South Wales. The place my heart has always returned to for my happiest childhood memories, and which I only ever thought of as home.

Many years later, when I was living in New York and Americans asked me where I came from, I explained that it was the same background as Richard Burton and Tom Jones. And, I would add, Dylan Thomas. Richard Burton represented to them at that time the loser, the pock-marked husband who had let Elizabeth Taylor slip through his fingers – not once, but twice. Pathetic! Dylan Thomas was dismissed as the lush who wrote maudlin poems, mainly about death. Who drank himself into his final coma there, where I was living, at that bastion of bohemian depravity, the Chelsea Hotel. But Tom Jones was something else; the guy who was knocking 'em sideways in Las Vegas, no less! So I was Welsh, the same as Tom, wow!

I boasted that whilst these three came from the bottom of the valley I came from the top where people were really wild and more wonderful than could be imagined, and because Pontycymmer was situated in a cul-de-sac valley no one ever bothered to go there since you couldn't drive through it, not like the Rhondda and the Ogmore. I told them there was a lot of inbreeding and everyone was crackers. Not only that, but the sheep walked around all day with a smile on their chops, and you could never buy Wellington boots because they'd always sold out.

I was off my rocker whilst spreading these rumours, but there remain in Manhattan various smart sophisticates and several anthropologists with serious intentions to visit this extraordinary place, Pontycymmer, and study the tribal customs. May my birthplace forgive my exaggerations.

My family, on both sides, comes from Pontycymmer. Since I have earned my living as a writer I am often asked whether I hail from a literary background. I answer, 'Yes, you might say so. My grandfather was a man of letters. His name was Sam the Post.'

This was my father's father, who survived a further fifty years after being pensioned off in his twenties, by the Post Office, for a chronic chest condition. We never noticed any wheeziness, except when he fell into coughing fits over his pipe-tobacco, the stench of which could have served as a secret weapon in either world war. My mother said some regarded him as a skiver, a con-artist. That there were real cases in the pits of miners with silicosis who were being devoured on their feet by the dust in their lungs, with no compensation from the Coal Board, none at all.

But I didn't care what anyone thought of Tadci* Thomas. He told me never to give tuppence for the opinion of twerps. The system was there to be milked and rules merely made to be broken. Anybody could have the life they chose – the trick was to swing it your way, and it was your duty to yourself to sidestep the dullards and the dreary order of convention. He was irresistibly mischievous, with the twinkling blue eyes and snow-white whiskers of everyone's Santa Claus. We recognized a quality in each other that bridged the gap of years, that nobody else could touch.

On his death-bed he mouthed my name as I bent forward to kiss him. I was an art student by then, with the appearance to prove it. Decidedly off-centre. He squeezed my hand in approval and I squeezed his in return. He crinkled his blue eyes and I burst out laughing, just to bring him back to life for a moment. Tears would have seemed inappropriate, an insult to the occasion.

Sadness never entered my soul with the passing of Tadci Thomas, nor does it now. I remember the long walks we took, never up the mountain, like with my other grandfather, Tadci Noyle. Nothing that required physical exertion. Always on the flat, along the disused railway track, down by the black, coal-brimming riverbed, a bag of toffees at the ready, the two of us winning against the world, buoyant at the sheer beauty of the whole bloody mess.

I had no paternal grandmother. She had died when my father was only four, at the birth of his younger sister, my Auntie Eleanor. My mother's mother, my Granny Noyle,

---

* The Welsh for grandfather, pronounced 'Takí'.

in her infinite wisdom, said we were always to remember that my father had been denied a mother's touch at a crucial time. His childhood had been blighted by that loss, despite all the aunties, for they were not the same, and it was because of this that he was to have trouble with intimacy all his life. And we should make allowances for this, always, whatever the circumstances.

She also said, but never in my hearing, that affable eccentric though he may have been, Tadci Thomas was not a fitting father. That his views were unsuitable for the ears of the young. That the boy had always lacked guidance, which could account for his difficulties later on. But by the time my own eager ears were open to Tadci Thomas, my granny was no longer around to temper the anarchy.

My Granny Noyle was special, there's no doubt about that. There are still elderly inhabitants of Pontycymmer who speak of her wisdom and the practical application of her spiritual beliefs. A lady of quality. That's what they say. And, even as a small child, I knew this must be true, because of the extraordinary effect she had on people.

She, herself, had been traumatized as a child by the loss of her home. That's what we were given to understand by my mother, who would regale us with the grim facts as we sat round the fire toasting bread on a special fork which doubled its own length when you pulled it out. Barbara and Sally and I would crouch close to the flames on soft cushions, with our knees folded beneath us. My mother would sit in the wooden rocking-chair, her stockings rolled down to her ankles, the gnarled garter elastic still inside. Her shins, from the knees down, were patterned with burgundy blotches, her toes were swollen with chilblains and the birthing of bunions. It was the same with all my aunties, and every woman in Pontycymmer. It would happen to us girls if we sat as they did on top of the fire. That's why we tucked our legs underneath us.

'Your granny,' my mother would start, 'was one of the Morgans, *the* Morgans of Abercrave. They were a cut above everybody else, the Morgans, and they owned the mountains and land stretching to Brecon for as far as you could see. As a little girl, Granny and her sisters lived in Craig-y-Nos Castle. But then her father, who was a drinking and gambling man, lost the home and it had to be sold. The Italian opera singer, Madame Adelina Patti, the greatest star the world of opera has ever known, bought Craig-y-Nos and your granny had to go and live in the little farm opposite. Get the photograph down from the mantelpiece, Sally, and mind your skirt, that it doesn't catch fire.'

We'd look in silence at the sepia study of the castle which lived in pride of place amongst the carefully preserved treasures on top of Granny's mantelpiece. Even Barbara would be subdued, not trying for once to pinch or tickle or catch the eye of Sally or me. Losing your home was serious stuff.

Granny never spoke of it herself, never. Just once I caught her in the rocking chair with the photograph lying in her lap, her face wearing an expression of great desolation, although her eyes were closed. It shocked me to realize that memories for adults could still carry such pain.

'He was a scoundrel, weak and dissolute.' My mother's mouth would tighten. 'The first responsibility of a father is to care for his wife and family, not have them thrown out of house and home.'

I would stare into the flames, sensing a deep bitterness. I could see the leaping turrets of a whole cluster of castles there in the glowing coals. As I watched them, one by one, they crumbled into the grate, reduced in the heat of the moment to just so many piles of ash. Like the dreams of grandeur in my poor granny's childhood.

He died, the wicked one, Granny's mother remarried – more than once, by all blurred accounts – and Granny ended up in Pontycymmer married to our Tadci Noyle. Her sister Anne, Barbara's granny, had married a German sea captain and bought the house that Barbara lived in now, just over the way. And further down our road lived one of Granny's other sisters, Auntie Jane. She was dead now, but her daughters, my Aunties Maggie, Eunice and Emily, school cleaners, as they were known, still lived in the street, Albany Road. My granny owned many houses in Albany Road by this time. It was important for her to become a landowner, my mother explained, to make up for what happened in her childhood.

'It was in the blood, land-owning. Just as it was important for your granny to see to it that I had a private education. That's why I was sent away to boarding school, to Miss Culverwell's Seminary for Young Ladies in Cowbridge. I mixed with the cream of the Vale of Glamorgan there.' My mother's voice would go all posh again. We girls would start squirming. Barbara always brought things back to earth.

'What did you say when these snobs asked you what your father did, Auntie Ronnie?'

'I said he was an engineer, Barbara.'

'But he worked in the pits just like everybody else.'

'It wouldn't have been wise to let them know that. Girls can be very cruel to each other, always remember that. In certain circumstances a small lie is permissible.'

'If it means saving your bacon, Auntie Ronnie?'

'Precisely, Barbara. And, in any case, it wasn't that much of a lie because my father was an engine-winder by then. Now, pass that toast over and let's get some butter and jam on it. Home-made gooseberry or Co-op plum, what's it to be? Hands up!'

So that explained my granny's air of distinction, and the chronic frugality that was practised in the house for her to scrimp and save enough to buy up her little properties one by one. It fell upon me as the most willing to collect the rent for her every Saturday morning from the tenants. She promised me money if I did this, what soon turned out to be unpleasant, task. More often than not I would be greeted with a slammed door and shouted abuse. Then I hit upon the idea of dressing up in my granny's old clothes from the little boxroom which contained everything that she couldn't bear to throw away.

I adored dressing-up. It was my favourite thing, next to painting and making up stories. The first door I knocked on, the tenant looked through the window to see this eight year old in a violet-ribboned hat as big as a bucket, with a man's flannel nightgown adorned with feather boas, and lady's pearl-buttoned, high-heeled boots. I stood, smiling beguilingly, clutching the rent-book. He came to the front door, calling all his family to have a laugh, the rent in his hand. From then on, every Saturday, I had no trouble at all. The rents were ready on the dot. They couldn't wait to see what get-up I would be wearing this week.

It was my first discovery of how to divert hostility with humour, of sensing that everybody enjoyed seeing someone dressed up, especially if it involved an element of ridicule. It was a lesson that was to stand me in good stead for the rest of my life; like my mother and her judicious use of lies.

My grandmother never learned of my weekly charade. My grandfather caught me at it once and said it was best that she never found out, understanding how much emphasis she placed on dignity. To a stranger she would have appeared detached, even distant, dressed in ankle-length black, her long white hair shaped into a smooth bun on the top of her head. Her eyes were pale grey, her features neat and small, with beautiful cheekbones and a chiselled mouth. The fine-boned body boasted a narrow waist, a still-full bosom, elegant ankles and wrists. Everything about her appeared graceful and pleasing to the eye. Her movements were unhurried, flowing into the rhythm of whatever she was doing: rolling pastry, washing her hands, brushing her hair, setting the table, peeling potatoes, shelling peas. Each ritual was imbued with its own richness; nothing ever appeared to be a task. All was undertaken with loving attention.

And so it was with the many who sought her advice. The same intensity, the total focusing on the moment of listening, obliterating all but the person and their problem. I loved watching her; being close. Ours was never a family who touched each other. There was a shyness bordering on horror at the very thought of embrace, of hugging, or the holding of hands. Stuff like that was considered very 'English', an ostentatious show of simple filial devotion that should be taken for granted. Simply to be in my granny's presence, content and without tension, was sufficient demonstration of love. Her spirituality shone like a lamp from within. When she moved from a room, it was as if the flames of the fire had grown smaller, or the lights had been lowered.

However, it wasn't all religiosity with her, as her chapel hats clearly demonstrated. I could never come to terms with that pious profile and the fairground confection balanced above. Was this her idea of a joke? I would not have placed humour on the list of her admirable qualities. But the millinery amounted to high comedy. Cabbage roses, sweet peas, violets, daisies, entire herbaceous borders perched on straw brims as wide as her shoulders, rivalled only by the headgear of that Latin spitfire of the silver screen, Carmen Miranda. Indeed, that no one other than me regarded my granny's hats as extraordinary was in itself remarkable. But such was her personal power that if she had attended chapel in the nude the congregation would have accepted it as further proof of her piety, an innocent celebration of Our Lord. She was as much of a law unto herself as Tadci Thomas.

Her husband, my Tadci Noyle, was as tall and commandingly handsome a spouse as granny's elegance demanded, and equally devout. He was senior deacon in the Tabernacle and so sat in the big seat, out front, beneath the preacher's pulpit. He had worked all his life in the Ffaldau Colliery, ending up as the engine-winder, lowering the men into the pit. One of the most responsible jobs, my mother said. He was known as John the Bump, for it was his idea of a joke to jolt the cage to the bottom with such force that he all but snapped the spinal columns of the entire night shift, as if they hadn't enough on their beleaguered backs. By the time I heard this I found it hard to equate such sadistic humour with the gentle giant obsessed with his garden, his copperplate handwriting and his genial joy in the words of the Good Book. But retirement can change people and I had never known him as a working miner. I can imagine at that time, when the fire was still fierce in his belly, that he could be as brutal as the next, with the fury of the frustrated underdog. A young father, helpless in a house mourning so many infantile deaths.

His final job paid marginally more than the pittance he'd earned in the mines since the age of twelve, and at the end of his fifty years he was presented with a gold watch. 'For services rendered – the evidence of one man's entire working life,' he'd say with a twinkle. He wore this on Sundays, the chain stretched over his best waistcoat. And on weekdays he'd have it propped before him on the table, ticking away as he worked at his immaculate handwriting, copying page after page of parables from the Bible.

He was a natural scholar who had taught himself to read and write. Whilst other children might loiter around the pubs waiting for their fathers, I sat on the steps of the Workingmen's Institute until my Tadci had tired his eyes out from studying, slaking a different thirst. Grown men had gone off to university from the reading room of the Institute. This yearning for intellectual enlightenment knew no parallel; no library books had ever been as thumbed or worn as those in the Welsh valleys during the depression. That's what my Tadci Noyle told me.

Education was seen as the only way out of the hell of unemployment and soul-destroying poverty. This was dunned into us from the moment we emerged from our mothers' wombs. Stick at it at school, come top at all costs, for only the brainy would find a way out of the valley to fulfil their true potential in the world outside. My Tadci Thomas's sunny combination of cunning and don't-care-tuppence held no water with my Granny and Tadci Noyle. Their ethic was industrious endeavour. Their favourite, oft-quoted, Bible parable was the one about the talents: ability was God-given, not to be buried in the ground for safe-keeping, or scattered on barren soil, but to be nurtured and coaxed into life so that everyone could benefit.

As soon as it became evident that I was a creatively gifted child, and no amount of fun and tomfoolery could distract me from writing a story or painting a picture, and I came effortlessly top in these subjects at school, I was given every possible encouragement. I was hailed as a family redeemer, the one who would achieve fame and fortune, by everyone, except my father to whom those things were the most important since he could never get a grip on them himself.

But though we were a Welsh-speaking household I was firmly discouraged from speaking the language. Both my mother and my granny insisted that I speak English. There was a widely held belief in this community, clinging to the spearhead of self-improvement, that it was common and working-class to speak in Welsh. I see it now as one

22

of the tragedies of my childhood, that I was denied the riches of my own mother-tongue.

My mother and father moved to England soon after they were married in the late twenties, although my mother returned to her mother's house in Pontycymmer to give birth to both my sister and myself. In fact, my childhood – my entire life – seems to have been split between Pontycymmer and London. It has never been one without the other, and both are still essential to me.

My parents' marriage was tempestuous from the start, and although I must have been aware of this from an early age, it was not until I was seven that events forced themselves into my consciousness in a way that was to have a grave effect on me.

My Uncle Bryn was getting married and my father was best man. We were waiting with the bride for the two of them to turn up. They arrived drunk, my father having spent all our money. We had no bus fare and had to walk home, me on his shoulders, enjoying the ride. I'd never seen him in such a jolly mood. He'd stop every few steps and hail strangers as friends. He'd burst out singing. He'd zig-zag across the pavement and lurch into the gutter. We lost sight of my mother, walking ahead with my sister; she was too embarrassed to be seen with us.

I liked it like that, just me and my father. He had always been my favourite, of the two of them, anyway. He was the one who taught me to swim, to ride my bike, to roll plasticine into a snake, to turn the painting of a pear into a person's face. He was the one who took us to the National Gallery to look at the Constables and Turners, with sandwiches and a thermos to last us all day. He was the one who made us queue for gallery seats, 'up in the gods', for the West End theatres. For plays which I couldn't begin to make head or tale of. *Lady Windermere's Fan*, what was that all about? Never mind, an abiding love of the theatre took root there in my infancy. That was my imaginative father's doing. The father I turned against when I was seven, after my Uncle Bryn's wedding.

His jaunty high spirits hadn't lasted for long. I lay in my small bed later that night, going over the puzzling events of the day. How the bride's veil had blown over her face for the photos and someone at the reception had said it was a bad omen, and that the two of them would never be happy together. (They were not, as it happened. He left her for a barmaid who served at his regular.) I could hear my parents quarrelling through the thin walls. I peered at my sister's bed to see what she thought. She was sleeping. She says now she can't remember the wedding and the subsequent events. I couldn't either, for many years.

But how could I have forgotten what I remember so clearly now? Living the rest of that week with no money until payday. No food at all, only bread and scrape. Neither parent speaking to the other. Then on Thursday, the final bust-up, the ultimatum. We two girls in the kitchen, shivering in our pyjamas. No money to put in the gas meter. No warmth in the house. My hysterical mother screaming for us to choose between them. She was kicking my father out. She could no longer stay with a man who cared so little for the welfare of his family that he would see them go hungry just as long as he could show off in the drink. She was going to leave him and go back to her own father and mother and we could stay with him if we wanted to. But we had to choose now, right away!

It was my sister's turn first. She chose my mother, which was no surprise. They were close, really close, at that point. Now it was my turn.

I looked at my father, his head hanging on his chest, his eyes shiny with the expression of an animal caught in the headlights of an oncoming car. I didn't know it then, but this had been a familiar scenario, this business of him and booze, years before I was born. He'd learned to drink in the airforce, or the RFC as it was known in the First World War. He'd lied about his age and his background and got a commission at seventeen, boasting of his prowess on horseback. He omitted to say that these were wild, top-of-the-mountain ponies, as far removed from proud stallions as the pit-ponies down the mines. But my father was an intelligent and attractive youth, as adept at getting what he wanted as his father before him. Tadci Thomas had taught him well.

And what he'd wanted most of all was my mother. My beautiful mother with her waist-length dark hair, her navy blue eyes, her slender shape. The electric presence of her nervy vivacity.

Those two were meant for each other in that impoverished valley. He, glamorous in his swaggering officer's uniform, she, freshly emerged from the smart and expensive boarding school to which she'd been sent, now home with nothing to do except play the organ every Sunday in chapel. Kindred spirits. Each living already what amounted to a lie, a false mask, caught in a trap of self-deception. Pretending to be what they were not. I got to be pretty good at that myself, too. Like father, like mother, like daughter.

They married, despite her parents' disapproval. My father had emerged from the war with grandiose ideas, but no plans to back them up. Nothing concrete, no signs of 'industrious endeavour'. His cousins went on to become doctors and teachers, treading the familiar path out of the valley through further education. But my father had tasted the fruits of an affluent life-style in the airforce, had mixed, as a commissioned officer, with a vastly different stratum. He'd fallen in love with my mother, that was certain. He'd also fallen for a way of life and the exciting edge of wartime camaraderie, the loss of which and his inability to recreate it would cause him envy and frustrated resentment for the rest of his days. By the time I had attained all that he aspired to and was in a position to share it with him, as I did with my mother, my father had, alas, long since died. His final exit the worst timing of all. The very man I most needed to impress was gone, robbing us both of the pleasure.

Years later, after we'd buried him, my mother sat me down and proceeded to enlighten me about my father. I didn't want to hear any of this, but it must have been her way of making a kind of peace with her own painful memories. She never referred to them again. She said that my father had lied about having a job so that she would marry him, and that he'd borrowed money up to the hilt and in fact spent his time at the top of the mountain.

'Doing what?' I asked.

'Dreaming,' she answered.

'Well, that's good, isn't it? He was probably trying to write. Or draw.'

'And drinking,' she added.

I said nothing. I was already drinking myself.

When things got tough after they'd married and the creditors were pounding on the door, he disappeared, leaving a suicide note. They found him before he'd committed the act, contrite and hungover, full of self-loathing. My grandparents came to their financial rescue.

It was at this point that he decided to make a fresh start, and he and my mother, now pregnant, came to London, seriously seeking fame and fortune. Dreaming again, but not drinking. He'd sworn off that stuff for life!

His first job was in a car showroom in Piccadilly, where he proved to be a hopeless salesman, more interested in chatting on a social level with prospective clients than getting on with the business (which he considered beneath him). He lost the job. Times were lean. He was lucky to get a job in a factory. I never found out what he did there, it wasn't regarded as a table-topic in our house.

And now, at my Uncle Bryn's wedding, he'd let my mother down again. The demon-drink hadn't loosened its grip, only temporarily inflamed his bravado. But there was nothing brave or swaggering about my father in our back kitchen that Thursday evening. He looked pinched with remorse in the face of my mother's ranting recriminations. He looked ancient and smaller somehow, as if shame had shrunk the very bones in his body. And, worse, there was something seedy about him. Something repulsive. A shabby dog with a quality of apology that made me recoil. A bitter mixture of pity and disgust moved in me as painful and powerful as anything that I had ever felt towards him. It replaced the adoration and trust that we'd built up over those first seven precious years of my childhood. I could never look at him again without lamenting the loss of what we'd once had together and experiencing again the deep discomfort and unfathomable feelings of that day of childish betrayal.

I too chose my mother. The decision was fuelled by the keen edge of hunger and cold, certainly. But it was more complicated than that. I was punishing him for having created the situation. If I could make him suffer, as I was suffering now, then perhaps we could return to some kind of truce. Equals again. Pals. But as soon as I'd said it I knew I'd made a mistake, that there was no going back. In punishing him I'd set into motion a reciprocal arrangement. We punished each other, my father and I, for the rest of his life.

My parents didn't split up. My mother didn't leave him, nor did she kick him out. But it was an uneasy truce. When the wages arrived on the Friday, my mother insisted that from now on she would hold the purse-strings. All money was to come into her pocket, every penny, and she'd dole out pocket money to my father, like a child. That's how much she trusted him. This wasn't unusual for Welsh households. Every one I'd ever known in Pontycymmer was doing this anyway. It was only because we were in England, trying to fit in with English customs, that my father had been allowed to handle the money matters. Welsh women understood the financial fecklessness of their men. Welsh women made better mothers than their English counterparts. They put their children first and foremost, they saw to it that they never went hungry, so my mother said.

By 1934, we'd fetched up in the seedy suburb of Willesden – Dollis Hill to be precise: the family's first stab at semi-detached English gentility, chosen as being a safe place to bring up children, bordering as it did on the leafy glades and green playing fields of Gladstone Park. Safe? It was there, a few years later, on the iron railway bridge leading into the park, that I was accosted by a stranger asking the way to the lavatory.

I still remember the cultured timbre of his voice, the tilted brim of his brown felt hat (a Trilby like the one my father wore; my father and the film star, Ronald Colman), the firm grip of his fingers laced in mine as I led him trustingly into the lengthening shadows. My sister, catching up, wrenched me away. She was furious and frightened, since I was her responsibility and we were already out after dark. But the scolding I got at home for going off with a stranger was more than compensated for at the police station. Huge men in uniforms swung me up in their arms and wheedled me with sweets for further information on what transpired to be a dangerous child-molester, with the entire police force on his tail.

We were at the station for hours. My parents wore

strained, anxious expressions. But all I could give them was how nice the stranger sounded, that and the colour of his hat. I couldn't add – how could I? – that some eagerness inside me had responded to the man and his request. I hadn't felt frightened of him, not at all. It was as if we were about to embark on an adventure together, hand in hand. I'd have been punished for sure if I'd said that, and how sorry I now felt for this hunted creature who had come so close to being my friend.

That was in 1939, the year I was seven, a year that was to be a turning point for me in more than one respect. In a matter of months I went stone deaf and was rushed, dying, to Willesden Green Hospital. Later that year the Second World War broke out. The events took place in precisely that order.

The medical explanation for my sudden deafness was acute mastoiditis, which could have progressed to the killer meningitis. My boy cousin had died nót long before of meningitis. He'd complained of earache, while eating fish and chips on a seaside holiday in Porthcawl, and the doctor had sent him and my auntie away saying it wasn't serious. Three days later he was dead. Another small coffin, another family tale of morbid fascination. So anything to do with deafness was thought to be pretty dicey, not to be treated as a joke.

And it certainly wasn't a joke as far as I was concerned. I'd gone deaf simply because I hated listening to what was happening in our house. This was the nagging that went on and on, and on and on, until I could stand it no longer and was taken in an ambulance to hospital, where I lay hovering on the brink of life and death in the intensive care unit. On admittance I was diagnosed as suffering from malnutrition. My father's fault, my mother said afterwards. But for years I felt to blame for shaming her so. She said she hadn't known how to hold up her head when the doctor had announced it.

I didn't miss my parents during those long months in hospital. They must have visited me but, confused in my illness, drugged and barely conscious, having no recognition or memory, I regarded them as strangers. I didn't respond to them at all. I was, quite literally, at death's door. They prayed to God for my life to be delivered back to me in our Welsh chapel at Willesden Green.

I still remember moments of that unreality in sickness, even now, over fifty years later.

I am sleeping out on a balcony of the hospital in the fresh air of summer. I watch the sky. One of the clouds has formed into an angel. She is smiling down at me and beckoning me to join her. I'd like to go with her, drift towards heaven, be with God where everything's happy. I whisper to a dark-haired woman who is seated beside my bed, who always seems to be there these days, though I don't know who she is. I whisper that the angel is calling to me. The woman starts crying, tears slide down her face. A nurse emerges and leads her away. I close my eyes. When I open them after what feels like a long sleep, the sky is full of stars. The angel has gone. So has the woman, who must have been my mother.

When I recovered I was sent by the council to a convalescence home in Yarmouth, the Dickensian horror of which was only alleviated for me by the outbreak of war, whereupon I was removed and shunted to my grandparents in Wales.

I changed character in that hell-hole in Yarmouth, simply in order to survive. I'd come there, in an ambulance along with other child invalids, straight from hospital where, presumably, some level of hygiene must have been maintained. Nevertheless we were all hosed down on arrival and our heads shaved, without exception. Just as if it were a concentration camp. We lined up, naked and shivering, for this. Some children started crying and never ceased until the day they left. But I was too numbed by misery to make any response. I had been in hospital for several months, so already I had assumed an institution mentality. This was yet another experience to reinforce my sense of utter aloneness, of there being nobody who cared what happened to me. I had long since forgotten my mother and father, or that other girl in the house, my sister.

We were given regulation green garments to wear of such coarse calico that you broke out in a rash the moment it touched your skin. It was freezing cold, and there was little to eat. The sole reason that it was considered a suitable place of convalescence for London children, I can only deduce now, was because of the benefits of the sea air. We certainly got enough of that. All morning and all afternoon we tramped along the esplanade in a straight crocodile, with all the rigid discipline of a school outing from Roedean.

As one of the smallest I was at the back of the line. It was my idea to cheer us all up one day by singing a song: 'You are my sunshine, my only sunshine . . .' In no time at all the others joined in. Amused, passers-by started throwing coins at us. We scrabbled to pick them up and were severely reprimanded by our minders.

I got into trouble for undermining the dignity of the institution. It was my very first clash with authority, but by no means my last. The incident ensured my popularity with my peers. I had relieved the boredom, and had actually made them laugh. I was the naughty girl prepared to take risks. Every evening from then on I was called upon to entertain before going to bed. I looked forward to the performance as much as they did.

My role as court jester, as clown, was conceived from the profound pain of my circumstances. Laughter was the way to transcend anything, anything at all. Everything.

But another avenue of emotional escape was about to be revealed, a life-line which would provide me with additional resources and further strength to see me through.

I had been in convalescence for several months and was making very slow progress. I had had no visitors, but I wasn't the only one. We were all from impoverished families a long way from home. Few of our parents could have afforded the fare. One Sunday, however, I was taken from the breakfast table and dressed in unfamiliarly pretty clothes. A white dress and matching cardigan, a ribbon in my newly grown hair, *polished* shoes. They said there was a treat in store, a lovely surprise, and led me into a small garden where I'd never been before. They sat me on a wooden seat, telling me not to move. That I was to wait there for my surprise to happen, which wouldn't take very long.

I sat there all day until twilight, never moving. At last, driven by hunger and fear of the dark, I timidly knocked at the door to be let in. All hell was let loose. What I hadn't understood, as nobody had explained it to me, was that I was all dressed up and put to wait in the prettiest part of the grounds because my mother was coming to visit me that day. She didn't turn up and everyone else forgot about me. But since I hadn't been expecting a visitor there had been no disappointment. I had assumed that the treat in store for me was this, sitting in this sunny garden, wearing these clean, beautiful clothes. I had closed my eyes and prepared for the further promised surprise, the one they said wouldn't take long to arrive.

It came slowly, but it came. First the sun on my upturned face seemed to melt something inside me, so that I felt that bruised hole in me gradually evaporate. Then the unfamiliar silence and solitude made me aware of other sounds which I hadn't paid attention to before. The humming of bees, the fluttering of butterflies, the songs of the birds. I could smell a sweetness on the air, a mixture of sea-salt and the fragrance of flowers. An unfamiliar sense of being in tune with everything around me, being a part of the world, instead of so painfully at odds with it – that's what I felt.

I opened my eyes slowly, but with heightened excitement. This was better than any game. I knew that from now on I would see the world differently, that my view was my own and special to me. My secret that nobody could ever take away.

I sat there all day, watching clouds move across the pale sky. I saw how the shifting sun lengthened the shadows and lit up the shades of the foliage at my feet. My new-found sight circled the tree-tops, tuning into the shapes. Shapes which it had never occurred to me to try to draw before when I had drawn trees at school. I stared hard into flower heads until my own brain hummed with the passionate hue of petal and stamen, colours leapt to life that I had not imagined before. I was dizzy with the world that had so miraculously been revealed to me. I wondered if any of the others knew about all this, or if I was the only one that God had chosen to show.

I wanted to get on my knees and say thank you to Him, but I couldn't because I had promised not to move from the garden seat. So I just looked up at Heaven and smiled instead. I reckoned He knew.

That night when all the fuss had died down over my mother's non-appearance and my abandonment in the garden, I refused, for the first time, to sing and tell stories. I went to the corner where the paper and paints were stacked and worked until it was time for bed. I painted birds and bees and butterflies and flowers. I painted a huge sun in the sky and me in the garden. I missed my bedtime cocoa because I was concentrating so hard. Everyone said I was a spoilsport and no fun any more. That I was turning into a swot, and aiming to be teacher's pet for when I got back to school again. They pulled my hair, they pinched me and hid my pyjamas.

I didn't care. I wasn't the first or last to suffer for following where God had shown the way. My granny said, 'He Travels Furthest Who Travels Alone'. She had pointed to Jesus Christ on the cross when she'd told me that. And now I knew what she meant. The Philistines were trying to stone me, to pull me down. That night, before going to sleep, I prayed, 'Forgive them for they know not what they do', which was the prayer my granny had told me to say when the people around you got on your nerves or made you unhappy with their jibes.

I understood now that entertaining others wasn't my only role in life. God had given me another. Now I was an artist. And always would be.

One day, not long after this, a man they told me was my father came to the home to collect me in a borrowed car and drive me down to the safety of the Welsh valleys and my grandparents. It had been so dunned into me, since my experience with the child-molester, not to get into cars with strange men that I took some persuasion. But just because I was getting in the car didn't mean I had to talk. I spent the journey in shy silence until the very end when I sang my entire repertoire of lurid music-hall songs, learned at the home, with such exaggerated vivacity and grotesque facial distortions that it was his turn to be silent. He was stunned, apparently, by the total contrast.

The Second World War was getting into its stride, and things were really hotting up now between us and the Huns. The convalescence home was deemed to be dangerous, Yarmouth being on the coastline and in direct line of attack from the enemy; so it was explained to me by this man who claimed to be my daddy. We drove through the night, and he departed upon arrival because he was on ambulance duty in London that day. He said that my mother was sad to have missed seeing me, but she had to stay in London with him for the duration of the war, and I was to be a brave little girl about this and understand that she thought about me all the time. I didn't know who, or what, he was talking about.

I still wasn't fully recovered, far from it. Constant pain-killers had affected my memory. I had little recollection of any life prior to hospital and the convalescence home. A portion of infected bone had been hacked from behind my right ear in one of my three operations and the gaping hole was not healing. I was to be permanently deaf in that ear and was starting to rely on lip-reading to make sense of what people said. The side of my head had been shaved, and I wore a dressing held in place with white bandages. I was white and emaciated, with the physique of a stick-insect. To compound my unfortunate appearance, my upper lip was swollen out of all proportion from a wasp sting, which had gone septic. Not a pretty sight. You'd have to be its parents to love it.

My sister, Sally, was already staying with my grand-parents in Pontycymmer, for the evacuation of London children had recently begun on a grand scale. My father carried me into the garden of my granny's house for the touching reunion between us. Sally was seeing me for the first time in almost a year. Her eyes widened with horror. She gave a small gasp and backed away. She hated me on sight, she still says it, for being so ugly. She honestly thought that I was some kind of obscene animal, with the skull of a monkey, dressed up in human clothing. Some-thing escaped from the zoo, the stuff of childish night-mares. My father left me there in the garden, for us to make friends with each other. Then he departed for London, my mother and the Blitz. My granny busied herself putting tea on the table, whilst my Tadci Noyle banked up the fire in the back kitchen.

Moments later they both rushed out, drawn by my screams. Screams of agony and fear which ricocheted around the valley. Thin, high and as piercing as a stuck pig in a slaughter-house. As terrible as the wails of stricken widows when their men perished in colliery explosions. Pontycymmer had never heard the like, not coming from the throat of a child.

They found me lying in a bed of thorns the other side of our garden wall. My sister had entreated me to smell the wild roses on the edge of the considerable drop down into the next door garden, and had pushed me over – from perfectly understandable feelings of distaste and revulsion.

My only memory of the rest of the day is of me stretched out, naked and semi-conscious, on the kitchen table, aunties hovering over me, easing thorns from my flesh. The sacrificial lamb, like some kind of Christ-child figure, the smell of strong tea and buttered toast in my nostrils. Incapable of uttering a sound now, unattended by professional medical care, because one of my aunties had suggested that Sally might be taken away as a delinquent. That this could be construed as a murder attempt.

So this time instead of calling the doctor the family closed ranks, as they had with Barbara, taking turns to attend to my bruises and festering wounds, dabbing me with the same disinfectant they used for the lavatory. It took days and days, which turned into weeks. I was so debilitated already that my body simply refused to mend. This business with the thorns was yet another set-back in a year-long saga of set-backs. But mend I did, with devoted attention. And all without recourse to outsiders.

But poor Sally was in disgrace with everyone until the last scab fell off; only then was she finally forgiven. They said it showed a spiteful side to her that they would never have guessed existed. Sally, of all children! Butter wouldn't melt in her mouth!

I would have forgiven my sister sooner. I bore her no grudge at all. In fact, I believe that I admired her for acting out her impulse. I had hated *her* too, on sight, when we were first introduced to each other. This took place in Dollis Hill, when I was two and a half, and she was almost five.

I never could understand why my sister hadn't lived with us before then. Why she had been in Wales with my granny for all those years before she came to live with us in London. A mystery! Sally says now that our mother simply couldn't cope with two children, and that when I came along it was all too much for her. At the same time, it could have been that my mother gave my sister to her mother as a form of placation, for company, perhaps, in lieu of herself. As an atonement for having gone against their wishes in marrying my father. Who knows, who can tell so long after the event?

This is my earliest memory, the memory of the day I met my sister. Everyone kept asking me whether I was excited to be having my big sister back to live with me. They asked in the kiosk, which sold papers by Dollis Hill Station. They repeated the same question in Davies, the Welsh dairy, and in the greengrocer's next door. In the sweetshop on the corner, Lionel, the son of the owner, gave me two Crunchie bars and said one was for my sister, so to be sure not to eat them both, and then he tickled me under my chin.

When we got home from the shops, my mother left me outside on the pavement, still sitting in my pushchair, and went upstairs to put away the shopping. While I was waiting for her someone else stopped to speak to me. They asked me if I was excited about my sister coming home today. I stared back, blankly. What did all this mean?

My mother came out again and we set off for the park. This was the normal pattern, this felt familiar. The same pavements, the same tree-lined streets, the same small gardens in front of small houses. Everything set out in identical order. Suburbia. Where nothing much happened.

Except today. We stopped at the edge of the park. My mother uttered a cry of recognition. A woman stood in shock, echoing the same sound. They fell upon each other in excited embrace. I had never seen this happen before, had never seen my mother so pleased to see anyone. Was this the sister that people had been asking me about? Should I be smiling at her too? I was confused. Even more so when they started conversing in Welsh, which I hadn't heard before – at least not outside the home.

We went to the woman's place, which was near the park. My mother drank tea and I was given milk and some biscuits from a small silver barrel, with the word BISCUIT on it. The woman spelled it out to me slowly, like a teacher. Which is what she was; a young teacher from my mother's valley. She asked me if I was excited about my sister coming to live with us today. So she couldn't be the sister.

They went on talking in Welsh and I looked out of the window into the park. I could see the swings from where I was standing on the sofa. I liked the swings. I wanted to leave and go to them. I turned around. My mother was crying. This wasn't new. I'd seen this before, lots and lots of times. Mama cried a lot, but not in front of other people, only me. Me and my daddy.

The woman comforted her in a low voice, speaking in Welsh. I stared at them both, registering the scene. Two women, one crying, her face crumpled and damp. The second bent forward in concern, her features distorted too. A mirror of the other's. At different times, in later years, I would relive this scene with these same two women. Again and again. But this was my very first perplexing glimpse of the force of female friendship. My introduction, also, into that dank swamp of my mother's neurosis and that of her Welsh friend, whom she hadn't seen since their teens but who now lived around the corner. This woman, too, would undergo psychiatric care in the confines of mental institutions. The two were, indeed, mirrors of each other.

Later, that evening, my sister arrived. She turned out to be a little girl, a pretty child with a long brown fringe, bobbed hair and a bright open smile. My mother and father, and the neighbours from next door and the landlady from down below, were all making a big fuss of her and nobody was talking to me. Not even to ask how I liked having her home.

I would have told them if they'd asked. I would have said that it was all right but now I'd like her to go. Enough was enough, so let's get back to me. I'm the one who's been here all along. That's what I'd have said. All I understood was that nothing was going to be the same again. *She* was always going to be there, with her friendly face and her neat ways and her clean clothes, sharing my room and my toys and my parents' attention. Understanding instinctively how to get on with everybody, reliable at all times. Kind and thoughtful. Good and quiet, placid and pleasant. Accepted as the nice one of the two of us, not difficult, or exhausting, or impossible, like me.

And worse – already knowing things that I didn't know. How to talk. How to dress. How to read. How to spell. How to write. How to cross roads. How to play hockey. How to pass exams. How to go to college. How to have dates. How to get married. How to have babies. How to be the mother of the bride. How to be a granny. There would never be any catching-up. My older sister would always be ahead of me.

On the other hand, now I had a friend. Someone to wake up to in the mornings. Someone to laugh with. Someone to pinch and to punch and tell tales to, and about. Someone to get into trouble with. Someone to share the blame and the blows, and the secrets. Someone to whisper with, to wink at, to pull faces to behind the backs of the grown-ups. Someone to dream with, to share

39

plans for the future. Someone to hold hands with, to nudge in chapel, and to kick under the tea-table. Someone to complain to about parental unfairness. Someone to steal jelly with, and jam, and spoonfuls of honey out of the larder. Someone to throw a ball to, and hold a skipping-rope, to race and to swim, and play snakes-and-ladders with. Above all, someone who shared my blackish sense of humour, who burst into fits of uncontrollable laughter, especially in the face of adversity. That was the very best thing about my sister. She was a giggler, like me.

And so it was and indeed still is. My older sister and me. So how could I blame her for pushing me over into the rosebush? Wouldn't I have done the same that day when she joined us, if there'd been a high wall instead of the side-bars of my cot? She'd sure as hell have found herself face-down in the thorns. I understood about sibling rivalry.

It's only in the last five years that I've truly learned how to love my sister with all my soul and at the very deepest possible level, without that crippling sense of competition. And to forgive her for all those school reports describing her as 'pleasant and friendly', while mine just growled 'disruptive influence!'

I remember that we moved to another flat after Sally came, and this new place was more to my liking since there were lots of other children in the street, and by this time Sally and I were out playing in the road, as rough and ready as the rest of them.

We were out in the road with our gang, the day my Tadci Noyle came from Wales. He wasn't expected. I think he was sent as some form of emissary, as a family peace-maker. It upset him to see us running wild, like hooligans, in that neighbourhood. Not long after we moved into a house in a nicer street nearer the park that he and my granny bought for us.

*

I went, not long ago, to have a look at this home of ours in Hamilton Road, Dollis Hill, where I lived on and off from the age of three to thirteen. I knocked at the door of a house in a street, both of which were considerably smaller and shabbier than I remembered. A young woman answered and regarded me with some suspicion when I told her I was writing a book about my childhood and that this house had played a major part in my development. I asked her if I could come in to refresh my memories. She led me through a narrow, tiled hallway to the kitchen and scullery. We stood at the entrance to the scullery for a moment and then went through, past the downstairs lavatory, into the glasshouse. I looked at the sparse garden, lamenting the loss of the apple tree. I peeped into the front room on my way out, longing to ask if I could take a look upstairs into the bedroom where I had started my first period. Surely every woman wants to relive that memorable moment of menstruation, that pain-racked step towards full adulthood and a lifetime's expenditure on sanitary towels. But I couldn't find the words, and she was getting nervous, I could tell. I left. It was a relief to us both. I never actually liked the house, or Dollis Hill, if it comes to that. I felt out of kilter in suburbia and I still do.

Though Sally and I found ourselves together in Ponty-cymmer for the start of the war, it wasn't for long. Perhaps the both of us were too much for my granny, but Sally went to rejoin her London schoolmates who had been evacuated to a rural place in England called Berk-hamsted. I joined her for a while but was sent away as being unmanageable.

The childless pair we were billeted on liked Sally very much, but they couldn't tolerate me on any terms. They claimed I was cheeky and not given to discipline, unruly, untidy; and that I had a foul mouth. They couldn't believe that Sally and I were sisters. Of course, Sally had been brought up with all the benefits of my granny's gentleness at an early age, whereas I had recently emerged from the hell-house in Yarmouth, mixing with the toughest of London kids, with the vocabulary and songs to prove it.

But when the couple entertained at night over their pink gins, they would haul me out of bed on a regular basis to sing these songs to the assembled company in the drawing room. I remember their favourite. I sometimes sing it today to make myself smile, recalling the yawning eight year old, so willing to ingratiate, who sang it for them then. Half-asleep, but like some seasoned old trouper giving it all she'd got, complete with American accent.

> Hey there, Mister!
> You better watch your sister
> 'cos the Fleet's in, the Fleet's in!
>
> Hey there, Brother!
> You better watch your mother
> 'cos the Fleet's in, the Fleet's in!
>
> They may be dark or fair,
> Those sailors don't care
> As long as she's wearing a gown!
>
> So – best take cover
> And hide away your lover
> 'cos the Fleet's in town!

But even my midnight cabarets couldn't persuade this couple to keep me, although they found me so convulsively entertaining. They only tolerated me with a drink in their paws. Come morning I was back on their blacklist again. More so, since now they had hangovers.

Sally remained, but I was returned to my granny and to Wales again, where I was to stay until I was ten. Home! I liked it that way. I loved my granny and my Tadci, and my Tadci Thomas best in the whole wide world. And all my aunties, and Barbara, especially her. But much as I loved these people, it was Pontycymmer, the place itself, and every single thing about it, that I responded to. When thoughts return to the idyll of my childhood, this is the time I remember.

My granny's house was only three doors away from the school I attended, Ffaldau Girls Infants. I already had intimate knowledge of it because my Aunties Eunice and Emily were the school cleaners. Sometimes they allowed me to go in with them after school hours and help them. I stood on a chair and wiped chalk marks off the blackboard. I mopped up spilled ink, and rearranged the teacher's desk top. I tip-toed into the headmistress's room, Miss Hill. Then I ran out again, filled with fear. Girls had been caned in this very room. I had seen them coming out of here, crying. Shaking their stinging fingers in the air. Blowing and spitting on them to reduce the scorching heat. Plunging them under the cold tap in the cloakrooms, surrounded by circles of silent pupils, mute in sympathy and the dread that some day this might happen to them. So far it hadn't happened to me. But it would, oh yes!

I worked diligently at lessons, though I was all at sea when it came to sums and stuff requiring good sense. While I was in hospital I had missed too much schooling in the basics to be able to catch up, it seemed. But I remember even before I was ill that sums were not to my liking. I had even gone so far as to challenge the teacher at my London school. When she claimed that one plus one equalled two, I wanted to know how she knew. Could she prove it, because I didn't believe her. I preferred to think that anything could be altered to my liking, such as the colour of the sky in a painting, or the choice of words in a sentence. Subjects such as mathematics, or geography, factual in essence, couldn't touch my soul and allow it to soar. I was singled out as an awkward little cuss, a Bolshie and on my own cloud nine, even then.

But it was in that same school that I learned I had *imagination*. The infant teacher, progressive for her time, asked the class to shut their eyes, while she described the scene of a forest storm to us. She then instructed those who had 'seen' the picture in their mind's eye to put up their hands. Mine shot up without any second prompting. We still all had our eyes closed. She told us to open them and count the number of hands there were in the air. Mine was the only one.

'Molly,' she announced, 'is the only one of you, out of forty in the class, who has any imagination.'

After that, nobody would play with me in the playground at break. They shunned me as if I had the plague, some disease which wasn't very nice. I learned, from this early lesson, to keep quiet about imagination until I'd sniffed out others with the same condition. Kindred spirits, in other words. And in order to court the popularity of my peers I started playing up in the subjects I didn't like, making everybody laugh. This was the case in every school I subsequently attended; this is what ripened my reputation – the number of hours I spent outside the door in the corridor. It was as important for me to court popularity as it was to distinguish myself in English and art, the subjects closest to my heart.

I spent all my free time at Granny's, drawing and painting. I loved going to chapel on Sunday, and particularly getting dressed in my special Sunday Best clothes, laid out the night before over the chair. Everything from knickers and vest, socks and shoes, skirt and blouse and cardigan. Then the Sunday Best coat and hat, gloves and umbrella. None of it was touched on any other day of the week, not even the handkerchief. All was whisked away on Monday morning to be laundered and spotless, made Holy again for our Lord the following week. I would have enjoyed seeing how I looked in this finery, but pondering on your own reflection in the mirror was not encouraged in our house. It was thought to be playing into the hands of the devil, vanity being one of the big sins. God could see what we looked like, and that was all that mattered. He gave us eyes to appreciate things other than ourselves. That is the way it was.

We attended chapel three times every Sunday, the afternoon being Sunday School, from which there was no escape. I liked the evening session best, when the chapel was packed to the gills and the hymn-singing ripped the roof to pieces. I loved standing up there on the big seat beside my Tadci Noyle to recite my verses, learned by heart from Granny's Welsh Bible.

I had no stage-fright, no nerves at all, then or ever since, not even in front of a packed gathering. Word perfect, never fluffing a line, big audiences never daunted me, quite the opposite. I thrived at any opportunity for exhibition-ism. My chronic shyness only surfaced in social situations, on a one-to-one basis, walking into a roomful of strangers. I was consumed with agonizing self-consciousness on the street, or travelling by public transport, certain that every-one was staring at me. Shyness on this scale indicates extreme self-obsession, I was later to learn. That made sense. Indeed it took the attention of a vast audience to satisfy my hunger for approval. The ego demanded it even then.

I was proud of my tall grandfather and his position in the Tabernacle, and loved the long walks we took together up the mountain, to the very top. He talked to me about God and about the meaning of good and evil. He told me lots of things about birds and animals and plants. He let me help him in the garden, where he grew rhubarb and roses. Everybody loved and respected him, he never let people down. He was responsible for his family. He never got drunk. My grandparents lived simply, just like everybody else in the mining village, but we always had enough to eat. There was never any shouting there. They were compassionate, gentle and deeply religious people.

I slept between the two of them in their big feather bed. I would sleep in many beds with many bodies, known and unknown, later in life, but these two are the ones I still recall with the most tenderness.

My grandfather always woke first in the morning. It was barely light, but he opened the curtains and I could see the rosy dawn breaking over the mountain opposite. He emptied his bladder in the big china pot under the bed, then washed his face in his own urine. He had the most beautiful complexion to the end of his life, which he claimed to be the result of this morning swill in his own bodily fluid, the only warm water in the house at that hour. He disappeared downstairs to light all the coal-fires in the house, and by the time Granny and I came down he had made the tea and toast and porridge. They were kept hot for us in the ovens each side of the kitchen fire. He did this every day of the week.

I lay in bed after he'd gone, staring at my sleeping granny. Hers was the oldest face I had ever seen, etched with a million cobwebs right down past her neck. I traced the lines with my finger poised inches from her wrinkled skin, then burrowed into her warm body and went back to sleep again.

Every Friday after school, I would sit down with my grandfather to write our letters to London, which was in the grip of something called the Blitz. This meant, my aunties said, that the Germans, our enemies, were dropping bombs to try and kill off the King and Queen and the government. But, in the meantime, a lot of innocent families, women and children, were also being killed, because the bombers could never hit the right spot.

'What does that mean, innocent families, women and

children – aren't the King and Queen and the government innocent too?' I asked my granny.

'Everyone's innocent, child,' she answered.

'The Germans, too?' I couldn't fathom this, it wasn't what they said at school. One of the London evacuees had news last week that his whole family had been wiped out in the Blitz and now all he could do was run from side to side in the streets shouting, 'Bloody Huns'. My granny sighed, shaking her head, and said that bombers were only boys, like our own boys, and couldn't be expected to know what they were doing. She said we should pray for our enemies, as we prayed for ourselves. That's what God wanted us to do, practise brotherly love. Though I never told anyone else what she'd said, in case they jeered, I believed my granny. It was what God wanted. So every night when I knelt to say my prayers and asked him to keep Mama and Daddy in London, and Sally in Berkhamsted, safe, I asked the same for the bombers. God's other children.

This asking, this praying for whatever you wanted to come true for you and for other people, was something in which I had implicit faith. My granny and Tadci and all the people in my chapel had said it often enough for me to trust it to be true. So, when each week passed and we had no news of a bomb being dropped on my mother and father, I understood it was because I was asking God to keep an eye on them. It never occurred to me that there could be any other reason.

Everyone was talking about the war and the bombing of London. My grandfather went down to the local hardware store in the High Street to buy a wireless, so that they could get the latest news. Our neighbours would crowd around the door to listen in wonder. Wirelesses were modern 'newfangled contraptions' which my aunties wouldn't touch in case they got electrocuted. It was a special treat for me being allowed to dust it each day, taking care not to touch the knobs and alter the position of the news station.

I saw a lot of my cousin Barbara at that time, and I regarded her as my older sister in the absence of my own. She was two and a half years older than Sally, who was two and a half years older than me, which made an age difference of almost five years between us. But you would never have known it. We were the same height for a start, since she was missing the inches that a neck would have given her. We had many things in common, she and I, particularly our love of drawing and painting, but above all our passion for the cinema.

Since Barbara was an only child, deformed and father-less, some strands of the family thought Auntie May had good reason to spoil her. The fact that she was obviously artistically gifted and clever at school was seen by my granny as compensation from God for Barbara's physical setbacks and the loss of her father. Our closeness was encouraged by everyone. We were considered kindred spirits, me having survived my early brush with death, which some thought had left me 'strange' especially when I spoke of angels beckoning from the skies, and my preoccupation with painting. We were two of a kind. Now this avid enthusiasm for 'going to the pictures' was seen as further proof that we were meant to be friends, that we could support each other in our individual abnormalities.

What I liked about going over to Barbara's was the time we spent in her bedroom. Mine at my granny's was spartan in the extreme. Polished brown linoleum, faded beige wallpaper, upright wooden wardrobe, a china pot under a hard-mattressed bed with one pillow and frayed flannel blankets, a wooden wash-stand with bowl, towel, and enamel candle-holder. And a picture of Jesus on the wall for praying to . . . No untidiness, no mirror, not a speck of dirt anywhere. Cleanliness next to Godliness. No wonder I always crept into my grandparents' bed.

Barbara's bedroom was the exact opposite. My Auntie May was not a chapel-goer. She didn't even go to church. I was given to understand that Barbara was being brought up as a heathen as an act of defiance on Auntie May's part, who was punishing God for depriving her of her husband and handicapping her child. And some said, who weren't believers themselves, who could blame her.

Auntie May was a professional woman, an arts graduate with a fine career before she'd met and married Uncle Tom. Now she was working again, so what with this income and Uncle Tom's headmaster's pension, she was regarded as truly affluent, and as economically impressive, in the eyes of our family, as Auntie Sarah, my own granny, who'd scrimped and saved to buy all those houses. The difference was that as soon as you opened the front door at Auntie May's you could smell the fact that money was being spent on the home. That money was regarded as being purely for pleasure, for life enhancement, in the shape of soft cushions and thick carpets, in sumptuous sofas and upholstered chairs, in lavish curtains and chenille tablecloths overlaid with ivory lace. This was a nest which smelled of fresh flowers and overflowing fruit bowls, of embroidery silks and mohair knitting wool.

While colour at my granny's house was so subdued as to be non-existent, at Auntie May's the assault of colour on the eye carried a physical message. You felt warmer as soon as you stepped inside. At the time her job involved supervision of arts and crafts for the Women's Institutes in the Garw Valley. At the end of her career she was honoured by the Queen with the OBE for services to South Wales. You could see her devotion to the work she was encouraging women to produce, for the house over-flowed with specimens on their way to be exhibited: handwoven rugs, embroidered tablecloths, patchwork

49

quilts, wickerwork stools, raffia baskets, knitted shawls, woven skirts, felt tea-cosies. The front room downstairs, the room my other aunties called the parlour, though never Auntie May, was used by her as a storage room for all these items. When you peeped in, it looked more like Aladdin's cave, the colours, patterns, textures, all dancing in riotous confusion.

But the real confusion lay up the stairs in Barbara's bedroom. This was probably my favourite room of any that I had ever been in, so far. I loved my granny's tiny back kitchen with its roaring fire and wooden stools because it represented the womb to me. I felt safe there, sitting against her knees, watching her perform her domestic chores. I felt as if I never wanted to leave, that I could stay there cocooned for the rest of my life. I didn't feel safe in Barbara's bedroom, quite the opposite. I wasn't exactly scared but I was certainly dazzled, certainly over-impressed and enthralled by so much evidence of all that the outside world had to offer me when I grew up.

It was very grown-up. Barbara's bed, for a start, was a double bed, the sort of width that it normally took two adults to fill. I counted her pillows once and there were six of them, in pillow-slips with lace at the edges or deep ruffled frills. The bed was never made. We were allowed to loll over it, or burrow under the sheets at any time of the day; Auntie May didn't mind. At Granny's you weren't meant to go upstairs after she'd dusted and made the beds, for fear of carrying dirt with you. Another big difference was Barbara's kidney-shaped dressing table and mirror. It dominated the room, the mirror. It was huge. In it, as well as seeing yourself and the bed and literally hundreds of glossy film-star pin-ups which covered the walls and which Barbara had sent for especially from the Hollywood Studios, it bore the reflection of all her paraphernalia. All her perfume bottles, her lipsticks, her powders, her rouges, her mascaras, her pimple-remover, her nail lacquer, and the Vaseline which she smoothed onto her eyelashes each night to make them grow as long as Hedy Lamarr's, who was noted for hers.

I was about eight when I first became intimately acquainted with this treasure trove, these forbidden fruits which my granny would have disapproved of so deeply, and Barbara must have been at the start of her teens. But I remember clearly when she had her first cigarette and that was when she was twelve, so I must have been down in Wales on a visit, just before my illness. The cigarettes were black Russian Sobranies which Barbara had sent away for, after seeing an advertisement for them in a magazine. She was always sending away for things; the postman called regularly with packages for her. She had the pocket-money and Auntie May never enquired what she did with it. Since the black Sobranies were so much to her liking, she ordered the same, only in colours. They came with gold tips, too.

'Look,' she said to me, 'how carefully I choose my lipstick to match my cigarette.'

She smoked the entire packet, one after the other, to show what she meant. Between each technicolour cigarette she wiped off her lipstick and applied another shade.

'Scarlet with turquoise. Crimson with blue. Cyclamen with fuchsia. Remember these things, Moll. It's very important if you want to be accepted in sophisticated circles.'

I'd nodded, mesmerized, so much to remember if I wanted to get ahead. Our cousin, Miriam, who'd never passed the all-important eleven-plus examination which I had still to try in order to go on to the grammar school, had just been sent away to work in service in England. She'd recently returned for a trip home and told us we were all drinking our tea incorrectly. She was fourteen and only the kitchen maid, but the butler had taken her under his wing and had been teaching her these important things.

Auntie May said it was rubbish, and so did my granny. But for a week Barbara and I had been practising in her bedroom with our little fingers cocked up in the air, as Miriam had shown us. They probably did things differently in posh English households. How would my granny and Auntie May know? They'd never been out of Wales.

Our cousin Miriam died in childbirth, still under the age of twenty. She'd met a sailor and married him and got pregnant, all in the one year. While our Auntie Maggie was waiting in the hospital to go in and see her after they'd come out to say that Miriam had just had a little girl, they came out a second time, now with tragic news.

Unbelievable, they said, the young mother had slipped through their fingers without a sound. The birth had been too much for her. She had the heart of an old woman, prematurely exhausted. What work, they asked, had this girl been involved in that could have depleted her strength to this extent? She's been in service, Auntie Maggie had answered. There was no reply. The pressure to do well at school was increased after that. Education was the only way to avoid the kind of job that Miriam had died from. Premature exhaustion at nineteen.

My special friend in Pontycymmer was not a chapel girl. In fact her family were quite the opposite. They didn't believe in God, only the power of politics. They were strong union supporters, always angry, always shouting. My grandfather said they were good-for-nothings, the whole pack of them. Rabble-rousers, he said, trouble-makers who hadn't got a good day's work in them. They were a hindrance to the union and not a help, and it was hot-heads like them who would undermine any progress for the rights of the miners. A cause that my grandfather, a respected figure in the colliery, had fought for all his life.

My friend Gwyneth had a large, sullen father and lots of grown-up brothers, who all worked in the mines. Her mother was always pegging out washing on the line, or ironing, or cooking, or laying and clearing the table in the big back kitchen where the whole family congregated around their coal fire. Fires were the focal point of all these mining homes; the coal by which the family survived, the only commodity that miners got free. Gwyneth spent all her time helping her mother, as the only other female in the house. She worked as hard as Miriam must have, yet she was only two years older than me.

I liked her because she laughed a lot; we laughed together. She had bright, carrot-red hair and matching freckles all over her face. Her eyes were green and shiny like two brilliant gooseberries. She was clever at school, the top of her class. She had been singled out by Miss Davies, the teacher, as 'university material', like me. This was another bond we shared. We loved going up the mountain, talking to the sheep, trying to catch the lambs, picking berries from the low-lying wimberry bushes, bringing them home to my granny to make into tarts. We talked of our futures. Gwyneth was going to be a doctor. That's what she said. She was going to travel abroad, go to America. I had decided to be an artist and if not then I would be a writer. We'd be friends forever, and might even live together when we grew up – if our husbands would allow it.

I'd been living with my grandparents for several months, when my parents arranged to visit me one weekend, making the long journey from London. I wanted to be well-behaved, but something in me rebelled. They talked of taking me back to London with them once the war was over, or even before, when the worst of the bombing died down. But I didn't want to go. I liked it in Wales. I couldn't believe that my grandparents would let them take me away. I preferred my grandparents to my mother and father. I hated their quarrelling, always about money.

I was rude and sulky over the weekend. My mother cried because I refused to kiss her and I was sent to bed early in disgrace. My father came up to my bedroom to punish me. My heart started hammering when I heard his heavy tread on the stairs. I was petrified of what was to come, but still I stared at him in defiance.

His grey eyes looked as cold and lifeless as the pebbles we'd used one summer to skim the surface of the sea in Porthcawl. As cold and lifeless as the day I'd chosen my mother instead of him in our kitchen up in London after he'd got drunk at Uncle Bryn's wedding. It was difficult to believe this distant, angry man was my own father. When he spoke to me it was with a voice that was full of dislike. He commanded me not to look at him like that. I continued to do so. But I was badly frightened and expecting the worst. I clutched my nightie around me, but it proved no protection at all . . . He stripped back the bedclothes and started to beat me.

I wouldn't cry. I wouldn't let him know how much it hurt. He was shouting, but I couldn't hear the words, my ears were ringing with my own pain and misery. He caught me by my shoulders and lifted me bodily from the bed.

'I'll break your spirit, if it's the last thing I ever do, you little demon!'

He was dancing with rage, shaking me like a rag doll as if I had no bones at all in my small body. It went on for a long time. He growled into my one good ear, the one unaffected by my mastoiditis, that he wouldn't stop until I begged him to stop. The tears seeped from my eyes and splashed down my face. The first sob wrenched itself from the bursting pain in my chest, to be followed by further racked cries as I lost all control of my body's response to his towering rage. The beating stopped. He had won. He demanded an apology. Again and again.

'Sorry,' I sobbed. 'Sorry, sorry, sorry, sorry . . .' Over and over again.

Then everything changed. The difference in this fierce and violent father of mine was remarkable, astounding, and in its way just as chilling. He lifted me out of bed again and cuddled me on his lap, crooning strange noises into my neck. He sheltered me in his coat. He kissed me all over my face, my neck, my shoulders. I fell asleep, still softly sobbing within the embrace of his arms. When I awoke in the morning, my eyes still swollen with tears, my body aching from adult blows, I knew that I never wanted to be alone with my father again. That we had crossed over a barrier that shouldn't be crossed between an adult and child, between a father and daughter. I was eight but I understood that it wasn't right to feel this uncomfortable, this uneasy, in this much pain. I had the power, I had seen that last night, to drive my father wild, to make him lose control so that he was beside himself. I contrived to avoid him all the following day, nor did he seek me out. He left for London without either of us saying goodbye.

The weekend changed me. I started misbehaving at school, seeking attention. I was naughty at home. I began to disobey my granny. Perhaps I was hoping for a repeat of the incident with my father, goading my grandfather to behave in the same way. Beating then caressing me, who knows. I thought a lot about the incident; something about it excited me, but I didn't know what. I went over and over it in my mind, until the memory became my closest companion. There was nobody I could tell.

One Sunday my granny caught me knitting trousers for my teddy bear out in the lavatory at the bottom of the garden. She was very cross. Sunday was the day of the Lord, it was meant to be a day of rest, and knitting was not allowed. She sent me to bed without my tea. I heard her going to evening chapel. Perhaps my grandfather would come up and punish me, like my father. He didn't come.

Later that evening my granny climbed the stairs. She gazed down at me, gentle and forgiving.

'Have you repented, little one?'

The same defiance rose in me that infuriated my father. I wanted to hurt her. She was letting my parents take me back to London. She was making no effort to keep me. I spat at her. I don't know where the words came from. I shouted in her sweet face, watching her kind eyes fill with tears.

'When I grow up, I won't need you and I won't need God. I shall do everything I want to do. I shall drink and smoke, wear lipstick and rouge! Have perms and wear red dresses and high heels! And I shall . . . *dance* . . . with *men*!'

'And will that make you happy, child?'

'Very! Yes! Be all good fun!' I spat at her again for good measure.

There was no punishment for this was a truly Christian household. I accepted her suggestion to pray, after a long silence in which my anger melted away and my granny's tears dried. I got out of my small bed and knelt beside it and we prayed there, with each other, asking for my forgiveness. I was restored again, my spirit in peace. I drifted to sleep but not before I overheard my granny whispering to my grandfather on the landing outside.

'John, I truly think that the devil has entered the child's soul!'

I retreated further and further into fantasy after that, daydreaming all week about Saturday night, when Barbara and Auntie May took me to the pictures with them. We would usually go to the cinema called the Hall, a dour building without decoration at the bottom of Oxford

Street, first popping into Greenslades' sweetshop opposite for a bag of sweets. We would sit upstairs, which cost sixpence, as opposed to downstairs which cost tuppence and was where I sat if I went with one of my other aunties, who all had less money than Auntie May.

Granny and Tadci never took me to the cinema, they disapproved of it heartily, regarding it as the seductive edge of the forces of evil. But Granny had great respect for Auntie May's judgement, despite the hedonism she displayed in her house. She didn't think an educated woman would knowingly subvert a small and impressionable child such as me.

The films we saw every Saturday night were highly unsuitable, mostly with an 'A' (Adults Only) certificate, which made no difference at all down in Pontycymmer. The place was packed with children, some even younger than me. There were babies there, still at their mother's breasts. You could hear them sucking in the silent bits, though there weren't very many of those; the audience believed heartily in total participation, especially in any kissing scene when the vocal frenzy would reach crescendo pitch.

Joan Crawford was a huge favourite and Bette Davis, with Betty Grable in her technicolour musicals the greatest draw of all. But the one we all wanted to look like, without exception, was Rita Hayworth. Rita Hayworth in *Gilda*. And my abiding memory is of Barbara's interpretation of this role some years later when that film came to Pontycymmer.

There had been a sensational photograph of Rita as Gilda outside the Hall cinema for a month before the film opened. She was wearing a slinky, strapless, satin evening gown with a slit right up to her thigh. Long shiny gloves stretched way up past her elbows. Her hair cascaded over one eye, right down to her bare shoulders. Her head was thrown back in an attitude of sexual abandon, with a long cigarette-holder carrying a smouldering cigarette about to enter her lips. Every time you passed the poster there would be a thick throng of boys of all ages, from eighty to eight, staring, spellbound, emitting moans and lip-smackings of keen appreciation.

Rita Hayworth as Gilda exemplified everything that those hours in Barbara's bedroom were all about. We had found our icon. Barbara even had the song; she'd memorized every word of 'Put the Blame on Mame' – Gilda's nightclub signature.

I'd sit on the bed, her enraptured audience, while she rehearsed every gesture in the mirror. She had the hair, thick and long, all right. I'd curl it for her with heated curling-tongs, to get the right look. But she had difficulty tossing it back from her eyes. The neck wasn't there, she hadn't the leverage. Apart from that and the guttural incomprehensibility of the actual words, incomprehensible to others, not to me, she was the perfect Gilda.

'You ought to get the proper clothes and give a concert,' I said one day.

'In the garage at the bottom of the garden!' Her eyes lit up.

That's what I liked about her; she always cottoned on right away to any suggestion. I sneaked an old shiny chapel frock from my granny's boxroom, and slit it up to Barbara's knickers to show all her leg. She pinched some high-heels from her mother and slathered her mouth with blood-red lipstick. We waited until Auntie May was out in her car for the afternoon and opened the garage for the public performance.

The entry fee was a farthing for little ones and a halfpenny for older children and adults. After half an hour, when no one had appeared, we sent word via the boy next door that there would be free chocolate biscuits and Tizer, and nothing to pay at all.

'The audience is the thing. Anything's better than nobody,' Barbara said magnanimously.

I'd brought my granny's toasting fork to prod anyone who looked like laughing, because it stretched further than an ordinary fork and gave me greater control. I didn't want Barbara upset. Not everyone would appreciate her splendid impersonation. She wasn't their cousin, there wouldn't be the same family loyalty.

Eleven children arrived, most of them from Bridgend Road where everyone always went hungry. I had to bribe the smaller ones to stay by passing the biscuits out as soon as Barbara appeared in her full costume, they were so frightened. I stood back, my toasting fork at the ready. But far from pandemonium there was total silence as Barbara swung into action, hoisting herself on to a kitchen stool and swinging one naked leg in its giant shoe.

'Put the blame on Mame, boys.' She raised one pencilled eyebrow and dragged on her shiny cigarette holder. Smoke spiralled through her tonged curls. She removed one of her gloves, a fur mitten with gauntlets (all the other gloves were too short) and threw it into the audience. It hit one of the toddlers in the eye, at which he promptly started bawling. I had to hastily pass the chocolate biscuits around again. We were only halfway through the first rendition of 'Mame', and Barbara had planned an encore whether they wanted it or not. I didn't think they would.

I led the cheering at the end. 'Encore, encore!'

But Barbara demurred, disappearing behind the towels that we'd hung up to form a curtain.

'Always leave your audiences wanting more,' she purred afterwards, a satisfied smile on her curly lips. 'Remember that, Moll, if you ever turn professional.'

My grandmother died suddenly. I woke up one morning alone in my bedroom, not snuggled between my grandparents as usual. I tiptoed back to them, alarmed by the unfamiliar sounds of voices in the house this early in the day. My mother was there, the doctor too. My mother barely greeted me. But who was she anyway, this white-faced woman with hunched shoulders and wringing hands, and frightening eyes in deep sockets? They barred the way to my grandmother's bed. I ran, crying, to my grandfather.

The kettle was on the boil, the porridge was simmering in the big black pot on the open fire, but my grandfather was not in his usual place at the kitchen table. I started wailing. What was happening? I ran into the garden. There I found my grandfather quietly pruning his beloved roses, lifting his face to the pink sunrise over the mountain, placing his hands together in prayer. He turned as I ran to him. He gathered me up in his strong arms.

'She has gone, *cariad*. My Sarah has gone.'

I held my tall grandfather tightly around the thick, powerful neck. My small hand patted his broad miner's shoulders, shaking now with grief. My granny and grand-father belonged together, they were a pair. How could he manage without her? Those thoughts went through my troubled mind. I had never known before that men could cry, but my Tadci Noyle was crying now, lifting his tear-stained face to the sky.

'Sarah, *bach*, what am I to do without you now?'

What did any of us ever do without my granny after that? Only lived our diminished lives as best we could.

Many people arrived for the funeral. My grandmother was 'laid out' in the front parlour. All the curtains and window blinds were drawn. I was frightened of the dark, more particularly with a corpse in the house. The boy down the road told me that corpses like to take a stroll in the night, and mind to lock my bedroom door. I woke up sweating in a nightmare, but was too scared to cry out in case my granny got out of her coffin to comfort me. I walked everywhere with a lighted candle. I was particularly terrified of the closed door of the front parlour. Relatives and close friends queued in the passage to pay their last respects to my grandmother in her open coffin, right up to the final hour before the funeral. They went in one by one, closing the door behind them so their final farewells were said in privacy. Each of them cried as they came out. My grandmother was a much-loved person.

Then it was my turn to go in. I pulled back in fear of the unknown. My aunties thrust me forward, pushing me into the darkened room, closing the door behind me. I was ten years old and had never before been in the presence of any dead thing, not counting the flies that fell off the fly-catcher above the kitchen table into our food. I caught my breath, I couldn't breathe. My heart was pounding in my throat, constricting the flow of saliva. I shivered with fear-filled excitement.

The air smelled of the wax candles at my granny's head and feet, of the arranged flowers along the mantelpiece and of the wreaths propped on the piano. But there was a scent of something sweeter too, sicklier. The smell of death.

I tiptoed over to the coffin and stared at my granny's face. She was absolutely still and so pale as to be almost transparent. The colour of maggots that live beneath stones. I touched her cheek and jumped back in shock at the sheer coldness. It was as if I had touched a marble statue, or a slab of hard snow. I was too numbed in loss even to cry. I ran from the room out into the garden, seeking my grandfather again. He wasn't there, but I knew where he'd be. I fetched my coat and set off up the mountain. It was the very first time that I had done so on my own. But I found my grandfather where I knew I would, under the hawthorn tree. The tree that we had sat beneath so many times on our walks, with the view of the cemetery and the school and all the collieries in the Garw

Valley. I sat down beside him and put my hand in his. And that's how we remained, not saying a word, until we were both ready to go down again. Hand in hand in the same silence we went, all the way to the house where the one we were missing so much already lay dead.

Many friends and neighbours and chapel-congregation crowded into the house following the funeral. The hushed festivities lasted all day and far into the night. One of my elderly uncles whom I had never seen before or since, took liberties with my underclothes after perching me on his knees. There in the front parlour, with my Auntie Emily playing a hymn on the piano and everyone singing. I wriggled away from him and his intrusive thumb, blushing to my roots, but he avoided my accusing stare and simply continued singing, gazing into the middle distance with a pious expression on his pinched face. This was my first actual physical sexual encounter. I pondered on it later, lying in bed, mourning my dead granny, listening to the hymn-singing and the piano-playing, looking at the patterns on my bedroom ceiling made by my spluttering candle. Sex and death, linked for the first time in my life. But certainly not the last.

PART TWO

Sex and the Suburbs

After the funeral, my mother packed my belongings and took me back to London with her. It was nearly 1943. The war was still on and bombs were still being dropped, but the worst of the Blitz seemed to be over. The all-important eleven-plus examination was looming up for me in a year's time and it was thought that I'd have a better chance of getting into a good grammar school such as Willesden County if I did the exam in London. Besides, my sister was back in London now, and already going to the school which made it more likely that they would accept me, providing I was bright enough.

I was bright enough in everything except sums, where I seemed to have an absolute blockage. The teachers couldn't understand how a child who had such a grasp of everything else could be so appallingly dense in this area. The only explanation could be that I had missed a lot of the groundwork while I was in hospital. It was hoped that I'd pass the eleven-plus on the excellence of my English work; that this would carry me through.

I hated the journey back to London on the train with my mother. She seemed permanently exhausted, this skinny, gaunt woman, huddled in the corner seat with tears streaming down her face. I was used to talking all the time to Granny and Tadci, to Barbara and Auntie May, and all the other aunties. I was used to neighbours stopping me on the street to have a word. I thrived on verbal exchange. It was why I was so good with words, because I was using them all the time. No one spoke on the train, although we were in a packed carriage. When I tried to talk to my mother she pleaded with me to go to sleep, to leave her alone, because my chatter was making her ill. I looked out of the window, watching Wales turn into England, trying to imagine what it would be like living with a mother who didn't believe in communication and a father who I was already frightened to death of, amongst people who were English and not Welsh. A sense of impending doom filled me from top to bottom.

From time to time someone would pull out a pack of sandwiches and pour a drink from a thermos. My mother had been too agitated after the funeral to have organized these things, so we had nothing and I was hungry and thirsty. Since I was the only child in the carriage people did offer me something to eat, but my mother refused for me. She whispered that it would be very rude to accept what you couldn't return. She said afterwards that the journey had been a lesson, a test of endurance. She was only referring to the food and drink. I saw it as more ominous than that.

That night she caught me sobbing into my pillow for my granny and Tadci and their soft feather bed. She stormed out of the room saying that I was an ungrateful child and she was sorry she'd brought me back with her. She would tell my father when he got home and he'd beat some sense into me. I lay awake, alert now for the dreaded step on the stairs and the flinging open of my door. I fell asleep still waiting, my heart hammering, all thoughts of my granny expelled from my mind in the palpitating terror of the moment. In the morning I awoke expecting to see the sun over the top of the mountain. Instead, there was my sister smiling down at me. I'd forgotten my sister, forgotten my playmate. She was already in bed by the time we got back last night, looked after by a neighbour until our arrival. My father had been on night shift in his new role of ambulance driver for the St John Ambulance Brigade, his job as part of the war effort.

'D'you want to play snakes and ladders?' Sally said cheerfully, sitting on the edge of my bed. I'd forgotten her good humour. Perhaps it wasn't going to be so bad back in London after all.

The differences between living in this house and my granny's disconcerted me at the start. But I soon got used to huddling underneath the stairs each time the air-raid siren went. Entire blocks in the street around us had been devastated. Bomb sites were a normal sight, but I couldn't get used to them at first. They exerted a fearful fascination, those bombed buildings, like teeth that had been wrenched from the socket of a jaw.

'Ten people died in that one, two families wiped out,' Sally would say, matter of factly. She showed me how to scour around these sites for highly valued lumps of shrapnel. She had eleven pieces of her own and I started collecting them with great enthusiasm to show off at school. All the other kids were doing the same.

The war lent an air of excitement to everyday life that was highly contagious. If someone wasn't at class in the morning, there was a good chance that they were dead. Though the worst of the Blitz may have been over there were still the lethal doodle-bugs to contend with. Most of our neighbours had air-raid shelters in the back garden. We had the startings of one, where the tiny lawn had been, until the roof caved in. My father wasn't too hot on construction. But one day he brought home a massive steel indoor shelter which he erected in the dining room. It was called a Morrison shelter. He painted an entire farmyard scene on the surface, with pigs and ducks, chickens and cows. Sally and I started sleeping in it at night with the cat to save us being dragged from our beds upstairs when the siren went.

My mother used the space under the stairs. So did my father if he was in the house. But we never saw much of him because his ambulance duty demanded his presence most of the time, day and night, it seemed to me. And I was glad. It was more peaceful in the house when he wasn't around. Nobody hit me, for a start.

The problems with my father had continued after my return home. Our only closeness was couched in physical violence. The beatings would occur whenever his mindless rages took over, but always started on the stairs leading to the bedrooms: a vicious swipe to the legs as I tried to run away from him, and then a relentless session while I lay on my bed, which always ended with fondles and kisses. When I misbehaved my mother would hold the threat over me.

'Go up to bed, you naughty girl! Your father will see to you when he gets home!'

I would lie there shivering in terror, expecting the worst. Welcoming the start, knowing that the sooner we got that bit over then the sooner the nice loving part would begin. The pleasure at the end of the punishment.

My mother turned a blind eye, but I can't blame her for that. She had her own emotional difficulties. Anyway, she couldn't understand my rudeness to him, and it wasn't as if I screamed for mercy during our sessions. I stifled all sound, only crying at the end, when I was black and blue, begging for him to stop. That was the moment we both hung out for, reaching the breaking point in readiness for the reconciliation.

I missed Pontycymmer more than I could explain to anyone. I ached to be back there, where I knew everybody and they knew me. The air was different in Pontycymmer. It smelled of rain and mountain earth, of coal dust and roses. The silence of the valley was alive with small tinkling sounds like babies crying, sheep bleating and the muffled workings of the colliery. Coal miners walked the streets on their way home from work, like the natives of a dark continent, black from top to toe, my Uncle Jack and cousin Emrys among them. You could only distinguish them by the whites of their eyes and the irregularity of their teeth.

In London, in Dollis Hill, everybody looked the same with their gas-mask cases on their backs. You didn't know their names or who they were. They were like the houses, and the streets they lived in – all the same. No individuality, no eccentricity, no fun. But the dreaded excitement of the doodle-bugs gave cause for celebration. Simply to have survived another bombing gave an edge to every waking day. Though I no longer lived within the warmth of a village, there was an air of camaraderie in our suburb which united us all. Even if we didn't know each other's names.

My greatest loss was my granny. I prayed to her every night. I prayed with my eyes shut tight throughout the air-raids, knowing she'd see us through, that she'd be having a word with God on our behalf. I'd lie awake at night thinking about her and my Tadci, understanding that a precious part of my childhood was now over and that it could never return. And the worst of it was that I had no one to tell, no one to turn to for comfort. Except God, of course, He was always there. He understood.

Sally and I had to share a room again because my parents took an elderly lodger to help them make ends meet. He was the air-raid warden from the end of our road, a 'real gentleman', my mother said, who had fallen on hard times, otherwise he wouldn't be forced to live in such a humble fashion. He gave me sixpence a week for cleaning his room. I would do anything for money, I was used to working. Hadn't I been my granny's rent-collector? I looked forward to doing the room, it was the first truly masculine environment I'd ever been in.

His name was Mr Hill. His room, my parents' old room at the front of the house, smelled of many strange things now, but predominantly of brandy; brandy and an expensive brand of pipe tobacco. His silver-backed hairbrushes reeked of scented oils, his clothes-brush had the aroma of ancient tweeds, his leather-bound books exuded a scholarly mustiness. Each time I entered to clean his room it was always in an unimaginable mess, but I didn't mind. It just meant I could linger longer over my task. I felt different in there, transported to another world. The world of sophistication and learning which I planned to join, the world that Barbara and I had spoken of, full of men who were real gentlemen like Mr Hill.

My mother said that Mr Hill was a public school boy, whatever that meant. She suspected he'd gone to Eton, and most certainly to Oxford University where Gwyneth was headed for. And me too, if I worked hard enough. I wondered if Gwyneth and I would come out of Oxford talking like Mr Hill, with a voice good enough to be on the BBC.

We didn't talk much, Mr Hill and I. We didn't have any actual conversations. I was too overawed in his presence to answer his genial enquiries as to how I was with any adequate answer which might have led us into proper communication. I overheard Mrs Marsden, next door, tell another neighbour that Mr Hill was 'three sheets in the wind more often than not'. But I kept that information to myself since it sounded vaguely critical of my hero. Whilst not quite knowing what it meant, the disapproving tone had been enough. They obviously didn't understand the behaviour of a true toff.

I passed the eleven-plus and got into the grammar school. All set for success in life now, so everyone told me. There were great celebrations in our house, all my Welsh aunties sent me cards. My father's cousins, Aunties Dilys and Enid, one a headmistress and the other a teacher, both living in Bridgend, now took a greater interest in me. It was an interest they had already expressed when Sally went to the grammar school. They would oversee our progress, scholastically speaking, from now on. In immediate practical terms this meant that whenever I wrote a letter to them, I could be certain of receiving it back, marked for spelling and punctuation. My birthday presents were always dictionaries, or text books on the use of the English language. They wanted us to follow in their academic footsteps.

Mr Hill presented me with a leather-bound volume of Longfellow's poetry. He said he hoped I'd keep it forever and remember him by it when I became rich and famous. I was starting to develop a crush – my first – on Mr Hill and his rich, fruity baritone. His was the last face that I saw before I drifted off to sleep. Every time I thought of him my heart lurched against my ribs. So this was what True Love actually felt like.

There was another cause for celebration in 1943, the same year that I passed my eleven-plus. I became a 'woman' like my mother and sister. Now there were three of us menstruating in the same house, though not for long. One of us stopped bleeding. My mother had a hysterectomy, but why, we never knew. I had too much to worry about on my own account. My figure was developing. Monstrous things were happening, like sprouting hair and burgeoning breasts. And the sudden and overwhelming attention of the opposite sex.

One Saturday morning, while I was cleaning Mr Hill's room, straddling the old armchair to polish the mirror behind, I experienced my first sexual arousal. I was still eleven, the arm of the chair was pressed between my thighs. Without thinking I started to rub myself against it, like an animal, a dog, a creature bent on pleasure. I watched my face in the mirror, fascinated by the change in expression. My lips looked swollen, my eyes were wild and shiny. I hardly recognized myself. I looked old and experienced. I looked like a film star in a close-up. I looked glamorous, the sort of person that men would die for!

That experience set a precedent. Each time I cleaned Mr

Hill's room I masturbated on his armchair. I took various objects of his, articles of clothing, a shoe, a shirt, and held them to my nose as I brought myself to climax. I kissed them, licked them, breathed their odour deep into my lungs. I never touched myself between my legs. That would have been too rude, forbidden behaviour of which the chapel wouldn't approve. The armchair did it all for me. I grew up in that room. I familiarized myself with my femininity. I couldn't wait for Saturday mornings.

Then, one Friday night, my father was called in his ambulance to attend a fatal heart-attack victim. The man had collapsed in the lavatory on Dollis Hill Station at the top of our road. He was with a prostitute. Both were very drunk, but she had managed to phone for the ambulance. The police were there when my father arrived. The man died in his arms. It was Mr Hill.

He didn't die as a gentleman should, my mother said solemnly. He died in sordid circumstances, with his trousers at half-mast. The worst aspect, she said, was that a man of such quality should have been in the company of a slut, a woman of the night.

The way she said it frightened me, the venom in her face.

'What does that mean?' I asked.

'A woman of the night, Molly, is the lowest of the low. Scum. Someone who sells her body for money.'

So now I knew what scum was. Sex and death. I was being punished for my pleasure in Mr Hill's room.

We kept all Mr Hill's things in his big suitcase because we didn't know what to do with them. He had never mentioned any family and there were no photographs. I moved back into my bedroom, but the masturbation didn't work any more. Not now there was no Mr Hill to think about. I lay in my bed instead, longing for his return and for the return of my granny. I remembered their faces. Mr Hill's curly moustache, his twinkling eyes when he'd been on the brandy. My granny's delicate tracery of wrinkles, fine like old lace. The warmth of her body in bed. And the tears slid down my face. The sadness. The misery of loss.

One day I came home from school to find a big, shiny car, a Bentley, outside our house. There was someone having tea in the front room with my mother. She was talking in a refined almost English voice, quite unlike her own. She called me in to meet Mr Hill's son. I stared up at him and couldn't tear my eyes away, he was so unbelievably handsome, so well-groomed, so suave, so ultra-sophisticated. His nose was straight, his jaw lean, his teeth even and white. I looked at his hands, at the neatly cut nails, at the smooth fingertips. Those hands had never done rough work. They weren't like the hands of any man I'd ever seen in Pontycymmer. But he was vulnerable, nevertheless. His eyes were full of tears, he had to clear his throat in order to speak to me. I fell in love with him on the spot; in an instant I had transferred everything I felt for the father on to the son. His voice was cultured and quieter than Mr Hill's, but the accent was the same. Upper-class, out of reach. A goal to be attained by fair means or foul.

He took Mr Hill's suitcase, but first removed the leather-bound volumes of Shakespeare and presented them to my mother. My mother had told him that I cleaned for his father, but she didn't say, because she didn't know, what else went on in those cleaning sessions. The son smiled at me and my insides floated away. I shall marry a man like that one day, I promised myself.

And then my grandfather, Tadci Noyle, came to live with us in London and a sense of magic returned to my days. He lived with us until his death at the age of eighty-three, on the first of October, 1945. The year I became a teenager.

We made him a bed, under the stairs at the start, because

73

he was over eighty now and couldn't be expected to move as quickly as the rest of us when the air-raid siren went. But gradually as the bombings died down we dismantled the indoor air-raid shelter and put him into a big bed in the dining room, where, when he became bedridden, he spent all his time.

His legs were already weak on arrival, so we bought him a wheelchair, and Sally and I used to push him around Gladstone Park. He spoke to everybody, it was astounding. When we walked in the park with our mother and father on Sundays after chapel, we didn't speak to anyone. It wasn't the thing to do. In England people kept themselves to themselves, my mother said. My grandfather thought that was nonsense. He made more friends from his first few outings in the park than my parents did for the entire time they lived in London. People were drawn to Tadci Noyle as if he were the Pied Piper. He smiled from his chair and said good afternoon to everybody we passed. They answered from sheer surprise, and one thing led to another. Before we knew what had happened he'd invited them home to tea. This led to arguments between my parents, especially over one of Tadci's greatest friends, an elderly Jewish academic as absorbed in ecclesiastical matters as my grandfather. My father was deeply anti-Semitic and didn't want Mr Lieberman in the house. He resented the hours that the old gentleman spent with Tadci, when he was bedridden, each comparing notes on their differing religious beliefs. But my mother stood her ground, trying her best to keep the peace. Tadci was allowed to have whoever he wanted in this house. After all, she retaliated, it was Granny and Tadci's money that had paid for it.

One summer we all went down to Jaywick Sands, outside Clacton on the Essex coast. Tadci had bought us a little holiday bungalow there. We looked a motley group on the platform at Liverpool Street Station waiting for the train, Tadci in his wheelchair with a Panama hat at a raffish angle, our cat in a basket, Sally, my mother and me with our belongings in assorted bundles, with a big trunk holding all our summer clothes. People stared, smiled and looked away. I stared back at them with a hostile expression. I was used to this, from being out with Barbara, used to dealing with people's rudeness. It didn't occur to me then that they were probably only staring and smiling because we looked so happy, happy to be getting away from London, to be going to the seaside. Happy too, that my father wouldn't be coming with us because he had to stay and work, which meant no quarrels, no telling off. No rows between him and Tadci.

Jaywick was an enthralling place for children, a typical seaside shanty town. It was built in rows of holiday shacks and bungalows, with brightly coloured façades covered in climbing roses and honeysuckle. As soon as you set eyes on the place, you knew you'd have fun there.

The people were interesting to me, too. The girl staying opposite us, a creature of mouth-watering glamour, was taking a quick break from her job in ENSA, entertaining the troops overseas. The family of the regimental sergeant major, next door but one, came from Hackney and spoke with the strongest cockney accents we had ever heard. The small granddaughter of the refined lady who lived in a sea-front chalet at the end of our road developed a crush on me and followed me everywhere. She was enchantingly pretty in the English way, with a long blonde fringe and hair which had been allowed to grow down to her small bottom. When I have little girls of my own, one day, I want them to look like this, I said to myself. And they did.

Tadci died when we returned to London. We took his body back to Wales and buried him in Bettws, alongside my granny. The funeral was spectacular. 'You could walk on the top hats,' my aunties said in awe. 'Everybody loved Uncle John.'

So it was back to my father being the only man in the house. It was never easy with him, but when my periods started the beatings stopped. I simply didn't react to him in the same way. I didn't goad him any more. I just avoided him altogether. An incident occurred once while my mother and sister were out shopping and I was in the house alone with him. He chose to take a bath in the middle of the afternoon. This was strange, because Friday night was bath night; we all shared the same water, one after the other, to save money. Nobody had a whole bathful of water to themselves. I heard the taps running, then I heard my father splashing and singing. Next his voice called my name, he shouted for me to bring the soap from the kitchen. I ran into the garden even though I was meant to be in doing my homework. My mother returned. The danger had passed, although I couldn't quite say what the danger would have been.

Now he began a much more wounding campaign of critical hostility which had even further-reaching effects, undermining my confidence over my talents and my appearance. He sneered at my paintings, he argued with my mother when she reported what the art teacher had said at the school's open day: that I was a gifted pupil and should go to art school for further study, and I should become an artist; it was my obvious vocation. My mother and father quarrelled violently over it. I used to creep to the top of the landing in my nightie to listen. But when my Tadci died my father's attention was diverted from me for the next few years. Tadci had left money for my mother, which meant that my father could give up his despised job on the ambulances now the war had ended.

It was 1946, Hiroshima had been bombed, the war was

over. All our lives would be changed from now on. We left the suburbs and moved to Paddington. This was to be the start of our many moves.

In the next five years, my parents moved five times and we had the same number of homes. The first move was the most exciting, from the so-called safety of the seedy suburbs into the heart of the much seedier centre of Paddington, which even then had one of the highest crime-rates in the country.

And it was doubly exciting for us now, because we no longer lived in an ordinary house. We lived in a business. My parents had bought a hotel in Sussex Gardens, which they were in the process of turning into a profitable bed and breakfast and residents establishment, to catch all ends of the market.

Paddington was then very much as it is today, shabby and tawdry but with a stimulating street-life and a sense of the unexpected. Sally and I thought it was wonderful, our first experience of cosmopolitan life! It was full of *men*, for a start, as opposed to mere boys. Men who stared at you with bedroom eyes as you waited at the bus stop in your school uniform. We turned, both of us, overnight into *femmes fatales*. We dispensed with wearing the vests that we'd always worn under our brassières for warmth and modesty, and helped each other yank up our bra-straps to turn ourselves into real Sweater Girls like Lana Turner, whose photograph was in my latest *Picturegoer*. Her titties were so high they looked like a double chin. Our shoulders tried to tell us that the leverage was over-steep, but we took no notice of the weals caused by the cutting-in of our straps. We wore wads of cotton wool or lint to ease the strain instead.

My mother was bewildered. She said that if we turned sharpish to talk to somebody they could be in danger of losing an eye. We took no notice. How could she know that 'the prow of a boat' look was in fashion? The big talking point in London was the towering photograph of Jane Russell's breasts obliterating the skies over Piccadilly Circus, advertising her forthcoming film, *The Outlaw*. The caption was already a catchword and we made sure it applied to us: MEAN! MOODY! MAGNIFICENT! We lived so near the centre of everything in Sussex Gardens, that we could walk, and did, to see all these treats. A real step up the ladder of sophistication!

Our first resident, full board, was a Scottish medical student from St Mary's Hospital in Praed Street around the corner. He was what my mother called 'a well-connected boy', with affluent friends who soon clamoured to come and live in our place, too. Then their sisters arrived.

One of these, a ravishing girl called Heather, with the eyes of a doe and the legs of a colt, had the most extraordinary retinue of male admirers. It was a full-time job, my father complained, answering the door and receiving the flowers, the chocolates, the party invites, sent by her swains. But one, more than the others, seemed to be her favourite. This was a gaspingly handsome lad called Christopher Lee.

Since ours was a moral house, unlike next door which made a fortune letting out to 'tarts' on a ten-minute basis – tainted money, my mother said scathingly – Heather was not allowed to take members of the opposite sex up to her room. Instead she had to entertain in the large sitting room downstairs. Sal and I used to take it in turns to carry tea, or coffee and biscuits in to the courting couple. Alcohol wasn't allowed. We were always disappointed not to find them canoodling. They sat, chastely apart, on our cretonne-covered settee. My mother had made the loose covers for this herself, with matching cushions and curtains, and was very proud of her machining. She made us examine the settee after these social occasions for signs of spilled tea. There never were any, and you wouldn't have seen them anyway since the pattern on the fabric was a dismal confection of autumn leaves. Little did we know that this same Christopher Lee would enter our dreams as Dracula in later years, the undisputed star of all those juicy Hammer Horror films.

That summer, Sally and I travelled to Wales all on our own for a holiday. We stayed at Barbara's in her absence. She had flown off with Auntie May for a trip to Switzerland in an aeroplane! Things were looking up for all of us. We travelled on to Porthcawl to stay with our Auntie Catherine, the wife of Tadci's older brother. This was the brother who had walked out of the house fifty years before and never come back.

'One of Interpol's few unsolved mysteries, my brother,' Tadci would muse. 'They had the police of five continents on the look-out, but he's still on their missing persons' file. My feeling is that he went because he couldn't stand Catherine's mania for tidiness.'

While we were at Auntie Catherine's we had a telegram from our father. Our mother had been rushed to hospital, haemorrhaging with a burst stomach ulcer. She was on the critical list and we must come home immediately.

Barbara had just got back from Switzerland and had planned to return to London with us. She joined our train at Bridgend Station. We were glad of her company to cheer us up. She was as irrepressible as usual.

'Our mother could be dying,' Sally said reprovingly.

'My father already has,' Barbara laughed back. There was never an answer for Barbara, she always had the last word.

My mother wasn't dying but she couldn't continue in the business, the doctors said. It was all too much for her frail strength. My father put the hotel up for sale and found an immediate purchaser. To my joy we prepared to pack up and move back to Wales, to Pontycymmer, back to my granny's beloved house. There my mother could recuperate and my father would decide what direction he wanted to take now. Sal and I would be able to see more of Barbara. I would attend the grammar school in Pontycymmer while Sally prepared to go off to college. Everything was working out fine. How lives can be totally transformed!

My best pal was still Gwyneth. I was fourteen now and she was sixteen. We shared every confidence, every hope and fear, except I didn't tell her about what I'd got up to in Mr Hill's room. And I didn't breathe a word about my father. I'd never tell anyone about that. Gwyneth was doing as brilliantly at school as ever, but there was trouble at home. Her family didn't agree with her going to university. She was needed in the house to help her mother, who was ailing under the strain of all the males still living at home. Her brothers had plotted to keep her there by introducing her to the colliery Romeo, a young miner with a growing reputation for drink and women.

Things started to change between us. She was no longer available to me; she was now full of Billy, this young miner. We giggled together in the same old way, but our times were snatched. She was with him whenever she wasn't helping her mother. But we did have one good session up the mountain before I left. She took me to a place, high on the hillside, up past the farm and beyond the brook where we used to paddle as children and found the dead sheep crawling with maggots, to a secluded glen where she went with Billy. Where they did unmentionable things to each other. Really rude and daring things, which involved taking bits of clothing off. I didn't want to hear. I knew that Gwyneth had never been a chapel girl, so she didn't know these things were forbidden and wrong, that they were the devil's work. It was not for me to tell her. I sensed she wouldn't listen, even if I did. She seemed caught in a kind of rapture. She didn't talk of her future any more, only of Billy and their lovemaking.

I had only spent one term at the grammar school in Pontycymmer, and was just rejoicing fully at being back in the valley with all my aunties, friends and family, not to mention the mountain, when my father decided to return to London. He couldn't 'settle', my mother explained. He was missing the bright lights of London. It was where he felt most alive. Sally and I both had boyfriends, but we had to bid them farewell. Hers was a college student, Elved, and mine was in his second year at Cardiff Art School. He was a painter called Peter Morris, whose father owned the garage in the middle of Ffaldau Square. When Peter saw all my sketch books he encouraged me to think about going to art school, myself. I'd always known that this was my future, but now it seemed like becoming a reality, not a pipe-dream. He was the first art student that I had met and his support fired my determination. If he could do it, so could I. I would apply for a scholarship, as he had done.

Our Tadci Thomas, with whom we had become very close, as he was the only grandparent left now, was sad to see us departing so soon. He shook his head when I told him.

'Your father has the roaming spirit, Molly. Always discontented, always on the move. The grass is greener in the next field, that's his belief. It springs from frustration. He was a clever boy, you know, but he's never found his niche in life. Nor will he at this rate. Pity.'

We embarked on a disastrous move to a suburb of London even more dismal than Dollis Hill. This was a real step backwards, socially speaking, for Sally and me. The ghetto was called Southfields. My mother referred to it as Almost Wimbledon, when people asked. Again we moved into a thriving business, a newsagent and tobacconist's, with a sweet and chocolate counter which ran the length of the frontage. We were to live above and behind this shabby emporium, wedged as it was between a greengrocer's and a dairy. My heart sank when I contemplated what was to be my bedroom, a boxroom overlooking the street with barely enough space for my bed. It was all right for Sally, she was going off to a smart domestic science college in Eccleston Square. This was my father's idea, not hers. He said it would be useful for the family for her to have this training for when he opened another hotel. She'd be *au fait* with the catering. He even drew the frontage of this swanky palace, right down to the geraniums in the window-boxes. Pie-in-the-sky plans. But at least it got her away from home, she said. Set her free to take on the world. She could always see the brighter side of everything.

I started at yet another school, one which was definitely not to my liking. It was an all-girls school, not a boy in sight! This was the first non-coed school that I had been to except for Ffaldau Girls Infants in Pontycymmer. The headmistress of Mayfields Grammar School for Girls on Putney's West Hill was a strict disciplinarian, legendary in scholastic circles for the splendid prowess of her pupils. I wrote vituperative letters to Barbara and Gwyneth telling them how she looked like a wrinkled walnut. How I was hauled to her study every single day of the school week for being late, and the length of the lines that I was forced to write out for punishment.

The reason for my lateness was that my parents had given me the heaviest of the newspaper delivery rounds to do before breakfast. It always took me far longer than I could have imagined, far longer than the other four paper boys, who were more familiar with the roads and houses than I was. I was paid for doing this work at a lower rate than the boys because my father claimed I was still a trainee, which didn't strike me as fair.

One morning, dreading another punishment from the headmistress, I put a spurt on at a busy crossing. A speeding car, not slowing down as it should have done at the junction, caught the back wheel of my bicycle. I was flung to the ground and the base of my skull hit the edge of the kerb. The car didn't stop. I was left unconscious in the gutter until an ambulance was called.

When my parents visited me in hospital they walked straight past the bed. I was unrecognizable to them, my face was so swollen. I had sustained a crack to the cranium which would cause me migraines for years. I was lucky to be alive.

We rarely went to chapel now; the business had taken over. This was God's punishment, my mother said. When I was better we should find a Welsh chapel and start going again.

When I came out of hospital, I lay for months in slow recovery, in my dismal cell above the shop, listening to the exchange of coins and the ping of the till. This was my mother's favourite sound. 'Money mends everything, Moll. You remember that.'

As a special treat, so she thought, she'd bring the day's takings up and empty it over my bedspread. Coins spilled everywhere, notes rustled like dry leaves.

'Learn to love the feel. Make money your friend, instead of your enemy, then you'll always have plenty,' she'd smile triumphantly. 'My mother always told me that. She always said that she wouldn't be surprised if I had business in my blood. But she died before it came into fruition. She'd have been so proud of me now, your granny.'

I looked at her from my convalescent bed. She was like a little girl sometimes, at other times like an old, old woman. The mood swings were becoming more manic.

But for the moment she was mostly up, dangerously so. I raged in adolescent resentment at both my parents. Didn't it occur to them that the reason I was in this bed and missing school at a most crucial time, with my matriculation examination coming up in the following year, was simply because she and my father had wanted to save money by using me for the early delivery round instead of a boy? That five-thirty in the morning was too soon to get up and do this kind of work before school? I knew perfectly well that my mother still wanted me to do well and go on to further education, but my father would have been just as happy for me to leave school and work in the shop. He was already asking if I was well enough to give them a hand. I wasn't. My vision was still impaired. I couldn't even see well enough to paint and draw. All I wanted to do was to lie in bed and eat chocolate, of which there was a ready supply downstairs. My weight spiralled to ten stone. I was fifteen with no place to go. The fun had gone from my life.

I also had plenty of time to think about the events leading up to my accident. On the morning of the accident, my parents had told me that Gwyneth had committed suicide. I had not been aware that she was on my mind, but she must have been. Perhaps I wanted to join her, who knows what the subconscious tells us?

My parents hadn't known how to break the news to me; they didn't tell me for a whole week after they'd heard. She'd had to leave school and marry when she'd become pregnant. Billy had taken to beating her, drunk, after the pub every night. He hadn't allowed any books in the house because, like her family, he viewed all education as a waste of time, said she was better off without it and he didn't want her getting any ideas that she could ever get back into it.

She'd given birth and, in post-natal depression and despair over her crushed career hopes, she'd gassed herself in the kitchen after putting the baby to bed. She was dead by the time Billy got home, drunk as usual. She was seventeen. Another part of my girlhood was lost forever.

We didn't stay long in this shop. My mother became seriously ill again. She gashed her hand on a metal toffee-breaker. The wound became infected and she was confined to her bed with a dangerously high temperature as the poison spread. It was time for me to vacate my sickroom and get on with a spot of work, my father suggested. I helped out in the shop, slowly at first, but my mind couldn't seem to concentrate on what change to give. We got embroiled with the police when one of the paper boys was caught absconding with a massive amount of cash which was due for the bank.

Suddenly the business went sour. My father said it had never been lucky and it was time to move. He started looking for a new place, another business like this, but more manageable, without a paper round.

We moved to Streatham in 1949, the year I passed my matriculation. If anything I hated Sunnyhill Road, a side street off Streatham High Road, even more than I loathed Southfields. But there was one compensation which transformed my life more than I could ever have imagined, so it didn't really matter where I lived. It wouldn't have made any difference to my elation. I won a major county award to go to art school for five years, at the end of which time I would have a degree. I would be an arts graduate, qualified to teach, which is what my mother wanted.

My father came with me to the interview at Goldsmith's School of Art. We travelled awkwardly together on the tram from Streatham, not knowing how to converse. There was a long line of applicants outside the principal's office. No one else had a parent with them. The principal talked like Mr Hill, kindly, courteously and was compli-mentary about my paintings, the very ones my father despised so much. I prayed to God to be accepted, crossing

85

my fingers behind my back the entire time. I passed the interview and was given a place at the college but all the way home on the bus my father could speak of nothing but my ineptitude in answering the questions. He said that I sounded like a kitchen maid, common and stupid. I must learn to talk properly if I was to be accepted in the circles that I would now be moving in. The best thing to do was never to open my mouth.

He was taunting me, trying to make me rise to the bait so that we would start quarrelling on the very day we should have been celebrating. There were no congratulations at all from him. Only from my mother, the neighbours, and the rest of the family. But I didn't care about him any more; he couldn't hurt me now; I was leaving him behind and entering a different world. I was to be allowed to paint every day of my life from now on. No one could take that away from me. I stared out of the window of the tram all the way home, my heart full of happiness and gratitude to God, aware that this unreachability of mine was enraging my father even further. By the end of the ride people were looking at him, he was shouting so loud. The conductor asked him to pipe down or get off.

My relationship with my mother had become very intense lately. More so than it had ever been. I only understand now the full extent of her dependency on pills. Uppers for depression, barbiturates for sleeplessness. A vicious circle. It explains her desperate mood swings, manic to suicidal. Her irrational anxieties and panic attacks. Her hysterical reactions to normal mishaps. It explains how sometimes coming home from school I would have to search the small house for her, not knowing what I would find: her unconscious, drugged, on the sofa; a note scrawled with the message that she'd taken the train to Wales; her sobbing on the kitchen table for no accountable reason, the place a total mess. Or, worse and deeply mortifying, a painted stranger dressed up in gaudy colours waving frantically at the school gates to take me 'up West' to 'tootle' around the shops.

The tootling was exactly the same every time, involving a horrendous traipse around the couture gown department of super-snooty Harrods store. I would be perched on a gilt chair watching my mother pirouetting in absurdly priced garments quite outside any normal purse. Supercilious assistants, sneering to each other behind her back, but not mine, smirked as my mother pretended to choose between each dress.

'It's the child I feel sorry for,' I heard one of them whisper. I was tied to my chair with deeply defensive humiliation. I loved my mother and couldn't bear the criticism. She wasn't doing any actual harm, she wasn't breaking the law. Why not humour the poor creature in her pitiable delusions of grandeur?

My mother was wary of what she'd heard about the bohemian life. Our neighbours, all working-class sceptics, had warned her about what could happen to a young girl among artists. Artists who, according to the tabloids which they all read, pursued the ethics of 'free love'. My mother had always stressed the value of a girl's 'good name'. She took it upon herself to corner me with moral platitudes. She quoted Gwyneth as an example of what could happen when a girl allowed men to play fast and loose, when a girl cheapened herself. When she, above all, meddled with men of a lower stratum, meaning to say men without education and advancement at the forefront of their minds. The only males I should bother with from now on, if any, she said, were to be of the 'professional class'. Otherwise all this striving would be a waste of time – this sacrifice that she and my father were making to give me a further education, instead of sending me to work like other families at our level to get the benefit of the extra income.

I was a virgin. No boy had been allowed anything other than a kiss. My mother insisted that I must never be alone with a male fellow-student. If one of them invited me back to his room, I was on no account to accept the invitation.

I caught sight of the art school Lothario on my first day. He was well-built, swaggering, confident, older. His hair was blond and curly, clinging to his scalp and the back of his neck like a Greek statue. He could have been Apollo, a golden-skinned god. He had a smouldering stare, and a chiselled profile. His full mouth turned up at each end in sensual invitation. His trousers were taut over well-muscled thighs, and there was a becoming bulge to the left of centre. All the new girls in my year sighed as he sauntered past in the canteen. He was obviously conscious of the effect he created. Every female craved acknowledgement, but his blue eyes singled me out, with such a blatant message that I blushed beneath my clothes. I was shocked by my instant response and the excitement springing up in my blood.

'Wow! You've made a conquest,' said the girl next to me. 'But beware of that one, he means business!'

His name was Rupert. He'd done his army service, which meant that he was in his early twenties already. I was barely seventeen; he seemed absolutely ancient to me, representing everything worldly and desirable. Forbidden fruit. I knew instinctively that my mother would mistrust him, that my father would hate him on sight, that my grandparents if they'd been alive, not to mention my aunties, would all warn me off. My interest increased, knowing that he was trouble of the worst kind. I was reminded of Gwyneth and her glowing face when she spoke of Billy. Now I began to understand. Though he didn't speak like Mr Hill or his son, his conversation was peppered with sophisticated American slang. He was an illustator, as opposed to a painter or a sculptor, meaning to say he was not a Fine Artist but one of the 'commercial crew'. This disappointed me, because, in addition to the social snobbery of my parents, which was now deeply ingrained in me, I had swiftly assimilated an art school intellectual snobbery. I understood that anything that smacked of the commercial was common. It was not the route I'd be wise to follow in my climb.

But my companion was right about Rupert meaning business. I was innocent putty in his professional seducer's fingers. Every time I emerged from a class he appeared in the corridor. Each tea-break in the canteen he happened to be lounging at the next table. He was surrounded by beautiful, drawling girls hanging on his every word. The sight of it turned my stomach and I tried not to look in his direction, instead engrossing myself in the conversation of my group. But his appearance was so compelling, his animal magnetism so absolute that my eyes were drawn back. He was ready, waiting with a predator's patience. He smiled at me through the crowd. I was stunned by the brilliance of that smile. What an invitation! What warmth! My heart jolted painfully against my ribs. It felt like falling head-over-heels in love.

His room was conveniently around the corner. I repeatedly refused his first few invitations to come for tea, explaining naively what I had promised my mother. He laughed for so long I though he'd never stop. I didn't like being laughed at and told him so. I walked away from him in the corridor, understanding that he would follow and try to placate me, try to please. I liked this game of sexual cat-and-mouse. Although it was new to me, I seemed fully at home with the moves. It was as if I had been here many times already. I was all set to win. And, I did win. I captivated him, to the envy of all the other girls. Their envy spurred me on, bolstered my ego, made me feel less of an inferior.

I was not an inferior, not as far as the work was concerned. Not in terms of energy and application and a determination to draw and paint as well as I possibly could. These qualities, of dogged persistence, of total dedication to the point of obsession, were as important as raw talent. That's what each of the tutors told us. And I had them. I had everything. Everything except class. I was common: the only grammar school scholarship girl in the group. The only girl in my year who hadn't gone to a posh private school, who didn't regard this time spent studying art as some kind of extension of finishing school. The only girl with a clear working–class accent. Willesden Welsh. My father was right. I was better off keeping my mouth shut.

My agony, and it was a kind of open-wound torture, this extreme self-consciousness over my humble origins, led me into aggressive behaviour from the beginning. I was on the defensive. I was shy. I was terrified that I would be made fun of, like my mother in Harrods. From that moment I became hyper-sensitive to criticism, reluctant to accept advice on any level, thinking I knew best. I was turning into a loner, although that might have been difficult for an onlooker to perceive because I was surrounded by people. I was the centre of the group. My raw vitality, my vivid gypsy looks, inherited from my mother, my irreverent humour in the face of authority, these had always ensured ready companionship. But the inner child was lonely, displaced, ill at ease.

Travelling through the dingy London streets, I yearned for the Welsh mountains. I missed Gwyneth and the long letters we used to write to each other. Faced with the open sexual challenge of Rupert, I was petrified, preferring the safety of sex among Mr Hill's suits and shirts. I ached for my granny and for my grandfather, for the serene reassurance of that part of my childhood. But when I thought of them I remembered the parable of the talents. How God-given gifts, like my ability as an artist, must not be squandered. And I was flooded with resolve to do the best I could, work harder than anyone else, be earlier, end up on top. Those were my decisions in that first week. Those, and the decision to capture Rupert, the prized idol. Win him ahead of all the horse-riding, yellow-haired, elocutioned, upper-class ingenues, with whom I was in such impossible social competition.

As soon as Rupert shut the door of his flat, he started in on me. He kissed me savagely on the mouth, his tongue thrust down until it was tickling my tonsils. He hurled me on to the bed and plunged his fist up my petticoats into my knickers. His middle finger and fore had speared me before I'd even drawn breath. He was strong, our struggle was unequal from the start. I screamed in agony from the pain; nothing had ever been inserted up there before. He clamped a hand over my mouth to keep me quiet.

I lay there crying. He looked at me contemptuously and told me to go and clean up. I stumbled to the lavatory, bleeding and panicking. What would I tell my mother? How could I tell her anything, for I had disobeyed her by visiting a man's room! He had broken something inside me; I was hazy about what it was exactly, but I was certain that now I could no longer claim to be a virgin. No one would ever want to marry me . . .

I returned to his room, after washing my hands. The soap was Imperial Leather. Throughout my life, whenever I smelled that soap, I would relive Rupert and his fingers; I would feel a sharp stab in my crotch.

He was kind to me now, dried my tears and told me that the bleeding was the start of my periods. I said they had finished a week before, but he explained that when girls are kissed passionately for the first time they often start bleeding. I believed him. I was relieved because now I didn't have to tell my mother.

I refused to visit his room again, though, so we took to roaming the dense undergrowth on the far edges of the college grounds, hand in hand, hugging each other a lot. I liked the other art students seeing this, the romance was high-profile stuff. I was Rupert's girl and it felt good. He told me that he had fallen in love with me and wanted to marry me. I was thrilled, but still didn't tell my mother. We kissed all the time, but he didn't interfere with my clothing, which made me feel safer. Then he informed me that he was actually engaged to another girl, a typist, who was expecting his baby, but now he was going to break up with her after their five years together. She would have to get rid of the baby. Because of me. I was scared by this talk. Things were going too fast! I didn't want a baby to die because of me. He coaxed me to his room again to talk it out in private. I hung back as he put his key in the door. We could both hear a girl screaming from the top of the stairs inside. It was a bloodcurdling sound, bowel-churning words.

'You want me to kill our baby, you bastard! OK! Just you watch this! I'll kill it and me at the same time! We'll both clear out of your life to make way for that precious bitch!'

The door swung open. Rupert and I watched in horror as the figure of a young woman with a swollen stomach hurled herself head-first down the long flight of steps, collapsing, to all intents and purposes *dead*, in a crumpled heap at the bottom. Rupert was galvanized into action. He whirled on me. 'See what you've done! This is your responsibility. If I hadn't fallen for you none of this would have happened – quick, run for a doctor, get an ambulance, tell them it's suicide. They'll come quicker than if you say it's an accident!'

I was frozen to the spot, paralysed. I thought my heart would explode. He saw my state and slapped me viciously across the cheek. My mouth filled with blood; he had broken a tooth with the force of his blow. I understood this language, the language of love, of stolen pleasure and punishment, and I did as I was told. I was responsible. I had played my part in this grisly scenario, in this tragedy. As I played it in Mr Hill's death, and Gwyneth's. I could have told Gwyneth that sex was the devil's work and that he would exact his price, but I didn't and she wasn't to know, not being a chapel girl. So she died as she deserved to.

Rupert's girl didn't die, but the baby did. The girl almost died too. They took her to hospital in the ambulance the doctor had ordered once I'd found him. I was so hysterical when I knocked on his door that he said I needed treatment, too, as I was clearly suffering from acute shock. But I ran away once I'd given him Rupert's address. I got on the bus and went home and sobbed to my mother; all of it came out. The next day she came up to see the principal of the art school and Rupert was expelled by the afternoon.

The principal summoned me to his hallowed chambers. I could barely knock I was shivering so much. He gave me a cup of tea which I couldn't drink, I was so afraid of spilling it on the carpet. He was kindness itself. He said that Rupert would have been expelled before but they'd given him another chance. Other parents had complained. Other new girls had been seduced, I wasn't the first. Then he wanted to know what had happened in the room in detail. I said that nothing had happened and I stuck to my story. But I couldn't look him in the eye because it was a bald untruth. And, though I wasn't going to the chapel as

93

regularly as I had in Wales, I knew that God was disappointed by my lie.

I was still praying then. I still asked for things and generally got them from God, but this incident caused a wedge between us. I'd been 'known' by a man, by his fingers at least, and I hadn't anyone to tell. I hadn't told my mother, not that part. I hadn't had many secrets before, only Mr Hill's room. Oh, and my uncle's thumb. And, of course, Gwyneth's secrets up the mountain with Billy. Now they were beginning to pile up.

But my first year as an art student changed me in more ways than one. Now I was in a different world, the world of art and all that that implied. I was transported by the work, by life drawing from the nude, by the study of architecture, anatomy, pictorial composition and perspective, modelling in clay and plaster-casting. I arrived early for everything and was the last to leave at night, taking advantage of any of the life drawing or portrait classes which were available to evening students.

I'd chosen stone carving as my craft to give me the feel of what it might be like to specialize in sculpture, although I knew in my heart that I truly wanted to be a painter. I had two years in which to make my decision. After that I would have a further two years' study until I sat my National Diploma in Design, my NDD, which would give me the equivalent of a university degree. A graduate, no less. But more importantly to me, a bona fide artist!

Since I was a scholarship student I was required to teach at the end of my training as a way of repaying the state. This was normal procedure then, so I would have to take a final teacher training year, which would give me, if I passed, my Art Teacher's Diploma, the ATD.

I couldn't wait to get out of bed every morning to embark on the complicated jurney which took me from Streatham to New Cross. I had to change buses at the Oval, or I could walk all the way up to Streatham Hill

Station and take a train. I was used to long journeys, so it didn't bother me too much. I liked looking out of the window, pondering on how magical my life had suddenly become.

The business with Rupert had shocked me to my very foundations, but it had made me realize that the opportunity I had been given to explore and extend my artistic capabilities must now be valued for what it was; nothing must come between me and my search for success. From now on romantic dalliances must take second place to my studies; if I allowed myself to venture into those treacherous areas ever again.

I was seeing everything with new eyes now, as I was being trained to. The drabness of my surroundings was gradually being transformed for me. I saw just how many actual colours there were in a grey paving slab, and that when a pigeon strutted on that slab, those same shades were re-echoed: the greys were actually amethyst, a blend of turquoise and slate blue, and the softest hint of pale heather.

I studied the faces of my fellow passengers, the parchment skin of the old man asleep opposite me on the train. The shadows around his eyes were made up of a fierce magenta, hollowing into an olive green.

When we were shown lecture slides of work by Van Gogh and Gauguin, and all the French Impressionists, I understood for the first time that now I was part of a privileged élite. I could see the world with their colours. Everything suddenly made visual sense. It was as if I had been given an extraordinary pair of spectacles and I'd never again see the world in any other way than this. Everything shimmered, and danced in a glorious cacophony of colour. This was a fruition of the glimpse I had been given in the garden of the convalescence home. Now that promise was being realized.

I didn't know then that God had a further treat in store

for me, that He was about to send me a soul mate, a kindred spirit, with whom to share my creative excitement. Barbara was coming to live with us! When Barbara left school, after passing her matriculation, Auntie May sent her to Bridgend Technical College to learn secretarial skills. While she was there she had become more preoccupied with the art course on offer. Now she wanted to come to London and become a full-time art student, just like me.

I was lonely without Sal; I missed having a pal in the house, especially since my mother and father spent every second in the shop. We opened early to catch the smokers on their way into work, and shut late to catch the peppermint trade, boozers on their way home from the corner pub, trying to mask their alcohol fumes from the wife.

Goldsmith's, which I'd only gone to because my Auntie Dilys went to the teacher's training department there, was full. So Barbara applied and was accepted at Camberwell College of Arts and Crafts, another good place which was actually nearer Streatham than New Cross. We travelled together in the mornings, and she just got off the bus twenty minutes earlier than me.

Trouble sprang up between Barbara and my father from the very start. We didn't stock her brand of cigarettes, the Russian Sobranies. There seemed no call in Streatham for such exotica, though it was clearly within my father's capabilities to order them specially for her. He refused. He tried to wean her on to Woodbines, untipped, which he smoked himself. She said loud and clear that she wouldn't be caught dead with such common things between her lips, that her entire life up until then had been devoted to style and it was bad enough having to reside in such a dreary hovel with such a tyrant, let alone adopt his sordid little habits.

I listened, enthralled, to this exchange, crouched at the

top of the landing, banished from the scene because it would be bad for me to hear such defiance, since I had a large quota of it myself. Her words rang loud and clear. Since the successful experiment with her dentures, it was now just about possible for anybody to understand Barbara's words. My father could be in no confusion as to their meaning. I heard my mother burst into tears. We were back to the daily dramas of life with my Tadci in residence. It seemed that my father could not live peaceably with anyone, I thought bitterly. I knew that Barbara wouldn't last long here.

She lasted a term, during which time cold war raged on an hourly basis. One Saturday morning, when Barbara was with her Camberwell fellow-students arranging a group show, and I was out shopping with my mother, she broke down at the haberdashery counter of Arding and Hobbs in Clapham Junction. She said she couldn't go on, the strife was wearing away at her nerves. My father was unliveable with and would continue to be so until Auntie May came up and found Barbara alternative accommodation.

I was outraged. 'You can't turn Barbara out,' I shouted. 'She's deformed. You can't turn a deformed person out on the streets. And she's a cousin. We love her. She's family . . .'

My mother collapsed and lay in a crumpled heap on the floor in the midst of the Saturday-morning shoppers. The haberdashery assistants hurried forward with a chair, chastising me with dark looks.

'Does she need an ambulance?'

'I shouldn't think so,' I replied coldly. I'd seen enough of this before. I'd had dramas like this with my mother all through my life. But now she was making Barbara the victim of her own ineptitude over my father and his bullying behaviour. She couldn't stand up to him, even in the defence of someone with no neck.

I was disgusted and wanted to leave home in protest, to go and share a room somewhere with Barbara, just the two of us. But it wasn't to be. Auntie May came to collect Barbara and settle her in digs near her college, a procedure which she carried out in strained and tight-lipped silence, to my mother's and my great distress. Things were never the same between the two families again. My father forbade any friendship to continue between Barbara and myself. He said to see her behind his back would be a gross disloyalty. There was no fear of that from now on, not in London, because he sold up the shop, yanked me away from Goldsmith's Art School and moved us all down to Brighton.

I was desperately disappointed to be leaving Goldsmith's. Now that the business with Rupert was safely behind me, I'd settled in wonderfully well. My work had improved out of all recognition. I had praise heaped on my head in every department and blossomed because of it. I was much in demand as a model. Members of the staff, painters and fellow students, were always asking me to sit for them. But I would never remove my clothes, I'd only agree to portraits.

Bridget Riley was the first to ask me. She was considered an extremely gifted student even then; held in awe, especially by me. She had two sizzling shades of lipstick, which she wore with great aplomb. One was sizzling pink and the other a startling sherbet orange. She was as slim as a boy and wore her hair cropped. Though the rest of us dressed in trailing skirts, with tightly tied belts, she sported trousers and straight-cut sweaters. She would have made a marvellous model for Coco Chanel, but it was a look that I was unfamiliar with in a girl at that time. Certainly nobody looked like that in Streatham, let alone Pontycymmer.

One day she stopped me as I was running along a corridor. 'Slow down,' she said. 'You're always running.'

I blushed, that was the effect she had on me. I was like a silly schoolgirl being reprimanded by her favourite prefect. But at least she'd noticed me, my inner voice whispered. I couldn't think why. I looked very much like a run-of-the-mill art student at that time. A pastiche of a Degas ballet girl, with flat pumps, a long fringe and a pony tail. I wore nothing on my lips then, only Vaseline, and a smudge of black crayon around my eyes. I considered make up to be trivial, tarty and obvious, except the lipstick that Bridget used, which I found enchanting.

'I'd like you to sit for me.'

'What?' Nobody had asked me this before. What did she mean, 'sit'?

'I want to paint you,' she said impatiently. 'I'll meet you on Thursday afternoon in the large studio, at two o'clock. Don't be late.' She walked away.

I was petrified. How could I tell her that I had an anatomy lesson at two o'clock on Thursday? Never mind being late for her – what about my tutor? Since the Rupert episode I hadn't missed a single class. I was never late. How could I blatantly miss a class now, just because Bridget Riley had snapped her fingers! But I didn't say this. I meekly turned up on the dot and sat while I was painted in semi-profile, seething in resentment all the while, with a dread in the pit of my stomach that the tutor, any tutor, might stroll through the studio and see me there, doing nothing except furthering a fellow pupil's studies.

My worst fears were realized when Mr Gardner, the principal, wandered past.

'Hello, young lady,' he smiled at me.

'Don't distract the model, please!' Bridget said sharply.

I was astonished. Did she know who she was talking to?

'Carry on,' he waved a genial arm. 'You've caught the

line of her neck beautifully, excellent work.' He smiled at me again and winked.

I was even more astounded. Where was the expected reprimand? More surprises were to come. The tutor whose class I was meant to be attending strolled by moments later. 'Ah, there you are. This is better, more fun sitting for your portrait than listening to me waffling on, eh?' He paused to study the painting, then stared at me. 'You must sit for me when you have time.'

Bridget groaned after he'd gone. 'They'll all be after you now, but remember that I saw you first.'

They were. Clifford Frith, the grandson of William Powell Frith (whose painting *Derby Day* was my father's favourite in the National Gallery), asked me to come to the studio in his house at Camberwell Green to pose for a full-length portrait. He painted me in a plush armchair in which an old tramp had posed the previous day. Within a week I was covered in flea-bites. My mother stopped me going again.

I sat regularly for a portrait class every Wednesday evening at the college where as many as forty students drew and painted me for two and a half hours. At first I was shy and couldn't stop giggling, but soon I became used to sitting still for extended periods and allowing my mind to float off as I had as a child in chapel. It probably sharpened my imagination, teaching me the first principles of the meditation which was to succour me later on, when pressures had become intolerable. In addition I was paid as a professional model, which made me feel less indolent and guilty for not going to my evening class. I never told my parents about this modelling. I knew instinctively that they would disapprove.

I met Quentin Crisp in his capacity as a professional model during that year. He was the most celebrated of the models, famed for his theatrical poses, his fuchsia hair, and his camp behaviour. He was my first male nude.

'What a tragedy you failed to treasure those early drawings of me, my dear,' he lamented years later when we'd become good friends. 'Drawings by you in your early-blossoming talent of me at the height of my physical beauty.'

I saw Barbara once before we made the move down to Brighton, which the doctor had recommended for my father's chronic chest condition. It obviously hadn't occurred to him that it would be as easy for my father to smoke as many cigarettes there as he'd ever smoked, and that we'd be selling them in our new shop in Brighton just as we had in London.

Barbara made the trip over to Streatham and waited until she saw my father go out before popping in to see us. I was flabbergasted by her appearance. She looked absolutely stunning. She had bleached her waist-length hair corn-yellow. She was brown, tanned and healthy-looking, which she boasted came from a bottle. Her green eyes swam mischievously in a smoky setting of grey-greens and turquoise shadows. Her garment was like Joseph's coat of many colours.

'You look marvellous!' I gasped, scared that my father might return and start a scene. He'd go berserk to see her standing there in his shop with the impudence to look so glamorous, so at ease, so utterly happy. 'What happened?' I gestured to her overall effect.

'Sex,' she whispered wickedly, so my mother wouldn't overhear. 'I'm living with someone. His name's Herman. He's the best painter at Camberwell, everybody says so. We're getting married, but for now we're living together.'

They returned, at the end of their studies, Barbara and Herman, to live with Auntie May who had moved to Bridgend. The wonderful haven in Pontycymmer had gone. But even if they had continued to live there, it would not have been the same as it was before. Auntie

May never forgave us for turning Barbara out and we never shed the guilt for doing so.

We moved to Brighton and I was accepted at Brighton College of Art. I mourned Goldsmith's for many months, and the loss of everything that I'd built up there. Brighton felt like taking a step back, somehow. All the students there were aiming to get to London, and here I was leaving it before I'd properly got started. Upheaval, as usual, and all because of my father. The only compensation was the sea. I'd never lived by the coast before, and it supplied what I'd been missing when I left the mountains in Wales. Now at least I had the elements, the raw elements, back in my life again.

For it seemed to me that I was losing everyone that I had ever felt close to, and now Sally, my own sister, was about to get married. She'd left her studies at the domestic science college and taken a smart secretarial course instead, to make sure, my mother said, that she wouldn't be without qualifications. To my joy, when we moved down to Brighton, Sally came with us. She'd done extremely well in the working world. Her secretarial career had taken off. She had worked at the House of Commons, in parliament, no less, for an MP, and in Brighton she got a job at the Sussex Hospital as personal assistant to one of the surgeons. I used to look at her in awe as she set off in the mornings, this sister of mine, with her groomed fingernails, her polished high-heels, her carefully shaped hair, her immaculate stockings.

We had been on one final holiday down in Ponty-cymmer, together. And that's where she'd met her future husband, at a Saturday night dance in Porthcawl Pavilion. She'd blossomed that summer, her twenty-first year. She looked really gorgeous; it was love at first sight. It seemed before I'd had a chance to grasp what was happening, she'd become Mrs Granville Gough, and I had for a brother-in-law this dashing, red-haired, rugby-playing hero from Blaengarw who had played, as a student, for Cardiff University. He was now an industrial chemist, working for the Distillers Company in Barry, which was where they started their married life. So Sal had married into the professional class; my mother breathed a sigh of relief. Now all that was left was me. She was hoping I'd catch an Oxford or Cambridge man, certainly public school. She specified this as something that would gladden her heart. I promised to see what I could do.

Sally had her first baby when I was in my final year at college. I was on my third fiancé by then – all had been art students – but so far they'd only ever been allowed to kiss me goodnight. No more than that. I was rarely on my own with them, preferring to stick with the gang. I had the reputation of being a *femme fatale*, a virgin prick-teaser who wouldn't give an inch. I wore safe-solid panty-girdles with long-leg gussets made of reinforced double elastic. If a prying finger ever strayed inside it would have snapped on the vice-like grip of my underwear. Thus were the fraying remains of my maidenhead kept intacta.

My mother went to stay with Sally in Wales to help her out with the baby. My father and I were alone in the house for the first time in years. His health was getting steadily worse as the smoking had begun to affect his lungs, and he held no terrors for me now. The night before my mother's return, I was awakened in the early hours of the morning by an earth-shattering crash. My heart leapt to my throat. The crash had come from the shop immediately below my bedroom. I got up in the dark and hurried down the stairs. I could make out two figures; one on the floor unconscious, the other lumberingly trying to lift him up. Two men: my father, comatose in drink, and Cliff, his Welsh drinking-companion, a publican, who was equally plastered.

My father's false teeth lay at my bare toes, the top denture snapped in two. The entire front shelf of sweet bottles had smashed to the floor. The mess was unimaginable. My heart sank. It would be up to me to restore this to some sort of order before my mother returned. My father was due to travel to London to meet her at Paddington, so they could spend a nice day up there together.

Cliff and I dragged my father up to bed. Cliff had to go home, he was useless anyway, but before he went he said to undress my father and see that he didn't soil the bed. I was to stay up all night, if necessary, help him with a bowl when he vomited, use a bedpan for his bowels and a bottle for his bladder. He held my face between his hands. The most important thing was *my mother should never, ever,* know. Another secret! The darkest of them all.

I had never seen male genitalia before. Our male models at art school always wore posing pouches. Once, travelling on the back of a bus in Wales, an old gentleman had sat beside me and tried to acquaint me with what appeared to be a lively, if bald, ferret in his lap. Now I was reminded of that and was absolutely revolted.

It was as much as I could do to heave my father's wrinkled flanks on to the bedpan, physically as much as I could do to hold a bowl at the same time to catch his vomit. I nearly vomited myself guiding his flaccid member into a bottle. I tried to erase the image of his sagging scrotum from my mind. This surely wasn't meant to be, unless as some macabre punishment for everything I had been to him in the past. Fate had stored up this moment as my introduction to male portions. It effectively put me off them forever.

By the morning I was shattered. But not in such appalling shape as he was. We tried to stick his dentures together with glue, but it was hopeless and he had to meet my mother without his upper set. I slaved away trying to restore the shop to normality. By the time she got back, questioning me cannily about my father's appearance, nothing appeared out of the ordinary. My father took me aside looking broken and ill. He had only a few years left, but we didn't know it then. My feelings towards him had reformed, a different intimacy had been established. I could never look at him again without a strong feeling surfacing. I saw him, vulnerable in his frailty, naked beneath my fingers. I was strong and young and vigorous. He was spent, his scrotum empty. I was addicted now to the switch between us. We were confidants. I wouldn't betray him to my mother. I would start boasting to him about my conquests before long. Of the ancient men of wealth and wisdom who were trying to purchase my company and love. My father could well become my manager, my procurer, my pimp. But he would soon die and that will be the end of that.

My last fiancé at art school was Malcolm, a black-haired, bearded repeat of Rupert. He wouldn't take no for an answer and finally I went to his room to give in. But what happened was a feeble fiasco. Penetration was impossible, according to him. Even when he located the hole, entry didn't occur. My body protected itself against his erection with a wall of sheer muscle. After years of defensive strategy my genitals were in confusion. Malcolm decided he needed a stick of dynamite to get anywhere. This from the swaggering stud of the year, leading-light of the fast London set who'd joined us at Brighton to qualify as an art teacher in the fifth year. My disappointment knew no bounds when he told me that I wasn't normal, that I was suffering from the symptoms of frigidity, from vaginismus. The engagement ended in ignominy for both of us, but the main difficulties were with our respective families, the difference in our religions – Malcolm was Jewish, my racist father's *bête noir*.

Even the breaking of the news that I was engaged to marry a boy that as yet I had not chosen to tell them about, even that was a farce. The reason I had kept quiet about him was precisely because Malcolm was Jewish. One of my father's early jobs in London was cleaning windscreens at a garage in Golders Green. An affluent Jewish businessman in a Rolls-Royce, smoking a large cigar, sporting a lot of gold jewellery, ran over his big toe before he'd finished the windscreen, and drove off without an apology. My father sustained a resentment for the entire race through this one incident. His anti-Semitism led him to support Oswald Mosley and his brigade of blackshirts, the Fascist political movement. A bunch of bully boys, just like him.

The night I told my parents, I waited until they were already in bed. I laced up my plimsolls, ready for running, then blurted out the news. I added the Jewish bit at the end, and then took to my heels and was out of the front door as my father's bellow of rage hit the roof. I ran around the block, through the deserted, dingy streets of our broken-down district. I was exhilarated. Running under the stars, I felt that my bravery had the blessing of heaven. By the time I crept in my parents were sleeping soundly. There was not a word of my engagement in the morning.

But my father started a campaign against Malcolm, against what he scathingly referred to as the 'chosen race'. He insisted that my mother mind the shop while he raided the till for ready cash, put on his Sunday best and took me to tea at the Grand Hotel on Brighton seafront. He pointed to all the wealthy, rag-trade, Jewish clientele, sneering that these were the 'brethren', my future in-laws. He made hilarious fun out of the fact that Malcolm's father owned a string of hairdressers (in trade, a Philistine, probably a poof!) in South Africa, where Malcolm intended taking me to live. Even my tutor at college was concerned about this plan. He said that I wouldn't be able to stand the political system out there. This was the mid-fifties and apartheid was already in place. I had never thought seriously about the politics of South Africa before.

Malcolm received a deeply distressed letter from his father, who claimed his mother was wearing black, was on a starvation regime and praying all day. He threatened to cut Malcolm off without a penny, withdrawing his financial support as from then, until he came to his senses and broke off the engagement to this *shiksa*. That was me, the *shiksa*. An unclean Gentile. The odds were insurmountable, especially since our sex life was such a cul-de-sac. I prepared to leave for my London teaching job and Malcolm sailed for South Africa. I'd split up with my third fiancé. I was twenty-two and ready to conquer the world.

The fact that I had secured a highly prized teaching post in London, where all of us wanted to be, was a cause for celebration despite the ache in my heart over Malcolm. I was the only student in my year to have achieved this and had every reason to feel proud, my principal told me. I wouldn't have got the job had it not been for my glowing testimonials. The interviewing art inspector at the London County Council had informed me of that. He'd viewed me with what seemed like suspicion as he'd looked through my application form, as if these superlative references were somehow too good to be true. I hadn't read them myself and don't know to this day exactly what they said, but Brighton Art School must have done me proud, because I was employed on the spot.

'And only what I'd expect after keeping you in free board and lodgings for five years. Why wouldn't they give you a blithering job – you're fully qualified, aren't you?'

My father was his usual gracious self on my jubilant return from the interview in London. It was late and he was itching to get off to the pub. He'd thought for one horrifying moment that I'd want to go out and celebrate instead of minding the shop so my mother and he could go boozing.

I took a short holiday before the teaching job actually started. My parents were allowing me to go to Paris with my friend Judy, a rich fellow-student. They actually encouraged me to go, as a treat for finishing with Malcolm. They didn't want me pining, they said. My father was ebullient. Victory.

This wasn't my first trip abroad. The previous summer I had won two awards at art school. One was a prize for outstanding achievements given by the National Union of Students. The other was an Italian travelling scholarship which took me to Venice, Rome and to Verona. I had seen the Sistine Chapel, the Giotto murals, and my first opera, *Aida*, in the open amphitheatre of the Colosseum. I had spent every moment drawing and painting for the thesis which I had to present on my return. The principal and the board of governors congratulated me on my achievements. They said I was a credit to the school and I had a brilliant future ahead of me. I hugged this praise to my heart as I had no one to confide it to, no one to celebrate with. My fellow-students would think I was boasting, and I didn't dare risk arousing envy; people-pleasing was too important to me. I wondered whether to tell my parents, but decided against it. They were drinking every day now, and the pub was uppermost on their minds. They wanted me to go with them, but I hated the change in them once they'd had a drink. My father especially. His slobbering revolted me.

But this was my first trip to Paris. It was Judy's first trip abroad. Her father, a local dignitary in Sussex with a law firm of his own, had booked us into a highly respectable hotel on the Champs-Elysées. Judy said we'd move, after the first night, to somewhere sleazy and exciting. She was very interested in low life, which is probably why I appealed to her.

I, on the other hand, was very interested in high life (which is why I was drawn to her). We were both equally keen for adventure though, and we laughed at the same things, which made her the nearest pal to Gwyneth I'd ever had. Life, upon leaving home, looked enthralling. I was glad that I was no longer an engaged woman. I needed time to hurl myself at life, but I was upset at being frigid and incapable of having sex, because I'd miss having children. I'd always wanted those. I hadn't let on to Judy that I was anything other than normal in the sexual area. She claimed to be livid with envy at me having lain nude beneath a blanket with a naked boy in the same bed. And I'd certainly done that with Malcolm, though pitiably little else! She came to Paris intent on losing her virginity. She achieved this aim on the very first night.

Within hours of arrival we, innocents abroad, were picked up by a smooth Turkish diplomat in the hotel. Right away, that first evening, we were thrown to the lions. He took us from one nightclub to another, plying us with drinks. We dumped him in favour of a predatory American millionaire who whisked me off to spend the night with him in the plush George V Hotel. This was against my will, but Judy had got her claws into what later turned out to be a Parisian gigolo, who was only too eager to deflower what he assumed to be an English heiress. I was out of a bed since they went back to our shared hotel room to accomplish the dirty deed. It was arranged that they would come around next morning to the George V to have breakfast with Robert and me.

I was scared, events were going too swiftly. The opulence of the hotel was overwhelming and I felt like an impostor walking through the lobby. Obviously I was not a guest, so what was I doing here with this old man? I could have been his daughter, no – granddaughter! But the look of me was all wrong, in my art student clothes, my black-eyed, pale-mouthed, existentialist make up. Clearly I was a prostitute then, here for sex. I sensed that the entire hotel staff understood this. I expected one of them, the commissionaire, the hall porter, the desk clerk, the hotel manager, all on duty in their tasselled uniforms, like troops guarding the fortress, I expected one of them to step forward and banish me, the immoral intruder. Command me to leave in front of everyone.

The image of my mother in Harrods came into my mind and my eyelids stung with approaching tears. Robert, perhaps sensing my alienation, pressed me to him in the lift. I wished he wouldn't do that, not in front of the bellboy. I stared straight ahead, stony-faced. Robert got out first. The bellboy winked at me behind his back. I glowered at him with as much dignity as I could summon. How dare he wink at me. I was an artist, not some cheap tart who'd left school at fifteen and whose parents didn't struggle to give her a further education.

When we reached his suite of rooms (all that space for one person!), Robert ordered champagne, smoked salmon and caviare over the telephone. I was amazed that there were people in the kitchens cooking at that hour – it was three o'clock in the morning. He asked me what my favourite food was, his hand covering the mouthpiece. I had never used a telephone; we didn't have one at home. I said my favourite food was bread-and-butter pudding with lots of hot, bright-yellow custard. He had never heard of that dish but I told him it was very Welsh. He asked the chef to make him some too. I added, 'Bird's custard is the best', but Robert didn't pass this on. He said they made their own custard at the George V. I said I was sure it couldn't be as good as my mother's. Robert chuckled and then guffawed, I couldn't imagine at what. He told me that quite apart from being the most exquisite little girl in Paris, my innocence and freshness had completely bowled him over. So refreshing in this jaded old world.

What 'jaded old world'? What was he talking about? And my innocence! I wasn't innocent – I had slept naked with a boy. Should I tell him that I was shoddy goods, not what I seemed, or would he throw me out before the bread-and-butter pudding? The last meal I'd had was at home with my parents. I was hungry. I kept my mouth shut.

Besides, apart from the ominous problem of being alone with a stranger and soon clearly expected to undress and sleep with him in the king-size bed, I was thrilled to be there. The rooms were like a film set, each leading into the other, all with ceiling-to-floor glass doors leading out on to a balcony. We stepped outside. I gasped at the view. Paris was a glittering carpet laid like a mosaic of priceless jewels at my feet.

Robert oozed wealth and well-being. He was sleek and well-fed, one of life's winners. He smelled of a subtle after-shave. His nails were manicured, his fingers soft. He was over six foot, powerfully built, athletic, with a wide, American smile, perfect teeth and an expansive air. He told me he was a supporter of the Republican party in the United States. He was a proud capitalist and despised everything to do with the Left. He said the poor brought it upon themselves, they didn't know how to work for success so they deserved their wretched poverty. I wanted to walk out right away. Instead I told him that my father once supported Oswald Mosley and his Fascist movement, testing him out to see if he approved. He approved wholeheartedly, as I knew he would. My heart hardened, I reassessed his face. Now his amused eyes appeared cold, rapacious, grasping. He was the enemy, the sort that Gwyneth's family were always ranting on about, an exploiter of my class. I hated everything about him and wanted to make him suffer, to show him that he had no power over me. He couldn't buy my nubile body. He wanted the purity that he thought was still mine, my virginity.

My blood boiled with suppressed hostility for all the underprivileged in the world who have been crushed by men like this. I was confused. My head was whirling with hunger, the champagne that I'd already drunk, fatigue, and the undeniable excitement of it all. Paris was everything it had been cracked up to be, and it was being handed to me on a plate. Robert pointed out over the view, pulling me to him, 'It's all yours, honey. You're my girl from now on. I'll buy it all for you, anything your heart desires. Tomorrow we'll start with the trinkets, some diamonds for here and here.' He fondled my earlobes and stroked each of my wrists.

I felt I'd lived this all before, in the front stalls of countless cinemas from the very start of my childhood. I should have been familiar enough with the expected response by now: a rush of gratitude and an impulsive flinging of arms around his neck and passionate kisses for the indulgent lover. But all he got was stubborn resistance. I explained that I couldn't 'do it', so please not to try, if that's what he was after.

To me he seemed ancient, well over sixty. There was a gap of more than forty years between us. I felt no desire for him, but he was still a man who desired me, so it amazed me that he respected my wishes, and allowed me to sleep on the farthest side of the vast mattress, curled foetus-like. A prickly hedgehog. This encounter led me to understand that older men might be the thing, that they do accept no as an answer, unlike young men, with whom sex was painful and impossible, anyway.

From now on I'd stick with old codgers. Rich old codgers! I could start to get accustomed to the luxury. There must be some who were not capitalists, whose generosity didn't mask the baser urges of lust. They couldn't all be my class enemies, could they? But an inner voice told me I was in a different world here. The values were not the same. Everything was about profit and loss, supply and demand. The standards of the chapel counted for nothing.

In the morning, at dawn it seemed – I'd had little sleep so anxious was I that Robert would ravish me, despite the reassurance of his loud snores – Judy arrived with her gigolo. She was radiant. He was avaricious, like a wolf, his dark, narrow eyes darting around the room, assessing the worth of Robert's belongings. Their arrival coincided with my taking a bath. I hadn't locked the door, Robert had promised not to peep at me, but wanted to talk from the bedroom. The gigolo had no such niceties. He barged in, cupped one of my breasts in his hand, and whispered that I could roll this American guy for a big, big, bank-roll. He sneered at my protestations of horror, splashing bathwater in my face, and said I was a stupid child, sitting on a gold-mine, picking daisies. I didn't begin to understand what he was talking about.

We left Judy and the gigolo in our bed. She couldn't keep her hands off this handsome reptile. Robert announced that he was taking his darling (me!) shopping. The gigolo grimaced behind his back, grinning like a wolf again, nodding his head at me, winking obscenely. He wanted me to roll the guy, obviously. I looked haughtily in the other direction. We ended up at Burberry's, much to Robert's absolute astonishment. But a new mac was all I would accept; I'd been needing a new mac for some time, and I didn't want him to think that I was a gold-digger. I was a gold-digger, I knew that well enough, otherwise I wouldn't have been accepting anything at all. But I wasn't proud of that streak in me, getting something for nothing, especially as I hadn't even come up with the goods, in terms of my body.

Robert tried hard to give me diamonds, but as I explained, I couldn't take them home to my mother. She'd have a fit! She'd imagine the worst! Robert appeared mystified by me, but became more devoted by the minute. He offered me the world, suggesting a visit to Dior, dinner at Maxim's. But I was in devastating awe of these places. My mother and Harrods burned in my brain. I wasn't in love with him, he lacked vulnerability, so I couldn't indulge myself by feeling sorry for him. I managed to give him the slip and although he tracked me down later in London, for the time being, in Paris, it was just Judy and me again. She was ecstatic, no longer a virgin. Her smile stretched across her face like a Cheshire cat. I was wistfully wondrous at her transformation. Sex never did that for me.

That afternoon, just for fun, we stood near the Arc de Triomphe thumbing lifts from passing cars. We chose the largest vehicles, Daimlers and the like. We'd just been to the Louvre, my idea, genuflecting before the Impressionists, but Judy was on heat, her loins aflame from her recent deflowering. Her gigolo had dumped her, hoping to latch on to me and make himself a fortune as my pimp. Bastard! Luckily, Judy was resilient; she'd achieved her objective. She was in touch with her sexuality and was raring to go!

She was sadly unimpressed with the male talent on offer in the Louvre. It was full of families or serious young men in sandals with wispy beards. She was 'thrumming with sex' – that was her refined way of putting it. Thumbing lifts on the salty pavements of Paris was another idea of mine, just to give spice and adventure to the afternoon. Just to keep Judy happy. It was the kind of thing Gwyneth would have enjoyed, leaping into the unknown.

Judy pushed me forward and stood behind. She thought my appearance was more striking. I took it to mean that I looked more like a tart. I was super-sensitive about this after my recent experience at the George V, but she showed such enthusiasm that I didn't want to be a wet blanket.

We didn't have to wait long. In a matter of moments an English Bentley drew to the kerb and a distinguished gentleman, with grey sideburns, a patrician profile and a film-star French accent like Charles Boyer, invited us to enter. He was so smooth and charming that suddenly it seemed safe. He asked us where we would like to go. We said anywhere really, we were new to Paris. He took us to Versailles and told us that he was a politician, a grandfather, a famous figure in the country. If anyone should approach us we were his nieces from England. Then he plunged his manicured nails into my knickers. We drove along, the three of us in the front seat with me squirming in the middle, while he 'played with my pussy'. Judy thought this was hilarious and was jealous that her pussy was not being played with. I suggested a swop, so he stopped the car and Judy got in the middle. That was better. We were all happy now.

He bought us dinner in a swanky restaurant. He didn't seem to be interested in intercourse, only playing with pussies. Judy knowledgeably informed me that after a certain age this was what happened to men. She said they liked licking pussies too; her gigolo did it to her. It made me feel sick. She told me this while we were still at the table, in the middle of the meal, as our host had excused himself to telephone his family. I couldn't eat any more. When he returned I didn't want to look at him. His tongue, as he ate, reminded me of a snake out to take a bite of my private portions. He asked us what we would like to do now and we said we'd like to go to a nightclub. He took us to one and paid the entry fee but refused to come in. He was too well known, he said, and the gossip columns would be full of it the next day. We were excited by this, but were already tired of him and his preoccupation with pussy. Judy wanted more action, I wanted adventure, so we kissed him goodbye and plunged into the dark depths of the club. The music was throbbing, couples were dancing. The club was called the Whisky-a-Go-Go. We were in the right place here! More risqué adventures followed, but I always managed to avoid physical intimacy. I was frigid, incapable of sex.

PART THREE

Enter the Demon

When I arrived in London I went to a nightclub, I had my first drink, I changed my perfume, and lost my virginity for good. Properly, or rather improperly, this time. All in the space of a week, no hanging about. I started as I meant to go on, full steam ahead. I was twenty-two already and had a lot of catching-up to do.

We all remember our first drink, those of us who get into difficulties with the stuff later on. We remember it down to the last detail as if it's the start of a life-long love affair. Which, of course, it is, with all the attendant delight and despair.

Mine takes place in the Studio Club, Swallow Street, Piccadilly. The time is seven-thirty in the evening on the second Friday in September 1954. I am wearing a sleeveless, clinging, midnight-blue, rib-knit dress, with a metal belt, gypsy earrings and matching gold sandals.

My hair is shaped in the currently fashionable Poodle Cut, short at the back and sides with a fetching confection of curls in a tangled-ball-of-string effect over the forehead. Much the same as Elizabeth Taylor's in *A Place in the Sun*. But mine is a home-concocted coiffure, without the undoubted benefits of a Hollywood studio hair stylist. The end result is a bit of a botch-up but not too bad considering.

I am equally ambitious when it comes to my maquillage. That's Elizabeth Taylor's too. My eyes are heavily encircled with ebony eye-liner, mucked out with matching mascara, just like hers. I have read in the *Daily Express*, my father's favourite Fascist newspaper, on their fashion and beauty page, all about Liz and, 'her exquisite angel eyes, set in place with sooty fingers'. This is the look I'm after. I have smeared the soot almost down to my cheekbones, until people are staring at me in the street. So I know I'm achieving my objective. You could say I'm very arresting.

I expect people probably wonder if I'm not Liz herself, who's in London courting Michael Wilding. Except she would hardly be toddling about the streets, queuing for the bus, or travelling by tube unless she was doing it all for a bit of a laugh. But this is not as far-flung as it sounds, me being mistaken for her.

We are the very same age, born within a fortnight of each other. And we could have been actual Astral Twins, born on the same day in the same year, because I was expected a fortnight later than my arrival. Which would have made me Pisces instead of an Aquarian, and everything about my life would have been different. I had my Auntie Lizzie Cats to blame for that, who was known far and wide in South Wales, and so called, for the forty cats she had crouching and crapping all over her floor and furniture. My mother, calling in for a nice cup of tea and a piece of cake at the very end of her pregnancy, found herself on all fours, skidding on the cat shit in the back kitchen, thus jolting me into action out of my womb-sleep falsely believing this to be the whistle-call for the start of the journey (only to give up from sheer exhaustion before I was halfway there, which is why it took me three days to arrive).

I had already been approached for my autograph by an ancient short-sighted American couple, who thought I was Elizabeth Taylor, on Brighton seafront, before even coming to London. Tourists from the Mid West, they said, between sighs of admiration and not believing their luck. I signed Liz's name, to give them a thrill. Something to show off about back home.

My lipstick is stinging pink, Lido Venice Pink by Lancôme. The very same lipstick as Judy's. Our dresses too are the same, only hers is a hot peach instead of blue. Later on in the evening, when we've really had a skinful and I can barely stand, we think it good fun to swop over dresses in the ladies' lavvy, just to test if anyone notices. No one does.

This lipstick is a new thing for me, because all through art school I wore nothing at all on my lips. But I was a kid then and didn't know any better. Now I'm in the big time, earning my own money. This week, tomorrow in fact, being Saturday, I'm off to Galeries Lafayette in Regent Street to buy some proper perfume, just like Judy wears, instead of the Yardley's Lavender my aunties give me for Christmas. I've put money aside for French perfume, all my own. Judy wears Miss Dior, which turns sour and smells like dog's piss on me, something to do with a chemical reaction, but I'll find something to suit me, I know.

I smoulder and pout a lot these days, since although I'm Liz, there is also a touch of Gina Lollobrigida in there. That's been commented on too, but only by silly schoolboys, or building-site louts, when I walk past wearing a sweater.

'Ooh, ooh! La Lollo! Look at it! Them tits!'

I ignore them. I won't give them the satisfaction. But I'm burning with embarrassment inside, and hot with a salty, acrid anger. They wouldn't begin to understand the sexual image I'm after. They never saw Rita Hayworth in *Gilda*. Or Jean Simmons in *Great Expectations*. Brigitte Bardot, who got it right in one, is yet to break in on the scene.

I try not to smile too much at the moment because the tooth in the front, which used to give me so much gyp that the nerve had to be removed, is now dead and I swear is going black on me. But if my angel eyes and sooty fingering aren't quite spot-on, then I can sit back and relax knowing that my belly and backside are as flat as a board, thanks to my roll-on (complete with gusset for protection against straying fingers), and that my burgeoning breasts in my up-lift Maidenform brassière will do the job for me, here in this club tonight. Knock men clean out of their skulls.

I am seated on the third bar-stool from the right. Judy is sitting to my left. The lights are dim and seductive, and Dill Jones, a fellow countryman of mine, well known in jazz circles, is fingering the keys with a little Art Tatum. Men hover around us. Life is about to begin. I look every inch the part. But now out of nowhere comes this sense of doom, a kind of dying inside. The warning, curdling voice of conscience suddenly spoils my fun. It's here, in my heart. My granny's face. All this is sinful, it's too good to be otherwise, too easy, too simple, too seductive by half. The start of the slippery slope. Devil's work.

I whisper to Judy, 'What'll I ask for when they offer us drinks?'

Sweet laughter trills from her exquisite lips. 'You are so quaint, darling! You ask for gin and Dubonnet. Large,' she adds firmly. 'A single's no good to anybody.'

I smile and nod in awe as usual of her social command, adoring the blasé sophistication. This must be how Princess Margaret sounds, with her champagne in her hand and her long cigarette-holder, sitting in nightclubs, lords and honourables all around her. I've seen the photos in the William Hickey column. The *Express* again. My father would read it out loud, shouting, sitting on our lavatory at the back of the shop in Brighton. Instructing us to note down the names of all these rich aristos, these silly asses, so we'd know who we were dealing with when we had the whole useless bunch of twerps eventually fawning for my favours. That was the most enjoyable part of his day, that and bollocking our beleaguered regulars who'd come in for a packet of fags only to go out with my father's advice on how to run the country ringing in their spinning heads. All hours of chronic boredom for him to fill until he started swilling the cider down his throat with my mother in the Seven Stars, every night.

But what I'm about to sip now is in no way apple cider. It comes in a different glass, for a start, a glass with a stem like a flower. It's the colour of blood, of roses and rubies. It's as rich to look at as velvet, and slides down my throat like slippery satin. When it hits my stomach, when it hits the spot, a thousand stars explode under my skin.

I have seen the film *Dr Jekyll and Mr Hyde*, with Spencer Tracy. How he changes before his own eyes after tilting that potion. It was obviously alcohol. The same is happening to me now. A shift in personality as powerful as the ocean pounding on to the shore. It sweeps over me in waves, and I have to lower my eyes so that no one can see. But when I raise my head I'm a different girl. No longer the Welsh chapel puritan, more the vamp of the valleys. My granny's face has gone, I can't hear my heart-voice. It's been swamped, literally drowned, in one gulp from my stemmed glass.

What's more, things are different. The whole world has changed towards me. I'm not afraid to open my mouth – far from it! My off-centre accent doesn't matter any more, nor the fact that I come from a scruffy sweetshop in the seediest streets of Sussex. Nor being working-class Willesden Welsh in the midst of these toffs, English toffs, and the product of a grammar school instead of coming from a boarding school in the Home Counties like Judy, with a tuck box and midnight feasts in the dorm and all those things that I read about in *Girls' Crystal*.

For with this drink inside me, the most extraordinary and marvellous thing is that now I can talk to anybody and it will be their privilege, not mine. I'm cultured and clever; I know about the finer obscurities of Art with a capital A. I can tell one painter of Flemish interiors from another. I understand the undercurrents between hot and cold colours, how to emphasize the throb of raw umber against a cadmium orange or lemon. I can knock spots off any other girl in the whole of London. Judy and I are equals, we always have been but I didn't see it before. There's nobody to beat us, not as a team. I see the shining excitement of all the men milling around us, jostling for position, for permission to dance. Avid for the undeniable delights of our nubile bodies. Perhaps tonight will be the night for me to have sex and actually enjoy it. Who knows what can happen? In drink.

I take a deep breath, my nipples spring to attention. I sense a shift in my groin as the insidious music gets to me, a delicious ooze of expectant lubrication in the sexual stronghold of my elastic gusset.

Judy leans over, her flirty eyes are afire. 'All set?'

'All set – I'll say!' I hear myself giggling. 'Christ! We'll divide this lot of cunts down the middle, no bloody trouble. Have their fucking guts for garters, every sodding one of them!'

This is a new thing too, the swearing. But I've never actually put it to such enjoyable use before, not since my childhood convalescence. The drink seems to give me a new way with words. Even Judy's eyes widen, and if I can impress her then I know I'm on the right track.

I learned the words on my very first day's teaching out at the Elephant and Castle. The children all swore, which was no surprise, but it was a shock to hear it in the hallowed confines of the staffroom and from a creature more charming and gracious than Grace Kelly, or Katharine Hepburn, or indeed the Queen Mother herself. And more upper class then anyone I'd ever actually spoken to face-to-face before. I'd noticed Sylvia Crowther-Smith in the corridor, in the morning, after the first school assembly. I was immediately drawn by the sense that she appeared as completely out of place in this dingy secondary modern girls' school as I felt. But I only needed a glimpse of her canary yellow twin-set and her two diamond rings, the very look of Judy's cashmere'd lot in Sussex, to have her down as another class enemy. Another to be lumped in with the leaden crew in the staffroom, with their lacklustre eyes and pursed lips and prim hairstyles.

Where the hell have you landed, I privately berated myself? Is this how it's meant to be after five glorious years at art school? Holed up here in the mean streets of the Elephant and Castle, the same stricken streets, drabness personified, like every street I'd ever lived in so far. Stuck in an all-female staffroom with this bunch of rule-abiders and regulation-upholders, every single one a stereotype of what a worthy teacher should look like. What would my Tadci Thomas have made of this lot or of my sorry situation?

But there would always be the children, the teaching, the Art. And though they would be the only consolation, I comforted myself with that thought. Because these girls, these eager, giggling, garrulous, shouting and screaming girls, ranged from the age of eleven to sixteen, were all me. Scraps of deprived humanity hungry for knowledge of how to cope with their lives. There was little enough in the way of aesthetics around them and it was my mission to open their eyes just as mine had been opened for me in that sunny garden, years before in the convalescence home. If I could do that for just one pupil in the whole of that huge school (in spite of having to teach over forty girls to a class), then all my years of training would have had some point.

I was as fervent and as idealistic in my dedication as that. But I couldn't see the same zeal amongst the rest of these teachers. Was it truly that impossible to keep the flame afire? Would I too sink into that same apathy, that terrible torpor, after a few terms of teaching in this place? The eventuality was too awful to contemplate. I determined to keep my head down and just get on with the job.

By the end of the first day, nobody had spoken to me except the children and one frightening apparition who looked like Tony Perkins' dead mother in *Psycho*. She turned out to be the mathematics teacher and strict Plymouth Brethren, the religious lunatic in this bunch of stiffs. In the staffroom morning tea-break I had just sunk into a fireside chair but jumped up immediately, startled by her bloodcurdling screams.

'Pardon me, that is *my* chair! I have sat in that chair for fifteen years, and have no intention of relinquishing it now! Thank you very much!'

My eyes filled with tears and an unaccountable misery. Was this the way things were in the working world? Was everyone this aggressive, this hostile, under the strain of holding down a responsible position? I could hear teachers shouting from every classroom, struggling to keep some measure of control over the kids. Tough little kids, down to the last one of them. Streetwise, though that term wasn't coined yet. I was lucky; I was young and dressed in contemporary clothes, which these young girls could identify with. They liked me, I liked them. We understood each other. I had come from the same place as them, I spoke the same language. I had no trouble at all in my art room. It was this staff which got up my nose, that was going to be the hardest part of the job.

But things were about to change. Sylvia Crowther-Smith exploded into the staffroom. Other teachers were dispiritedly donning their coats and hats, preparing for home, depressed that the summer holidays were over and they were back in the hell-hole of yet another appalling term's work. The doom-laden atmosphere was contagious. I shrugged myself into my own overcoat, dreading the fact that I'd have to be back here again tomorrow. The silence was broken by the trained tones of a voice intended to embrace the back stalls and upper circle. A thrilling voice coated with centuries of privilege, of theatrical command and total confidence. An Edith Evans voice, imperious and rich, holding everyone in thrall.

'Has anyone else here had the ghastly misfortune of teaching effing 4C today? What a perfectly bloody bunch of cunts! Honestly!'

The effect was electrifying. The room emptied in seconds. Except for me, only I remained, rooted to the spot. Laughter, glorious laughter rose like a bubble from the centre of my being. God had taken care of me, yet again. He could see what was needed and had sent me this kindred spirit, this simply marvellous infectious soul, this destroyer of pomp and circumstance. This fellow Aquarian as it turned out. This person, thirty years my senior, who was to become my closest chum, my mentor, my surrogate mother, my nourishing source of intellectual and emotional sustenance for the rest of my life. Even, eventually, the godmother to my own children.

'I took 4C this morning.' I grinned to show her that in me she had found an ally.

She spun round, her eyes shining, and broke into a husky laugh that warmed the cockles of my numbed heart.

'That deserves tea, darling thing – a jolly tea in Soho! Grab your things and let's get out of this Godforsaken hole. Just look at that dreadful gas-ring, positively Dickensian. How these poor little squashed tomatoes are expected to learn anything in these surroundings beats me. The lower orders pigeon-holed for life, you see. Crushed from birth. Where do you hail from? You look Mediterranean, a Latin for sure.'

'I'm Welsh.'

'A Celt? How amusing! I was born in Brazil; my

mother's family are all Brazilian. My father was English, I'm afraid. When I was sent to school over here as a girl, something withered inside me. The coldness, the grey people, all so ghastly compared to the tropics. I never quite recovered—'

She didn't stop talking the whole way to Soho. I had never heard anyone speak so spontaneously on public transport, or laugh so loudly, or refer with such relish to private parts. This last topic cropped up as she told me about the book she was currently reading. 'So important to have a book on the go at all times, darling.' This book was by an anthropologist called Margaret Mead, which propounded the theory that western women wear their wombs on their forearms in the shape of shopping bags. And that the men parade their penises in the guise of furled umbrellas.

The entire busload of passengers in this the rush-hour, the busiest time for London transport, craned their necks around as Sylvia enthusiastically pointed out examples on the streets. They would remember this enlightening conversation for the rest of their lives, as I have. The hitherto normal sight of housewives shopping or city men walking with the aid of their umbrellas, even on days when the heavens were free of rainclouds, would never seem the same to them again.

We descended on Berwick Street Market, passing Dansey Place, off Shaftesbury Avenue, which Sylvia pointed out was where she co-founded the National Council for Civil Liberties with Ronald Kidd, her lover. That was in the twenties and thirties, as far back as that. Before I was born even. And she lived with this man, without being married!

I looked at her with a new regard, an even greater awe. I couldn't, in a million years, imagine living with a man without being married. What would the neighbours have said – or done? In Pontycymmer once when two people shacked up outside wedlock, the whole street rose up in fury, pelting their bedroom window with pebbles from the stream. The pair of them were hounded from the place. My Auntie Emily, school cleaner, told me that.

But I understood that normal morals didn't apply to people like Sylvia and Ronald who had been on the stage. When we got to know each other better and I visited her home she showed me his silver-framed photograph and I thought that I had never seen anyone so handsome. A true matinée idol, with a slouched trilby hat, just like my father's and the man in the park. Sylvia said that the females used to fall for Ronald like ninepins, but she was the one who got him, who held him spellbound until his premature death over a decade before. Her normally laughing face saddened when she spoke of him. She said she had never found anyone to take his place. I said, 'Yet,' believing, as I still do, that you never know what's around the corner.

She laughed and shrugged the suggestion away. 'No, my angel, you don't understand. That side of my life is over for good. It's all finished. No more sex, no more lovers.'

It was my turn to laugh. 'Mm, let's wait and see.' It didn't enter my head that anyone could live without sex, because by the time we held that conversation my virginity had gone up in smoke and sex was all that I could think of. I was in the grip of an obsession which threatened to border on love. But I refused to allow myself to fall again. Malcolm was still secretly there in my heart. A permanent scar.

Sex didn't happen that night in the club with Judy, and if it had I would certainly not have remembered. I drank to total oblivion that evening, which set the pattern of my drinking for the subsequent thirty-three years. The next morning I had no memory of what had happened, or with whom. I was sick in the ladies', but that didn't stop me staggering out for more. I knew that I simply couldn't get enough of the stuff. Apart from the vomit and the dizziness, I adored what it did for me. I was floating, my feet didn't touch the ground, it was the fantasy feeling I'd always wanted. As to sex, there was some kind of blurred image of an old groper in the back of a big car, but I had passed out by then and was no good to anyone. Unless they went big guns on necrophilia.

I was sharing an underground basement flat in Earl's Court with another ex-student from Brighton, a beautiful, leggy, creature who put everyone in mind of Audrey Hepburn. Her name was Betty, and she was teaching art, too, in some school out in Surrey, which meant she had to get up at sunrise to catch a train.

Every morning I would lie in bed, luxuriating, with another few hours to kill, curiously watching her get dressed. She had the body I wanted: no breasts, just nipples. She could wear four sweaters at once, which she did to keep out the cold at that early hour, but still look as lean as a racehorse. She had studied fabric design at Brighton, rubbing shoulders mainly with the fashion crew. Aliens. Ultra-sophisticates, groomed to their fingernails. Daunting to the scruffpots like me in the painting school.

I examined the nonchalant manner in which she munched the three Mars Bars which made up her breakfast. How she managed, and I particularly marvelled at this, to mix each mouthful of chocolate with a massive drag on her fag. Betty smoked as much as my father, which meant one filter-tip between the lips and the next already out of the packet and halfway to the lighter.

But if this was the diet for a shape such as Betty's I'd best start puffing myself, because as yet I hadn't started. My father's coughing had put me off. The sound of his surging phlegm every morning, and the subsequent spit-and-snot clearance for the past twenty-two years had put paid to any desire that I might have had to smoke. But this early-morning sneaky surveillance of Betty and her ever so *soignée* silhouette, fag in mouth, smoke curling lazily above the cloud of her shoulder-length hair, munching her Mars Bar, was beginning to change my mind. I'd like to look like her.

Betty went home to Sussex at the weekends, taking her sheets and all her washing for her mother to do. I was amazed. On Sunday nights she brought them all back again, clean and ironed. And she brought back cakes that her mother had baked for the flat, and home-made biscuits and marmalade. I was more than amazed, I was flabbergasted. Was this what normal mothers did for their children, grown-up or otherwise? I supposed it must be. It was what was called 'mothering'.

My mother and father were no longer in Brighton. They had sold the shop and skidaddled down to South Wales, to Barry, to be near my sister and the baby. They missed me too much now I'd left home. My mother found the nest empty and unbearable.

Judy had intended to come and stay with me this weekend, my first on my own in London. But at the last minute she had to cancel and remain where she was, still living with her parents in Brighton. She planned to get a job up here too, and live with Betty and me. But this hadn't happened yet. I was all alone.

I sat in the kitchen of the basement wondering what on earth to do. It was Friday evening and the weekend stretched ahead. I knew nobody yet in London, no boys, no girls except Betty and Sylvia at school. Self-pity started creeping in. Then the telephone rang.

My life was about to change as fundamentally as it had when I met Sylvia Crowther-Smith. Tonight I would meet the other most formative influence in my life, the British actor James Robertson Justice.

Oddly enough, and I must have had my reasons, I never introduced these two to each other although I was so closely bound up with them both. I kept them in separate compartments. I think it was because I couldn't bear the thought of either of them being critical of the other. I probably thought they would cancel each other out in a head-on collision, such was the charismatic force of their personalities. In truth, I preferred to keep both on their pedestals. It was less confusing that way.

To the rest of the world James Robertson Justice was one of the leading lights of the British film industry, a bosom pal of Prince Philip, a keen practitioner of the art of falcony. An enormously popular anarchist currently enjoying prestigious personal publicity as the bearded, witty, irascible, eccentric Sir Lancelot Spratt in *Doctor in the House*. It was a larger-than-life character that he barely had to bother to act, requiring little effort, for Sir Lancelot was James Robertson Justice. But to me they were both Mr Hill.

The voice on the telephone was exactly the same. It enquired pleasantly about Judy, understanding from her father that she was to be in town that weekend. Oh, so she wasn't here after all. That was a shame because the plan was to take us both out to dinner. Would I accept the invitation although we hadn't yet been introduced? But he felt as if he knew me already, he'd heard so much about me from Judy and about what a simply marvellous, naughty holiday we'd so recently had together in Paris.

My stomach leapt to my throat. I was thirteen again, masturbating against Mr Hill's armchair, my mouth swollen, my eyes wild in the mirror. Transported, I dropped the receiver. It slithered out of my sweaty hand. But the voice was still there when I picked it up. I had to sit down to stop my knees shaking. He would be round to pick me up in an hour.

From thenceforward that would be my reaction every single time James telephoned me, every time I heard his name, or saw his face on a cinema poster, or set eyes on him when we met. In recent years, now sober, I have allowed myself the intense pleasure of watching James in television reruns of his old movies. I can do that now without lapsing into maudlin sentimentality, without indulging in churning emotions and taking a further drink to quell deep-felt regrets.

For James was married and loved his wife, Dilys, dearly. They had supported each other through the tragedy of the drowning of his son, an only child. The question of divorce never arose. But, almost immediately, he wanted to set up home with me in London, to buy me a house and start a family together, so that I could give him another son. Instead of feeling overjoyed by this proposal, it triggered off an unsettling anxiety. I felt guilty enough about having an affair with a married man, married to a Welsh woman, what's more, which made my deception and treachery to another female even worse. I didn't enjoy the secrecy of the relationship. I couldn't brag about James in the way that I'd like, to my mother and father, to Sally, to Barbara, not even to Judy.

Judy knew that we'd met, of course; that I'd been to bed with him. But she didn't know how very often or the full depth and passion of the relationship. Nobody did, not even Sylvia. The fact is that deep down I was ashamed. Ashamed of the hole-in-the-corner aspect of the affair, as if I was betraying myself and everything that I'd been brought up to believe. My inner voice told me what my granny would have said, that this man has no respect for you, or he wouldn't be making such immoral suggestions.

But I had no one to tell, nobody anywhere to consult about it. Least of all James, I couldn't begin to tell him.

Think how pathetically parochial, how nauseatingly naive I would have sounded to a man like him. I'd lose him forever! He'd already been teaching me how to think for myself, encouraging me to read more widely. He'd given me Dylan Thomas's *Under Milk Wood*, and Frank Harris's *Memoirs of a Victorian Gentleman* for my journey to work, on those mornings when he couldn't drive me in his scarlet sports car. A pillar-box red Carmen Ghia. He said that poetic prose and pornography were the perfect travelling companions, in life as on a journey. And if there was any grain of wisdom to be learned from his experience, I was always to remember the vital importance of satisfying the equal demands of the soul and the senses.

I welcomed reading a book on public transport in the morning. I dreaded him driving me to school anyway. But my reaction to this too would change. The very first time he did, dropping me off on his way to Pinewood Studios, where he was filming, I pleaded with him to park around the corner. I didn't want anyone to see me with a man at that time of the morning, let alone with the famous James Robertson Justice. They might jump to all sorts of conclusions and think there was something going on!

He ignored my pleas, throwing his large head back and guffawing at my obvious discomfort. He filled the sports car to capacity with his six-foot bulk and abundance of energy. I looked at him, my eyes ate him up. Over fifty already, but at his peak, in his prime. I thrilled to the potent male power of him. And – let's face it, the sheer gut-churning glamour of sitting in a sports car with a film star. Fuck what people would say! I was learning fast!

He put his foot in its lemon-yellow sock on the pedal, building up speed so that when he slammed on the brakes the streak of scarlet metal screeched to a halt, halfway up the kerb at the very edge of the school playground. I cringed at the contrast between this absurdly swish car, this expensive symbol of affluence, and the rubbish-strewn, broken pavements of those impoverished streets. The intensity of the colour, like a concentration of geraniums, attracted a swarm of gaping girls who flung themselves and their satchels all over the bonnet. It was like being inside a hive covered with buzzing bees.

James honked the horn to scare them off, but this only attracted more, which actually delighted him. We were surrounded, like visiting royalty. James was used to this kind of situation with autograph hunters, but I'd never been the centre of such a crowd before. It could very easily give me ideas above my station. I prayed that Mrs Macmillan, the headmistress, couldn't see this. She was a committed member of the Communist Party and would view the whole incident as a corruption of minors, in which case I could be out on my ear. I nipped out sharpish to escape James's farewell embrace, which I knew he was planning for the benefit of the over-excited audience. I gave a hasty wave from the school gates as he swung the car around and zoomed off down the Walworth Road. The girls squealed with delight. They made a nightmare of my whole day.

'Is he your boyfriend, Madam?'

'Course he's not Madam's boyfriend! He's Madam's grandad, ain't he Madam!'

'Nice car, Madam!'

'Ever so nice. I'm after a bloke wiv a nice car like that!'

'Chance'd be a fine thing!'

'If Madam can do it, then so can I – can't I, Madam?'

'Madam's beautiful. Madam looks like Elizabeth Taylor. You look like the back end of a bus!'

'You don't 'ave to be beautiful, do you, Madam?'

'Nope! Our mum ain't good-lookin'. She gets lifts in cars like that all the time, she does.'

'Yer mum's a tart, that's why—'

'She ain't!'

'She is too! She's on the game! My dad says he doesn't want me and my sisters endin' up like your mum . . .'

All pupils were required to address us as madam. In morning assembly when they chorused, 'Good morning, madams!' it sounded as if they were addressing a convention of brothel keepers. I always winked at Sylvia across the large hall, then held my hymn book in front of my face to discourage any girl hoping to join in the fun.

When James dropped me off, around the corner from now on, I was always in time for assembly. Otherwise, I'm ashamed to say, I had to slip in late at the back. Hardly setting a fine example of punctuality; my headmistress hauled me over the coals for this. She asked me what on earth I got up to at night, as some mornings I looked so exhausted she'd like to give me the day off. She warned of the perils in burning the candle at both ends. And in the middle, I could have added. I managed to suppress the urge to supply her with an exact answer. Instead I studied her big blouse, gauging the weight of her breasts. Wondering what James would do in bed with a fine, handsome woman like her.

I knew he still noticed other women although he said I filled his every waking and working thought. That very week he was reminded of my body while filming, and was so overcome that he almost forgot his lines. The French girl on the set had breasts just like mine, apparently. Years later I saw the film, *Doctor at Sea*. The French girl he referred to was Brigitte Bardot.

My Tadci Thomas would have thoroughly approved of this man. My father already did – James Robertson Justice was one of his idols. I longed to tell him that his idol was screwing his daughter until the cows came home. That on our very first date we dined in chandelier'd elegance at the legendary Ivy, with stars of stage, screen and radio at every table. And there, within inches of everyone, James had his fingers in my Marks & Spencer knickers under the table, almost all through the meal.

It was a bold decision on my part to dispense with my elastic gusset that evening, but from then on it was stockings and suspenders all the way. I liked the louche vulnerability beneath my skirts. If my mother had known she would probably have sustained her first coronary. She would have died of anxiety and dread worrying whether the draught was going to give me a cold in my kidneys.

My kidneys were the last part of my anatomy on my mind at that moment. James had an uncanny knack of folding and refolding the flesh of my clitoris. For such a huge man he had a deceptively delicate touch, treating it as though it were fragile tissue paper. My body responded with a longing and lust that I had never had with anyone else. Neither of us could really be bothered with the meal, but we both enjoyed this, the foreplay. And all the better for being in public, as if his hand wasn't playing with me at all.

We spent that first night in the Cadogan Hotel. I had acute difficulty in walking past the desk clerk. For a moment he looked like our chapel preacher. But as soon as we were in the lift James started kissing me and I returned with a passion to equal his own. We couldn't stay apart. He tore my knickers off in the corridor and tossed them in the fire bucket. Later, when I sneaked out to retrieve this item of underwear someone had stolen it already, complete with soaking crotch. I was surprised. You'd expect better than a bunch of thieving perverts in the middle of Belgravia.

It took over five hours to actually arrive in bed and when we did get there, it was at approximately the same hour that my grandfather would have been getting up to start the fire and the porridge, if he'd been alive. I thought of this as James lay asleep and snoring in my arms. Apart from Robert in Paris, and Malcolm, I had never slept with a man before. Not as lovers. James was my first. My first in more ways than one. I told him this but I think he guessed and, far from finding me a bore, he seemed delighted by my inexperience.

We started off on the floor just inside the bedroom door. The carpet fluff got up my nostrils, so that I sneezed my way to the supreme importance of my first orgasm. But there was something so pleasing about the informality of the position, down there seeing the undersides of all the chairs, that it didn't matter. Indeed, James said, without even knowing of my frigid history, that the sneezing would have helped release hovering tension.

Next we screwed in the bath and flooded the entire bathroom floor, which had me on my knees mopping up with dripping towels. James was driven to a frenzy by me in this position. He said I had the most erotic arsehole this side of the Arabian Desert. He asked me if I understood what he was talking about and for a change I decided to come clean and be honest. I said no. So he took a toothbrush, smothered the handle with soap and stuck the tip of it up my bum. When he asked me if I was enjoying it I took the honesty even further and admitted that I wasn't. Not at all. He said that's the chapel for you and left it at that. I didn't feel I'd pleased him as much as I'd have liked.

When we eventually got into bed, having almost broken the arms of an easychair and the legs off the bedside table, in short wrecked the whole room, James kissed my bruised mouth and said he worshipped and adored me and if we were not careful we would devour each other to extinction. He told me he had a final treat for me. He pulled the neon strip-lighting from the bedside lamp and inserted it into me, telling me not to move or cough or sneeze, just to continue breathing as gently as possible. I lay there petrified. Isn't this what happened to that girl with Fatty Arbuckle? God Almighty, look after me now, if You can bear to look! I trust James with my life, but don't let this thing splinter inside me. How would I have my periods – it would be gushing from every seam. I'd spend all of my life paying a fortune in dry cleaning. I'd be doomed to red skirts for the rest of my days . . .

James withdrew the sixty watt light and encircled the width with his fingers. 'This is your capacity in cubic inches,' he said lovingly. 'If you ever feel less than sexually satisfied, you know where to reach from now on.' He replaced my latest lover in the light socket, cuddled up and fell fast asleep.

We returned again and again to the Cadogan Hotel. We thought of it as our special place. James said that one day it would be famous, with a blue plaque hanging outside to inform the general public that this is where we made sexual history together. He said that eventually my life would be far more celebrated than his, long after he was gone and forgotten. Painters, like writers, are in the privileged position of leaving their work behind them, whereas the actor's art is essentially ephemeral by its very nature, the performance over and done with once executed. We argued about this. I cited the cinema to carry my point, that film entraps the performance for all time. But he disagreed, especially when it applied to his own career, which he considered child's play.

I couldn't bear him talking about being gone and forgotten, or the difference in our ages; to have to imagine a time when I might be alive without him. It obviously preoccupied him far more than it did me. He maintained that the greatest pain between couples such as ourselves was jealousy, sexual jealousy. I assumed he meant mine, because yes, I could see that becoming a chronic problem. My jealousy ripped me apart whenever another woman even looked at him, which they did all the time, of course they did. But I thought I concealed that pretty well. It took me decades, indeed not until I'd reached his age and was involved with a younger person myself, to realize that he was talking about his own jealousy. Poor lamb.

James and I shared three primary enthusiasms. Eating, drinking and fucking. Like most couples in an obsessive relationship we did these alone. He kept me hidden away, all to himself, apart from the food-and-finger-foreplay pantomime which usually took place in the old Pheasantry Club on the King's Road. He liked it there because it was arty and dark, which encouraged him to take risky liberties with my lingerie whilst eating and exchanging coarse comments with the painter Annigoni who was usually at the next table.

Pietro Annigoni's work was not to my liking, but his sycophantic portrait of the Queen was much to my father's traditional tastes. The *Daily Express* had given it great coverage, claiming it to be on a par in terms of artistic achievement with the ceiling of the Sistine Chapel. I had actually seen that ceiling, so knew better. But when I told my father I'd met this artist, his dentures (new) almost dropped from his gums. He boasted to anyone who would listen that his daughter was moving in the top artistic circles of London. He said that all the sacrifices to educate me were now proving worth it. He told my mother, and she told me, that the chickens were coming home to roost and to sit tight and wait for them. Whatever that was supposed to mean.

James failed in his objective of getting me to dine out with no knickers on at all. What would they say in the hospital if I got run over, that was my main reason. But I didn't tell him that. Instead, just to please him, I took them off in the ladies' at the Pheasantry one night. He roared with approval and got over-excited as his fingers touched the spot. He told me I was a model pupil, forked up his rice, creamy with chicken, and bellowed over to Annigoni how it reminded him of 'come'. My come.

I wondered what they would have made of me in Pontycymmer, Tadci Thomas and all my aunties, sitting here with these celebrities and talking this kind of salty talk. I steered all thoughts away from my granny, or God. I didn't want to spoil a good time. That evening I luxuriated in James's approval and the novel naughtiness of my own bare buttocks under my petticoats. We were chatting to Annigoni at the bar, with our post-dinner brandies, when a young man invited me to dance. I was on my third brandy already and unduly dizzy with drunken desire, a state that James viewed with genial amusement. He said that every man in the room was lusting after me, but he was the lucky bugger who would be getting it; my body scent alone was enough to drive an army gladly to the brink of death. And that kind of adulation which no one had given me before was creating a special excitement in me. Although I only wanted James, I now cast my eyes around, just to check out whether what he was saying was true. It was.

I was a vision of voluptuous loveliness. He was right there. I was wearing a waspie underneath my dress, a fashionable foundation garment that I'd sighted in Fenwick's Bond Street window, like the one Scarlett wore in *Gone with the Wind*. I'd fastened it on the tightest hook-and-eyes so that my waist was no more than twenty-two inches and my 34C uplifted tits were tumbling, nearly to nipple level, over the strapless top of my C & A siren-red taffeta dress. The skirt was a full circle when you laid it on the ground, so it could take up to three bouffant petticoats underneath it at a time. Those red and black petticoats were a real prize, stolen property as it turned out. Christmas presents from the kids at school whose dads were all on the thieve in between doing time at Wormwood Scrubs. They could get me anything I wanted. I had only to say. A car, a bicycle, a refrigerator. I acted stern, when I realized what the score was. I could get done for receiving stolen property, I told them. I tried to return the petticoats when I realized how they came to be mine, but I'd worn them by then. I put them back on straight away in the staff lavvy for the next lesson. You couldn't swop back soiled stolen goods, apparently.

My hair was shiny black and in mint condition, having been sawn off in tiny tendrils at the Maurice School of Hairdressing at Piccadilly Circus, who advertised for models on which their students could practise. I went there every week and was in the forefront when it came to the latest styles. And all for free. This cut was called the Italian Look. Even Elizabeth Taylor hadn't got around to it yet.

I had never danced on the minute dance floor adjoining the Pheasantry bar before. James viewed dancing as a waste of good drinking time. He didn't see the point of shuffling his bulk around a bloody postage-stamp when he was better off conserving all his energies for the bedroom.

But I adored dancing, it was one of my passions, and I was actually brilliant at it. When I was only thirteen, Sally and I used to go to cheap dancing classes in Cricklewood. We went every Saturday and learned everything, nothing was too complicated because our hearts were in it, the Rhumba, the Foxtrot, the Tango, you name it. So when this young chap asked me to dance I must have looked at James with such poignant longing that he gruffly said he supposed it was OK but not to be all fucking night at it. Well, once I got started, I couldn't stop. That chap was nifty on his feet, more Gene Kelly than Fred Astaire, which was how I liked it. To tell the truth, I lost track of time. I forgot about James, I barely noticed the crowd which gathered to clap each time a dance ended. I hadn't danced like this, not since I was out last with Judy at the

Studio Club, or with Betty at a students' hop. I hadn't been out dancing with young men, not since James. When I returned to the bar, hot, happy and laughing, James silently handed me my drink. He overheard the young man ask for my number and I could feel the sudden atmosphere, icy cold. I put my arm through James's and snuggled against him. I shook my head and said that I was sorry but I was already in love and didn't give out my number. The downcast young man drifted away. I stood on tip-toe to kiss James on the mouth. He was seething. We didn't ever go back to the Pheasantry again. After that, he only chose places which had no dance floor.

That evening marked a turning point. From then on I had a sense that something was missing. My times with James were not enough. Unbelievable though it was, and for the very first time in my life, I had a hovering sense of loneliness, a sense of alienation. Now I looked forward to a drink to escape this. I couldn't understand why because since I started this sexual stuff I was like a bud that had suddenly burst into blossom. Men actually followed me like dogs on heat in the street. When I travelled by tube in the rush-hour, hanging on a strap to remain upright, I could feel their hands crawling all over me. I would take a deep breath and stare at the ceiling, pretending it wasn't happening. I told James, and he nodded his head saying I was a witch, and in olden times would have been burned at the stake for driving men mad. He meant it as a compliment, but I didn't construe it as such. I felt it was all my fault, that something about me must be proclaiming my availability. Now I was dissatisfied. I didn't like the way things were going for me. I truly hated the sense of being a sexual object adrift in a sea of rapacious predators.

All my other friends were starting affairs which led to marriage with men of their own age, while I was stuck, waiting for James. Hanging about when he was off on location, filming. Waiting in until he arrived late, after roistering with the Thursday Club, a group of raffish eccentrics, which included Prince Philip and Baron, the society photographer. They were the ones my father read about out loud, longing to be part of that world. And here I was, neither in it nor out of it, nibbling at crumbs from their table. I didn't say any of this, though. Like any girl in an affair with a married man, I had to sit tight and keep mum, taking what I could get. This was the first and last time I got embroiled on those terms with an unavailable man. I learned the hard way that it was a mug's game, too painful a lesson on which to waste my youth. But I was unable to break away yet.

Sally had another baby, which meant she now had a husband, a girl and a boy and a mortgage. I had nothing, not even a fiancé. My mother and father came to London for a day-trip to see for themselves how I was getting on, why there was no talk of a boyfriend. I was going to take them out to an early dinner at the Stockpot in Knightsbridge which was one of the new French-style bistros. They were having a cup of tea in my flat before we went, when the telephone rang. I was dreading it would be James. My father answered enthusiastically, winking all round. He put on a posh voice and said, 'This is the London residence of Molly Thomas. The butler speaking. Who shall I say is calling?'

James was perplexed and displeased to hear a male voice. He was ringing from Scotland, checking up that I was in reading on Saturday night instead of gadding around.

He exploded. 'Who the fuck's this? Tell the tart that it's James and to get her bloody arse over to this telephone!'

My father bristled. I could hear James's voice clearly from the other side of the room, but was helpless, rooted to the spot in fear.

'James who exactly?' My father lifted his hand to me as if I was a small child, as if he was going to swipe me one

Above 'Sam the Post' – me with my grandfather, Tadci Thomas.

Above right My granny and Tadci Noyle visiting their children in Bettws Cemetery.

Right The photo on the mantelpiece: Craig-y-Nos Castle, my granny's home.

Left 'It was always the three of us' – Sally and me, the baby . . .

Below left . . . and cousin Barbara.

Right My mother (right) was an acknowledged beauty.

Far right The best days of his life – my father in the First World War.

Below right Things changed when I was seven. My Uncle Bryn's wedding. Middle row, l to r: my father, my mother, Uncle Bryn, his bride. Front row: Sally and me.

Above Art School days (me centre with Judy to my left).

Right James Robertson Justice. My sexual Svengali. (*BFI*)

Opposite page, above Judy and me on the toot in Paris. That's my red mac she's wearing.

Opposite page, below My form photo at Silverthorn School, with Sylvia.

Above The bride's veil had blown over her face – a bad omen. L to r: Sally, Mama, Granville and me.

Below A loving father: Michael and Sarah.

Above right Preparing my first exhibition in our front room, which I used as a studio, in Palace Gardens Terrace. (*John Timbers*)

Below right 'Darling Mollikins – after the whisky. (*Belinda Barr*)

I was sent to Paris for haute couture but I chose Paco Rabanne's plastic clothing instead. This photograph stunned the fashion world. (*Jeanloup Sieff/Nova*)

across the chops for consorting with riff-raff who referred to his daughter as 'tart' and used bad language into the bargain.

The answer thundered back. James at his most pompous. 'James Robertson Justice, of course, you bloody ignorant little swine! What other James would it be for Christ's sake!'

'*The* James Robertson Justice?' My father's dentures were on the move. His eyeballs embarked on a nifty swivelling act as I nodded miserably from across the room. My mother started wringing her hands in excitement. I now knew what the chickens coming home to roost meant.

'The one and only James Robertson Justice, of course, and indeed is there any other James?—' My father assumed a Uriah Heep stance, shoulders bowed, jutting arse, bowing forward at the waist. His tone was offensively obsequious, a bully-boy meeting his match. My fear was now larded with embarrassment. Further cringe-making conversation was about to take place.

'Allow me this opportunity, as Molly's father, sir, of saying what enormous pleasure your performances have afforded me in the past. I know my good lady-wife wishes to join me in my sentiments. Here she is, sir, to have a bit of a word herself. I'm putting her on—'

I left the room. This was too much. There was something grotesque about my father calling James sir. I was furious at the situation I had got myself into. I knew the dinner ahead was going to be ruined by recriminations and accusations as to my life-style, my morals, my conduct. I stood outside the room in the corridor, seeing the set-up for what it was in all its shabbiness. James, some kind of Scottish toff, who acted a bit on the side, when he wasn't kow-towing to royalty, sticking his randy dick, and whatever else came to hand in the way of electricals, into a pathetically eager snob from the lower orders. An absurd

145

girl on the make, desperate to scramble up the social ladder, by fair means or foul, in justification of her parents' endeavours and sacrifices to educate her out of her class. I thought of my granny and God, and being on top of the mountain with my grandfather. I thought of how long it was since I'd painted, really painted, for myself alone. I tried to remember when I last went to chapel. And I swore that if I could get through this evening intact and in one piece that I would never again turn my back on those things which were most precious to me.

My parents emerged, both beaming, from the room.

'Mr Robertson Justice would like a word with you. We'll wait in the kitchen to give you some privacy.' My father had never spoken to me with such pride and tenderness before.

'Hello,' I said into the phone. My voice was dull. I was on the defensive. I didn't care what James thought, these people were my parents. I loved them, even if they appeared to him to be a pair of provincial prats. If it weren't for their hopes and aspirations on my behalf I wouldn't be here at his beck and call, stuffing my luscious breasts into his greedy mouth, two at a time; sucking his scrotum, pumping his prick dry of seminal fluids; posing bare-arsed in my waspie for a photo to give him something to focus on when he was wanking off in my absence. I could have said all that, it was on the tip of my tongue. But all I managed was a dreary little hello. He soon won me round, of course. He wasn't born yesterday, and he knew me well enough by now to understand every possible inflection of my voice. He had told my parents that he was a great admirer of my paintings, that he was planning to purchase one and was ringing to ask when he could do so. He enjoyed supporting young painters, especially Celts. He liked the sound of my father, and wanted to meet him sometime. He left that for me to arrange, that's what he told my father. I was back eating out of James's hand. Again. But now I was joined by my parents. He'd got the whole family by the goolies.

I had not been entirely faithful to James in all this time, but since my other swain was even older than him I didn't think sexual fidelity came into it. Lennie Plugge was seventy and had been Errol Flynn's best friend. They used to hunt as a team in his more active years from Lennie's luxury yacht in Monte Carlo. I met him through Judy and her connections. His son, Frank, who had recently left Eton, had become a beau of mine. He was a charming boy and I was fond enough of him, but on my part it was not a romance. He invited me to his family home in Lowndes Square and I became friendly with Anne, his mother, and his younger twin brother and sister, Greville and Gail. Anne was a chic and charming hostess, a green-eyed beauty with a lithe body like the Duchess of Windsor. When she kissed me on arrival and departure I could smell her perfume lingering for hours. I wanted to be like her when I had children and lived in my own home. I was as intrigued with them as they seemed to be with me. They had a television set, for one thing, which I'd never seen before. There were millions of grand rooms and marble bathrooms in that vast mansion, and a butler to open the door. They obviously looked on me as Frank's girlfriend, someone to be grateful for, proving that he was clearly not homosexual, despite his schooling. That's what Lennie told me anyway, when he got me into his bed. It was quite appropriate apparently for a father to steal his son's girlfriend from under his youthful nose. They had a different way of carrying on, the upper classes.

Lennie had initially rung me on a professional pretext. He memorized my phone number from seeing his son dialling it and rang one evening to invite me to dinner at his apartment in Dolphin Square, where he lived on his own, away from his family. He collected me within the hour in his huge Buick, the American equivalent of a Daimler, he said. He wanted me to meet an important television producer who was married to one of the famous TV Toppers, *the* blonde dance troupe of the small screen. This producer commissioned artists for backdrops and scenery; I could make a name for myself and a lot of money. I embarked on one of the most boring and unproductive evenings of my life. One of the most enlightening, also.

This enlightenment didn't occur until almost the end, by which time I was gagging for more drink with a desperation that would become even keener as the years progressed. The producer had already asked me for my telephone number, quietly so that his wife wouldn't hear. I was surprised. If he only wanted to get hold of me for work why wouldn't he want his wife to know? He saw my hesitation and whispered not to worry, he would get it from Lennie. He said he was encouraged to meet me at Lennie's, because it showed that I had a weakness for the more mature man, such as himself. I stared at him. I asked him what he meant by that. He patted my knee under the table, saying that Lennie had always been a sly old dog and had the pick of the prettiest girls.

I was very angry by then because I thought that he believed me to be on the game. I stood up to go and the producer saw that he might have overstepped the mark, so he left with the TV Topper before I could even get my coat. I was left alone with Lennie, a revolting, fat, bald, old man. I spun round on him, my fury fuelled by disappointment over the failed job opportunity and sheer lack of booze. I shouted at him.

'You cunt! You got me here under false pretences. That pig had no intention of passing design work my way – he obviously thought I was your prostitute, hired for the night. Does your son know what kind of fucking bastard you are?'

To my utter amazement he collapsed on the carpet. I stared down at him, completely taken aback. The fall was so swift and dramatic. He didn't move. Seconds ticked by and there was no sound at all. I could hear my heart pounding against my ribcage. 'Blimey, girl,' I said to myself, 'you've bloody gone and done it now! This lump's had his first coronary! He's a former Conservative member of parliament, a distinguished citizen who visited his constituents in his yacht for Christ's sake! He invented the car telephone. He's a millionaire. His family have had you to Sunday tea and let you watch their television. He's not used to gutter-talk. You've shocked him to the core. This is tantamount to murder!' I could certainly lose my job over this. And how would I explain to James what I was doing alone with this man, anyway? Let alone Frank and the family.

I raised a cautious toe and prodded him gently with one of my patent-leather Lilley & Skinner stilettos. 'Lennie . . .' I whispered.

He was galvanized into action as violently as he had effected his sudden collapse. 'Molly darling, oh, my sweetheart, dearest child – forgive me, forgive me! I am just a foolish old man who would go to any lengths to have you in my company, so that I can tell you I have had no sleep since I first laid eyes upon you with my son. Your beautiful face and lovely body have haunted me. You are truly the girl of my dreams, my darling. I would give you anything you asked for, anything, anything . . . just say you'll be mine, that's all I ask.'

He scrambled to his knees and wrapped his arms tightly around my legs, burying his face in my skirt. I couldn't shift for the weight of him. I looked down, bewildered. And moved.

All I could see from this far up was the top of his bald

head and his halo of silver hair. The hair of my grand-fathers. He was as old as they were and probably knew as much and more. He'd have a lot of interesting things to tell me if I gave him the chance. He was not glamorous like James, not a film star in the public eye. But he'd made his mark in the world. He was a man of distinction, in *Who's Who* and all that. He'd educated his sons at Eton, and had provided his family with one of the best houses in London, in one of the most exclusive squares in the world. Why he wanted me of all people when he could have anybody was a mystery that I couldn't begin to under-stand. But want me he clearly did. So who was I to deny an old man some pleasure to lighten his dwindling years? I would have said that about either of my grandfathers wouldn't I? Those two marvellous men who taught me so much.

A feeling welled up in me as tender as when I held my sister's new baby. It wasn't the same as the excitement at the prospect of sex with James, but perhaps it came from a more profound source. I saw our bizarre reflection in the beautiful gilt-framed mirror which spanned the far wall. Something about it thrilled me. The contrast between my youthful power, my robust health and his aged frailty. It was like a painting by the German Expressionist Otto Dix. I thought of Mr Hill dying in the gents' on Dollis Hill Station, dying in the arms of the prostitute. She must have been kind to him, as I was being kind now.

'There, there,' I said gently, stroking Lennie's bald head. 'There's nothing to cry about. I forgive you.'

My life assumed its own shadows for the next couple of years as I embarked on a pattern of secretive half-truths. I kept my men in separate compartments from each other, pretending to each of them that they were the only one. James shocked me one day when he warned me about

Lennie. He said to beware of ever falling into the clutches of that man, Captain Lennie Plugge, who gobbled up little girls like me for breakfast.

I asked him innocently what he meant, and he said that Lennie Plugge's power was insidious, and could change a girl's life, in the same way as a chap called Stephen Ward, who I was also to steer clear of, should we ever meet. I wasn't to hear Stephen Ward's name again, not for many years, but when I did it was in connection with Christine Keeler, Lord Astor, and John Profumo.

Lennie never took me out; he rarely left his opulent 'love nest', as he called it. He explained that his function in my life was to serve my best interests, always to be there, the one I came home to after spending the evening with other boyfriends. He advised me against going to bed with anyone else. All that would happen was that I'd get myself pregnant, or catch some awful disease like VD: the twin horrors. It was best to sleep with him and keep myself pure for my future husband. He was going to train me to catch the biggest fish and make the best marriage. The trick was to be brilliant in bed and that was what he was going to teach me; just as the continentals taught their young girls to make their husbands happy.

He said to look at Mrs Simpson, the only way she got the Prince of Wales and nearly became queen was because she was so flabbergastingly good at cock-sucking. Her skills in that direction tied the Duke of Windsor to her apron-strings forever and if I got even a tenth that good at it, then I could make just as fine a match. But it would take a hell of a long time, patience, and a lot of practice. I was up for grabs, ready for whatever it would take to make my family proud of me. It was no good getting educated if I ended up marrying back into where I'd come from. My mother had told me that a thousand times, citing her own misery as an example.

However, I was less than enthusiastic at the prospect of

chewing on Lennie's limp dick for hours. It seemed to me that it wasn't the best use of my youth. But apparently fellatio was the name of the game and the trickiest to master. Sometimes, mid-mouthful, my head jammed on his plump stomach and gagging for air, I thought guiltily of James and wondered if this was what he meant by Lennie's insidious influence. And yet something about the situation made it hard for me to leave. I had fallen into a pampered trap. I was a faintly struggling fly in Lennie's seductive spider's web.

There were various components which lured me there. From the start of the relationship it became clear to Lennie that I needed alcohol and a lot of it to 'relax' – meaning to say I couldn't strip off until I was completely sozzled. With James this had never been a problem because we consumed at the same rate, neck and neck. But Lennie was a teetotaller and always had been. So from now on his refrigerator, the first I had ever seen in a private home, was stocked from top to bottom with chilled champagne especially for me. The minute I arrived he popped the cork in celebration and the bottle was all mine. He told me to remember the label, Krug, because that was the best and the only champagne that his darling girl should ever drink. The snacks he provided were always the same. Caviare and smoked salmon, both of which took some getting used to for someone more at home with tea and toast with jam, for those sinking moments of hunger, as my mother called them.

I pulled a face at the caviare, when he first gave it to me. 'Ugh!' I spat it out over the Persian rug. 'What kind of muck's this?'

He looked faintly reproving and pursed his mouth.

'Try again, slowly. Savour the flavour. Think of it as spunk.'

I spat again. 'Horrible! I don't like it!'

'Darling girl, it's an acquired taste and part of your

social training. Now try again for Lennie, sit on my knee, that's my sweetheart. Let's slip your little panties off while I feed you . . .'

So I was assured of my alcohol supplies when I went to Lennie's. And I was assured of the drugs that he introduced me to as well. For it was there that I got hooked on to sleeping tablets for the first time, extra strong knock-me-outs which he'd found in America. I never knew what he got up to in bed with me when I took those pills. One minute I was on the pillows, drunk and drowsy, trying to respond to a bout of what he called cunnilingus which involved him munching for hours on my minge, and the next I was waking up to the alarm clock which summoned me to teaching.

Lennie was up already, with my morning tea and my bath running, as solicitous and dependable as my Tadci Noyle. The same age. I lay, fuddle-brained from drink and sleeping-draught, in the scented vapours of the bathroom. A room like no other bathroom I'd ever seen before or since. I focused on the jewelled bath taps and the tasselled, padded velvet walls, on the painted nude in its gilt frame on the ceiling. I studied the big toe on the Rubenesque body, how it was curled up in ecstasy while her companion played with her pussy. Lennie explained that this happened to all girls, that it happened to me when he excited me in the same way. I didn't tell him that whatever he did to me I felt as dead as cold mutton, and that I purposely pointed my toes up in order to please him.

Part of me wanted to lie in this theatrical luxury all day and be like Lennie, never going out. This is what he tried to persuade me into doing every morning as I prepared to leave him. He would have liked me to stay and continue our game of backgammon, lying on his exquisite Marie Antoinette bedspread, which cost him a fortune. There in the fetid atmosphere of dying flowers, French perfumes, and silken drapes, with never a glimpse of daylight. When I described it to Sylvia, she all but exploded. She remarked on my pallor, my waxy appearance and was determined to yank me back into the land of the living. I arranged for her and Lennie to meet.

He couldn't understand how I could love teaching, especially in what he referred to as the slums. He shuddered as he said it. I explained that my parents had sacrificed a lot for me to get this far, and I was a source of great pride to them. And, in any case, we should all give back to society what we had taken out and help those who were less privileged. He as a former politician should support that.

He pointed out with a patient sigh that I had much to learn about politics and had only been subjected to a ghastly socialism. I told him that I was certainly not interested in listening to a Tory arsehole spouting on about capitalism. And it was at those moments that I longed for James, who would have been halfway through a bottle of Napoleon brandy for breakfast by now and regaling me with reasons why anarchy was the only way to go, politically speaking.

Those conversations with Lennie usually took place while he was soaping my back in the bath. Sometimes I hated these talks and his viewpoint so much that I deliberately splashed bathwater all down his silk Jermyn Street dressing gown. But I had to go a bit easy because I was waiting for the next stage of our ritual. The money. The five pounds which he would press into my hand to pay for the taxi to the Elephant and Castle. He would order the taxi in advance and it would be already waiting when I emerged, but I always told the driver to drop me at the bus stop around the corner and I pocketed the fiver. I needed this money to send to my parents. This was one of the reasons I returned with such regularity to Lennie, two or three times, sometimes more, a week.

A fiver in those days was a lot of money when you consider that I was being paid the vast fortune of twelve pounds a week as a graduate teacher. Nobody in our family had ever earned as much. I was already sending five pounds of this to my parents and had been since I'd arrived in London. But they were in appalling financial chaos again. Unpaid bills from the Brighton shop were dogging them now in Barry. Cash that my father had gambled with behind my mother's back. The Littlewoods' betting slips arrived to give him away. There were horrendous rows about this, and my mother wrote that her life was a nightmare.

They'd made a terrible mistake, moving when they did – another error of judgement on my father's part. The seaside bed and breakfast business was non-existent in Barry for the winter months, until the summer season took off. There was very little other work, but my mother managed to get various jobs doing casual labour in kitchens, or factories, and my father was working all the hours that God created on a building site. At his age, he was the oldest there.

His chest condition was as chronic as ever, my mother wrote. That week he'd had to take time off work and lose wages, laid low with an attack of recurring bronchitis. His cigarette intake hadn't slackened off at all, despite the fact they had little spare cash for fags. Now they'd no longer got the shop, he was really missing the ever-ready supply of Woodbines. They couldn't get out for drinks as much as they used to, there just wasn't the money, so she'd taken up smoking. It was their only treat. That and looking forward to seeing me in the forthcoming half-term holidays. My donations were really appreciated, but I must mind not to go short myself. She couldn't sleep a wink for worrying. My father *hated* it in Barry and wanted to move already. A man on his building site had fallen off the top scaffolding into the cement mixer with his first coronary, and another dropped dead as he was hauling the bricks, all in the same afternoon. My father said anything to relieve the boredom, anything for a laugh. Write soon – and send what you can. Every little helps!

Lennie's sleeping pills were really getting to me. It took until the mid-morning break for the numbing effects to wear off. My imagination didn't function for teaching until then, so the girls in the first double-period found themselves with their favourite art lessons instead of the truly creative ones which produced the spectacular work from them. Their favourite was pattern-making, zigzag-zigzag-dot-dot-dot-circle-circle-circle. They told me excitedly what pattern would go where as wallpaper when they got married. Getting married was all they thought about. Getting married and playing at sex while avoiding it. The working-class morality of my background, with the same filthy sense of humour. I had to censor my conversation every step of the way with these kids. I learned this to my cost in the very first days.

'We'll be making handpuppets next week, and for the heads I'd like you to bring some balls.'

A titter ran round the room.

'Large or small balls,' I continued, falling right into it. 'If you haven't any of your own, borrow your brother's.'

The class erupted. Amidst the hilarity, a voice choking with laughter shouted, 'Can't do that, Madam. He'd be lost without them!'

We sat in circles weaving baskets in my craft lessons. I explained that we would have to start with the base and that it was important that all their bottoms should have neat little holes in them. Bedlam broke out.

'Mine's got a nice little hole in it, Madam!'

'So's mine – look, look, Madam!'

The sauciest stood up and dropped their drawers,

156

poking their small bums in my direction. It was at times like this that I prayed the art inspector wouldn't drop in, or the headmistress be on her rounds. Because much as I tried to show a stern face, I couldn't help but enjoy their exuberant high spirits.

But however popular these pattern-making classes were with my pupils, I could see that my jaunts over to Lennie's were going to have to be limited to the nights when I was not teaching the next day, so I needed another source of extra income if I was to be any kind of solid financial support for my parents. No sooner had I come to this decision than two money-making opportunities presented themselves.

Another old codger, William, came into my life, one who required private painting tuition, and I agreed to pose in the nude for the artist Alistair Grant. Both paid the same money, five pounds an hour, the identical sum as Lennie's taxi fare. That was obviously my worth in whatever area I chose to operate. I didn't tell anyone that I was posing in the nude. It wasn't what any decent girl did, even ex-art students. We left that to the professionals.

I certainly didn't tell my mother or father. I just said that I had found a wealthy patron who required painting tuition as often as I could spare the time to fit him in. Which was absolutely true. What I didn't say was that William's money was as tainted and as shame-making as the other two sources. And even harder to earn, because I had to work my bollocks off attempting to mould his slender artistic gift into some kind of shape, as well as putting up with the same old sexual harassment at the end of it.

He would pin me against his stack of top quality, six-foot square Green and Stone canvases, which cost as much as I could earn in six months, and tell me I drove him wild with my animal magnetism. As I struggled to escape from his portly embrace he would get so over-excited that he'd ejaculate like a pubescent boy. The man was in his sixties, for Christ's sake! I would spit at him in disgust, and his cock would start twitching again. So soon!

After some time of this, I demanded my tuition money in the coarsest possible way, saying that if he continued to treat me like a tart we'd have to renegotiate my fees. His eyes shone in adoration. His entire body went into violent spasm. He timidly touched my mouth to prevent me saying more. Then, in a trembling voice very close to tears, he asked me to be his wife.

I would have many proposals of marriage in my life, but few as unexpected as this. Though I had no intention of granting him this, his heart's desire, I agreed to visit him at his country estate. He sent the chauffeured Daimler to collect me and when I arrived he had the entire house staff waiting in a line-up to bow and curtsy, eleven in all, from the butler to the tweeny maid and the gardeners.

I told Lennie all about it and he said I'd done well and he'd check this chap out as to his background and qualifications. It was a pity there was no title, he said, but obviously the man was upper class otherwise he wouldn't have succumbed to me in what was clearly a sado-masochistic way.

He was surprised that an actual marriage proposal had come into it. But I was and always would be a girl that men lost their hearts to. A witch, in other words. He told me to keep William on hold until something better came along. I knew Lennie would have termed James as something better, because when we were in bed one night James appeared on the TV screen and Lennie turned to me. 'That's my idea of a good man,' he said. 'Got the right attitude to life.' I grinned into my gold goblet of champagne and said nothing. It appealed to me, hood-winking these pompous bastards, these swine who thought they knew it all. That's what my Tadci Thomas would have said. But a shattering event was about to happen which would alter all this forever.

I was twenty-four when my father died. His death took five days from start to finish. Five days from his first heart attack at home in bed, to his last in Llandough Hospital.

Mrs Macmillan, my headmistress, summoned me from my classroom saying my sister was on the phone with bad news. I automatically assumed it must be my mother. She was the one who was always at death's door with some complaint or other. The hypochondriac crying wolf again. But I could tell by Sally's voice that this time things were serious. It was my father who was in hospital, not my mother, and I must travel to Wales right away.

I took a bus to the hospital from Cardiff Station. My mother and Sally were already there at the bedside. My father was unrecognizable, shrivelled and small beneath a welter of tubes taped to his arm from a Heath Robinson-like contraption alongside. We spent the next few days at the hospital, only going home to snatch a few hours' sleep.

The news came in the middle of the night. My mother stumbled into my bedroom to tell me.

'He's gone,' she wailed. 'He's gone, he's gone . . .'

We clung together, crying in the dark. I sat her on the side of the bed, holding her with one hand while I put on my dressing gown. It was three o'clock in the morning, the bleakest hour of the night, and we'd just had the worst news possible. I was half an orphan now and my mother a widow, but there was an unopened bottle of brandy in my bag, bought by me in case. James had always told me that brandy made any pain bearable. By dawn I couldn't remember what we'd been drinking about.

We took the bus in the morning to collect his belongings from the hospital. I waited outside. I didn't want to go in. A wintry sun was trying to shine through a sky the colour of dirty sink water. I was nauseous from a hangover and not having had breakfast. It would seem obscene to eat at this time. I thought of my mother and what it would be like for her from now on, and how my father wasn't so stupid to make his getaway from the circumstances of their lives.

I had stood in this same spot two nights previously, when my mother and I had remained by the bedside in vigil. My father had regained consciousness and I had left the two of them holding hands, to be by themselves, while I took a walk in the grounds. I looked up at the sky then, scattered in stars, trying to imagine how it would feel if my father died, if he didn't recover. I put my hands together and begged God not to let it happen. I'd give up drink and sex and everything if that was what he wanted, I said. But it hadn't felt right then. I couldn't make contact, not in the way that I'd always been used to. I was out of practice and God had refused my prayers. Understandable.

A desolation swept through me like a keen wind. I was alone. Forsaken. In my own wilderness. Things could only get worse from now on. I couldn't wait to get a drink down me to kill that feeling.

We sat on the bus going home, my mother and I. Neither of us spoke. Tears rolled down our cheeks. I wanted to think about good times that I'd had with that dead father of mine. I wanted to think of all the laughter that we as a family must have shared over the years. But all I could see, mourning him now, was his face in the kitchen when my mother threatened to leave him all those years ago. That, and him lying naked in my arms, his upper denture in fragments on the sweet-shop floor below, his lower denture lying on the pillow beside him, and his scrotum dangling over the edge of the pisspot, which I was holding.

I didn't want these images. I would have liked to wipe them away as I wiped my drawings from the blackboard at school. But they wouldn't shift. They had taken root, becoming stronger and stronger over the years until the weight of them was unbearable and had to be seen to.

We buried him in Bettws Cemetery with my granny and Tadci Noyle, in the family grave which contained the corpses of their dead babies. My mother was so distraught, so demented, that she had to be restrained at the open grave from hurling herself in. She kept screaming my father's name and, collapsing, had to be carried from the cemetery. Sally and I knew that our lives would never be the same ever again. Our mother had become our child.

That sudden, shocking, and premature end to my father's life in his mid-fifties had an immediate and dramatic effect on my life. It destroyed the spell of my ancient old men. I finished with every single one of them. Even James. I never saw him again.

I broke their hearts, so they claimed, especially James. But it was something that I simply had to do. The death of my father lifted a kind of curse. That's how it felt to me, though I was not able to pin it down. But it explained the sense of freedom, and the fact that I felt able to get on with my own life, with people my own age, at last.

To my surprise, now that I really needed them, my closest pals were no longer so readily at hand. Every single one of my girlfriends was married! I looked around and saw that I was now totally on my own and would have to start all over again in building a life for myself. I hadn't realized how much time I'd been spending in the grave!

Betty was married and living the colonial life out in Kenya. Judy was also married and living in London. Sylvia had fallen in love and was due to marry a friend of Lennie's, John Scaffardi. These two, Sylvia and John, would be like family to me in the future, but for the present they were wrapped up in their late-blossoming romance. She was in her mid-fifties and he in his late forties. This was a love affair that Lennie and I had arranged. Everyone was thrilled to bits with the outcome.

I was living by myself in a bedsit in Drayton Gardens. When I returned to my tiny room after the funeral in Wales, my landladies were waiting to hear the news of my father.

I choked on the words, 'He died,' and bolted upstairs. I stared at the red gramophone he'd helped me to buy and I played both my records: 'Pavane for a Dead Infanta', which backed 'Air on a G string', and Elvis Presley's 'You Aint Nothin' But a Hound-dog (crying all the time . . .)' – the other side was 'Heartbreak Hotel'. All suitable stuff. Tears seeped down my cheeks. The pain was excruciating. Had I really loved him that much, after all? I didn't understand anything any more. I hurled myself on the bed and sobbed into the pillow. I ached to be with my mother, to comfort her, knowing that she felt even worse than this.

There was a gentle tap on the door. I opened it. My cheeks were drenched, my eyes swollen. I didn't care who saw me like this. It was one of my landladies with a drink in her hand. She set it down on the table and put her arms around me.

'I know how it was for me when my father died, darling,' she murmured into my neck. Time hung, suspended. I had no idea how long we stood there, the older woman and me locked together; she in the past and me in the present, both gripped in our agonies. We let go at the same time. She pointed at the whisky, full to the brim. 'This will help.' She left the room, quietly closing the door. I smelled the musk of her long hair lingering on my skin. I stood, alone, not moving from where she had been, and it was as if she was still with me, in the silence, waiting for dusk to fall. My consolation.

She was an Indian princess and she lived here in their house with my other landlady, her lover, an American actress. At this time in the fifties lesbianism, to someone as unsophisticated as me, was something you only read about in the *News of the World*. The female equivalent of a 'queer'. We had two 'pansy boys' at Brighton Art School in the fashion department. And there was 'a big girl's blouse of a man', at our Radnor Walk Welsh chapel, who used to beg to make teas with the women instead of volunteering to play Rugby for the London Welsh.

I had never, knowingly, met a lesbian before. Now the house was full of deep-throated females dressed up as men. Nancy Spain, the writer and broadcaster, was a regular visitor, until her death in a two-seater plane crash. I didn't have any contact with this marvellously raffish set. I just heard them in the hallway. I would peep down through the banisters, as they arrived, waving their bottles of booze, and watch them disappear into the basement, from which laughter exploded all evening long. I felt this was a forbidden world to me. An alien world where women had learned, indeed chosen, to live without men. I would have liked to join in because I didn't enjoy the feeling of missing out on anything, anything at all. But I was not qualified, I didn't belong.

I started going out on my own for the first time since my arrival in London. For the first time ever I was doing what I wanted, without referring to somebody else's whims. I felt good, independent at last. I began seeing exhibitions at the weekends. I made a tour of the galleries and in the evening I went to the theatre. I saw Beckett's *Waiting for Godot*, at the Criterion Theatre, Piccadilly, standing at the back of the stalls all the way through because the seats were sold out and, in any case, I couldn't have afforded them, even if they'd been available. Men tried to pick me up, but I was used to it by now and knew how to deflect the situation without getting paranoid.

I didn't drink on my own. I would go for a cup of tea and a poached egg on toast before the theatre at Lyon's

Corner House in Coventry Street, just like Sal and I did when we were teenagers. It wasn't the same as the ritzy restaurants I used to go to with James. It wasn't the Connaught or Brown's or Claridges, where William used to take me. But it was more fun, doing what I liked, more comfortable.

I sought out obscure foreign films in tiny fleapits in an endeavour to widen my cultural view of the world. One night I walked home in the rain, down Park Lane which was then the centre for prostitutes. One threatened me with her brolly, thinking I was strolling her pitch. I had just seen a French film about a famous orchestral conductor in the grip of heroin addiction, played by the current continental heart-throb, Daniel Gelin. It felt appropriate to be mooching along, soaking wet, isolated in a kind of intellectual misery, frowning morosely as men kerb-crawled in their cars. The same kind of men who until so recently I would have been doing my best, in a baby-doll way, to delight. My childhood diet of Hollywood musicals didn't really satisfy me any more. I was drawn to gritty realism now.

I was still first in the Leicester Square queue for *A Star is Born*, with Judy Garland and James Mason, though. I'd always been excited by James Mason, ever since he'd whipped Margaret Lockwood to death in *Fanny by Gaslight*, and slammed his stick down on Ann Todd's piano-playing fingers in *The Seventh Veil*. I could imagine how intensely enjoyable it would be to make him suffer, to have him in my thrall, as I had William and the rest of them.

I struck up a conversation with a pretty girl in the queue. It was Saturday night and she was on her own, too. She was killing off a few hours before starting work, she said. We sat together and had ice-creams. I told her about my father dying and she said that she left home years ago, when she was just a kid, because her father was such a bastard. She said she hated men, but was getting her own back now. She milked them for every cent they'd got. She had regular clients, but she worked hotel lobbies as well by slipping the lads at the desk a tip. She asked me how much I earned and hooted with laughter when I told her. It was as much as she could make in an hour.

I refused her offer to join her that night, though she was eager to show me the ropes. But all the way home on the underground I wondered who was the twerp, her or me. One week on the game would see to all my mother's worries. What was the difference between that and what I'd been getting up to?

I began to familiarize myself with what was going on in the jazz world. Dill Jones, my Welsh pianist pal, urged me to go and see Louis Armstrong who was appearing live at Earl's Court. I whined that I couldn't afford it and he got really cross. He said that some things were worth making sacrifices for, and if it meant not eating for a week to buy a ticket then that was too bad. To see Louis Armstrong perform in the flesh was to take part in history, for a jazz giant like this didn't happen every day. And just to be in his presence, hearing him play, would change me forever. I realized what a gulf there was in my life, what extremes. On the one hand, I knew all these wealthy geezers who wouldn't shift themselves to see a black jazz giant, even if they'd known who he was, and, on the other, the artists and teachers that I moved amongst were like me, without the price of a ticket. Surely there must be people for me to meet who shared my interests, but didn't live with a crippling fear of financial insecurity?

I went to the concert. It did change my life. It showed me that from now on I must strive to be as pure in spirit, as innocently open and as spontaneous as Louis Armstrong. Forty years on the experience is still with me.

I saw Hoagy Carmichael, I met him after his show, when I waited backstage for his autograph. He kissed me on the cheek, his eyes shining. I was empowered by his charisma, by his magic. I bought his music, and Louis Armstrong's, and played them in my bedsit looking out of the window at the tree in the garden. I sensed a wholeness, a completeness, the same as I felt when I painted, or coaxed paintings from my pupils. Seeing something grow, like the sounds from these musicians. Honouring the flame, both my grandfathers would have said.

Under Milk Wood was on in Shaftesbury Avenue, with Donald Houston as the commentator. A longing swept over me, listening to the language, for Pontycymmer and all things Welsh. I thought lovingly of James, who had introduced me to the works of Dylan Thomas. His body came into my mind, followed immediately by the body of my father, his withered flanks in the coffin, the dead flesh hanging around his stiff neck. And all I knew was that I didn't want any ancient reminders of my father's skin anywhere near my own.

I hung my red mac up by the sink when I went to spend a penny in the ladies' at Lyon's Corner House before going to the theatre. The red mac that American Robert bought me in Paris. Somebody pinched it. It had gone from the hook, vanished, stolen.

The attendant murmured her sympathy. I shrugged and started laughing.

'Easy come, easy go!' I said, without elaborating.

Something about it felt like rough justice, I explained to Judy on the telephone. She was in Paris when I acquired the garment, and I thought she'd like to learn of its loss.

'I am laying the ghosts of my past,' I said wisely. There was a mystified silence at the other end. But I knew, something told me, that these things were happening for a reason. Important changes were taking place in my life.

Robert came to London a week after the red mackintosh incident. He rang me from the Westbury Hotel off Bond

Street. I told him what a coincidence it was that he should pop up just after the disappearance of the mac, which is why he was in my mind. I didn't say how briefly or with how little love . . .

'We must replace that little raincoat,' he said with immediate generosity. 'How do you feel about diamonds now? Are they still unacceptable, honey?'

The old me responded eagerly: the greedy one, the other me, the one who I despised and thought I'd dumped along with all my old wealthy swains. He sent a taxi to collect me right away. He told me he hadn't stopped thinking about me since Paris. No other girl had affected him this way. We went straight to bed. He had put on a lot of weight. He heaved and humped on top of me, missionary position. I'd forgotten how hairy he was; it was like being fucked by a polar bear. I started laughing in the middle of it and couldn't stop. It was so awful.

I imagined what a hilarious tale I could concoct for Sylvia and John and for Judy, especially for her, and tears ran down the side of my cheeks. I was hysterical. I smacked his vast buttocks to speed up the action, and he shot off in surprise, with a roar which caused the management to ring up discreetly and enquire if everything was all right. But it was over. At last. He rolled on to his side of the king size and got down to business. The stuff I'd been waiting for. Two bourbons on the rocks, American style, right up to the brim as I liked it. Then I didn't care what he did to me. When I was 'out of it', everything was OK.

He asked me to come to live with him in America. He had two ex-wives already but if I wanted to we could get married. A life of Luxury, with a big L. I told him about my mother and how I couldn't leave her on her own now that my father had died. He said she could come too. I said that my mother wouldn't like leaving her grand-children, or my sister. No problem, the more the merrier.

All he was interested in was me and if that meant exporting the whole of Wales and its population, so what. He could afford it.

He was obviously astonished when I told him I would think about it. Money bought anyone in this world, in America. But my mind was already made up. Anyone who needed me that desperately must have something wrong with them. He must be as second-rate as me. The answer was no.

In any case I was now having more fun on my own. More satisfaction at a deeper level. I was going to St Martin's Art School in Charing Cross Road one evening a week to a portrait class which was taken by Herbert Holt, a favourite tutor of mine from Brighton. He said that my presence in the class was a great help to him. That I brought a breath of fresh air and that it was useful for the other pupils to see how vigorously and fearlessly I tackled a canvas.

He invited me to his studio in Chelsea for my opinion on his latest works. He had been commissioned to paint various portraits of chairmen of the board and other worthies. I said he should break free of these, for they were stunting his growth. My candour was becoming invaluable to him, he claimed.

He took me to the Chelsea Arts Club. He was a member there and made me a member, too, because he felt it was important to mix with other artists after leaving art school, otherwise someone like me could get swallowed up in teaching and lose sight of their own work. Just as he'd got swallowed up in society painting, losing sight of the real goal.

I didn't much take to the Chelsea Arts Club. It was full of old farts to my mind, and the décor was depressing. I lunched there one day with Herbert and was held spellbound, with the rest of the table, wondering whether the drip from Sir Charles Wheeler's nose would touch his soup spoon before it reached his mouth. The food was appalling, just like school dinners – the only edible part was the pudding. Pink blancmange or sponge pudding, smothered in my old favourite, Bird's Custard. I made my excuses and didn't go back. Herbert paid my first membership fees, and I let them lapse for some years before I returned. But when I did I was married and a very different person.

It was at Herbert Holt's portrait class at St Martin's that I met two young architects, Noel and Roy. They introduced me to the York Minster Pub in Soho, known as the 'French', with Gaston behind the bar. Through them I met Mary Holland, a young Irish writer, who became a lifelong friend and confidante, and she invited me to the party which changed the direction of my life even more dramatically than my father's death. It was there that I met Michael Parkin, my future husband.

It was my first London party since the funeral and I bought a party frock in the January sales from Fenwick's in Bond Street. It was a real Brigitte Bardot number, with a twirling skirt and scooped neckline which shamelessly flaunted my cleavage. This was the fashion now, so that girls like me with plenty to flaunt were really top dogs. It was taffeta, this dress; a strange shade of khaki, almost olive green, cunningly chosen to match my eyes. I looked like a pouting Pekinese that evening, my hair a tousle of wayward curls, with tendrils curving over each cheek. I had lost a stone in weight after my father's death, so that my waist looked tiny, and I plastered so much opaque, worm-pink-to-white pastel lipstick over my mouth that the eye was immediately drawn to it as an openly inviting and somewhat obscene orifice. Jayne Mansfield in Hollywood and all the factory girls at the Elephant and Castle were currently sporting this same mouth.

Michael said later that he fell for me on sight. He had been reading an Anthony Powell novel from *A Dance to the Music of Time*, in which a character called Gypsy Jones just added up to me, and when I flounced into the room looking so exotic, he couldn't see anyone else from then on. I felt the same about him. He was the first one to speak to me, and I liked that. I liked his confidence. I didn't think for a moment that I stood a chance in hell with him, simply because he was everything that I'd ever wanted. More to the point, he was what my mother wanted for me, and what my father would have astringently described as a 'step up'.

At the end of the party he asked to drive me home. He said, 'Mine is the Riley outside', with such pride that I thought a Riley must be grander than a Rolls. I said yes. I didn't allow him in that first night, not from any feelings of morality, but because I didn't want him to think me too sluttish to marry and I knew my bedsit was in a mess. We sat in his handsome vehicle, a collector's item, more covetable than a mere Rolls any day, he told me. We sat for hours outside my front door in Drayton Gardens. I told him everything there was to tell about me, everything I thought he would want to hear, leaving a lot out. I spoke very carefully, trying to imitate Judy's accent, trying to match his own. My voice was unfamiliar to my own ears and would continue to be so throughout our marriage. It was a measured delivery which couldn't sustain itself in moments of high excitement so those had to be watched.

I accepted his invitation to go and stay with him at his country cottage in Wivenhoe, outside Colchester. We went to bed together within hours of arrival, after we'd had enough to drink in the picturesque country pub. I liked his method of love-making. He drove his erection in without foreplay. His penis was long and thick and large and very hard, the opposite of all the old men I'd been with. It didn't take long before it was over and done with, and then we'd start all over again. Sometimes he got hard again before he'd even withdrawn from the ejaculation.

We couldn't get enough of each other, it was like a fever, this need to devour. But it hurt every time and that reminded me of what little experience I'd had with Rupert, and Malcolm. I supposed this was what sex with young men was like. But I was never sober when it took place. I couldn't contemplate doing it without a drink to loosen my inhibitions. And the pain which felt like punishment was all mixed up with delirious pleasure. Exactly what I wanted and deserved.

Michael proposed to me on our second date and I accepted without question. I knew he was right for me. The news of my engagement flew along the Welsh valley back home, fuelled by my aunties.

'Have you heard of our Moll's triumph? She's not only marrying English, but public school and Oxford University! Imagine!'

Those same aunties were still referring to Michael all through our seven-year marriage as, 'How's the Oxford graduate, Moll?' They never bothered to learn his name. Not ever.

My mother had mixed feelings about my marriage. She was delighted with Michael; he was a real gentleman and had lovely manners, the son-in-law she'd always hoped for. She spoke as if she had reared me for this moment, for this magnificent match, as if I was marrying into the crowned heads of Europe. She was relieved to see me 'off the shelf'. I was nearly twenty-five already, which was ancient enough to be considered an old maid. Most of the girls I was at school with had got married at eighteen, and even those who went on to college were usually engaged by the end of their studies.

On the other hand she dreaded me leaving the country, dreaded the loneliness she would suffer. Michael and I would be going on honeymoon in the South of France before going to live in Germany. He had a high-flying position in the Armed Forces at their headquarters in München-Gladbach.

But she got excited about the wedding preparations, once she understood that, although the mother of the bride, she would be relieved of the financial burden. Lennie and Michael both knew of her lamentable position and undertook to organize everything. I didn't care one way or the other, but everyone seemed to want the full works. We were to be married in my local church, around the corner from Drayton Gardens. St Mary's, The Boltons, one of the most beautiful churches in London, as it happened. I had never been in it before my wedding day and, deep down inside, I would have preferred our Welsh chapel in Radnor Walk, but I didn't dare say so because in terms of grandeur it was not a patch on The Boltons. The reception was to take place in Lowndes Square, Belgravia. Lennie was giving it for me in his house as his wedding present. Nobody guessed how I'd earned it. Or perhaps they did. Frank was one of my ushers and Gail, his little sister, was my lovely flower-girl.

When my mother came up from Wales to meet Michael, I took her round to Lowndes Square to introduce her to Anne Plugge, Lennie's wife. Anne told her how fond they were of me, as a family. I squirmed as my mother put on a posh accent, though it was only what I was doing myself. My discomfort went further than that, though, I felt like an impostor before this charming creature. Did she know what had been going on between me and her husband? She offered us a sherry. The feeling passed. Thank God for social lubricants.

Since cash was so short we shopped for the wedding dress while the sales were still on. My mother favoured Harrods, as she always did. But I bore a grudge against the place since the assistants' cruelly derisive treatment of her in the past. I anticipated the same assistants snarling at me in a similar fashion. I was enough of a fraud already.

We went to Woollands in Knightsbridge, my favourite department store. My mother immediately asked the assistant to bring us the cheapest wedding dress she had. I knew I'd been right to resist Harrods! We were brought the one worn by the model in the white wedding finale at their recent fashion show. The girl had obviously been the size of a stick insect. It was going at a throw-away price because it was so ludicrously tiny. I couldn't even get my arms into the sleeves, let alone do the zip up at the back.

'We'll take it,' my mother said.

The assistant and I were speechless.

'It's too small,' I groaned. The assistant nodded vigorously.

'It's under a fiver.' My mother opened my purse.

'I can't get into it, not even my arms.'

'You will. By the end of the summer, you'll get into it. At this price I'd get anyone into it.'

I gave up my teaching job, and London life, to spend the summer with my mother helping her to run her bed and breakfast business down in Wales. And to lose enough weight, under her supervision, to get into *the dress*. She approached my diet with the maniacal enthusiasm of someone who barely ate at all, except to pop laxatives morning and night. The summer was an unqualified success even before we embarked on it because we were jointly involved in my mother's twin obsessions – making money and losing weight.

I turned my back on the successes I had recently garnered in the teaching profession. In my few years of teaching, the work of my pupils at Silverthorn School had increasingly caught the attention of the LCC Art Inspectorate. Since the death of my father (and now that I was no longer sleeping-pilling it with Lennie) I had poured all my prodigious creative energy into my lessons and the girls had responded in similar measure. The results emblazoned every corridor in the school. Six-foot murals pitched and patterned in all shades of yellow: lemon, canary, ochre. Animal panels in pounding earth colours. Rich brown wolves, soot-black bears. Ginger tigers with orange eyes. Passionate seascapes in sombre purples and sullen blues. Cobalt blue skies, brilliant with screaming gulls. Menacing eagles, hovering blackbirds, silhouetted against storm-clouds. Self-portraits of every single pupil in the entire school, they lined the stairs, the doors, spilled on to the ceilings. The very best of children's art greeted me every morning when I went into work. We were running out of wall-space.

This fact hadn't escaped the notice of the art inspectors. Two, instead of the usual one, arrived unannounced, which was always the case, when I was constructing giant-insect mobiles with Form 3C. I barely noticed their intrusion, we were having so much fun.

A month later the same children and I were on public display in County Hall, demonstrating our art to the public for a whole week. In the meantime, three of my pupils had won the leading prizes in the *Sunday Pictorial*'s Children's Art Competition. Their paintings were reproduced in the newspaper and were soon to be exhibited in a Piccadilly gallery. And the headmistress had given the school a half-day holiday to celebrate our having won *every single* prize in the Children's Art Competition, sponsored by Cadbury. Twenty huge hampers of chocolate bars were among the prizes, which, when distributed, meant every child got one.

I held extra classes after school for an hour or more, for the especially gifted children, and the ones who only offered their enthusiasm. I cherished those with a burning desire to express themselves as much as the ones with outstanding talent. And it always paid off in the end. The work was, in its own way, as magical. The result was that, in the face of dire parental opposition, three of my girls got into art school and embarked on their chosen careers as artists. Not many out of the hundreds who passed through my hands, but as enthralling to me, as a teacher, as my getting into art school must have been to my teacher, given the same unpromising background.

I met one of those talented girls in a hospital, years later, when my youngest child was having her tonsils and adenoids removed. A handsome young husband was at her bedside. He followed me from the ward to tell me that she would always be indebted to me for changing her life, for opening her eyes to the beauty in the world, for helping her to become an artist.

'What is she in hospital for?' I asked, conversationally.

'She's going blind,' he said. 'Which is why she so values what you enabled her to see while she had her sight.'

It was suggested to the Higher Art Inspectorate, following these successes, that I be given greater responsibility in a larger school. I was offered such a school, in charge of my own department, in Camberwell – a step up from Elephant and Castle. I would have been the youngest head of department in an LCC School, but I threw it all up to get married.

I can hardly believe now, looking back, that I could have disappointed everybody who'd encouraged me in my teaching career in this way. That job was offered to me as a positive honour. I had worked hard for such an opportunity, and yet there was no thought of this at all when I turned it down so casually in favour of marriage. To understand myself and this incomprehensible attitude I must remember what the climate was like for girls in the fifties. Even educated ones like myself were expected to relinquish all thoughts of a career when they got married. Their future was to be husband, home and babies from then on, as soon as the ring was slipped on to the finger. And, in any case, the most pressing problem on my mind at that moment was getting into *the dress*!

I enjoyed working with my mother. It felt good,

virtuous, loving, to be there when she needed me so much. And she certainly needed me! The business was in chaos. I had to remember that she had been attempting to organize the summer bookings just after my father's death when she was all over the place, mentally and emotionally.

The first time I realized that she had over-booked in triplicate for the coming week was when three different families arrived on our doorstep from the North. All for the same sea-facing bedrooms. That happened with varying frequency throughout the season from then on.

Each time, faced with irate travellers, my mother had the same reaction. She drifted out to the backyard to study the roses. Nothing could distract her. She refused to face the reality of the situation. I had to run through the back lane to the house three doors up.

'My mother's done it again,' I gasped. 'Can you help out?' The neighbour came to like the income so much that she opened up in the B and B business herself the following season.

We didn't drink at all that summer, and I didn't miss it one bit. I liked working hard and pulling the business into some kind of manageable shape in order to clear off the debts. In the process we got really intimate. My mother did the cooking and I did everything else: the shopping, the cleaning, the laundry, the serving at tables. We did the washing up together. Now that we were doing full board instead of just B and B, there was a lot of washing up. That I really loathed. Breakfast, lunch, and evening meal. But on the other hand it was when we talked the most, my mother and I, over the washing up.

We went over old ground, details of her childhood, of her days at boarding school, how she was the head-mistress's favourite although her family didn't appear to be landed gentry like most of the pupils. The headmistress obviously recognized quality when she saw it, and she certainly saw it in my mother's mother. 'She knew without asking that Granny, your granny, Molly – was a true lady. Bring the photograph, let's put the photograph of Craig-y-Nos Castle here on the kitchen window-ledge where we can see it every time we do this wretched old washing up. To remind us that we haven't always been skivvies in this family.'

We stared at the photograph together. It had accompanied us always, wherever we had lived. The first object to be placed on each successive mantelpiece upon moving in. The same photograph that my granny had in pride of place above her own hearth, over which she must have so often sighed.

'Will you come with me one day to visit the castle, Moll? It's a hospital now, but they'd let us see over it, if we say who we are.'

I turned away from her eager face. I didn't like this business of Craig-y-Nos. It seemed wasteful that the lost dream should still be invested with so much longing. I never did go with her to the castle.

Sally and Granville lived very close, so we saw a lot of them and the little ones, Sian and baby John. It was strange to see the change in my sister, so much the young mother now.

'You'll be next, Moll,' she said to me as she changed the baby's nappy. I took him from her and held the back of his tiny head as she'd shown me how to do, so that his fragile neck didn't snap in two. Wonder rose in me at the sheer fragility and unfathomability of this exquisite structure. I placed him high on my bare neck, his faint breath brushing my flesh. New blood, new bodies, the next generation. The biological clock ticked on imperceptibly. I now yearned to have babies of my own. I was ready.

I had no time at all for my own work, for my paintings. I started to feel a sense of loss about this, keenest after I bumped into Gwyn Thomas, who lived in a bungalow opposite my sister.

Gwyn Thomas, at this time, was still teaching at the local school, but his reputation as a leading Welsh novelist and contributor of mordant, humorous pieces for *Punch* was already established. In time he would become a major personality, a trenchant wit, on television and the radio, a national institution, still sadly mourned and missed to this day since his death in 1981.

I had first met him when Sally moved to Barry and I did a drawing of him, commissioned by a communist magazine in London. He liked the drawing so much that he asked me to paint a portrait in oils of him. These, the drawing and the painting, were my first paid professional commissions on leaving art school.

In later years we performed on television together, each egging the other on to bolder verbal excesses, but whenever we met he never failed to voice his regret that I was no longer painting. My soul jolted when I saw him.

'Turn your back on your talent at your own peril,' he said darkly. Gwyn represented my artistic conscience.

Michael, my fiancé, had already taken up his new job in Germany, but before our proposed wedding in the coming September he came back to England just once. I was nervous of seeing him. We had been out together just six times; I was marrying a man I barely knew. I drank until I was legless when we all went out. So did my mother.

Purged almost to extinction with the help of accumulated laxatives from my mother's drawer of pills, I wafted, sylph-like, up the aisle in the under-a-fiver wedding gown. I was twenty-five, the year was 1957. Old pals, like Sylvia, who hadn't seen me all summer, gasped at the transformation and said I was not looking my best. I seemed peaky and out of sorts. I had flu. I was debilitated, and crucifyingly hungry but unable to keep anything in my stomach. My bowels were in chronic confusion, not knowing whether they were coming or going, they'd been coaxed to evacuate themselves so relentlessly in recent months.

My brother-in-law, Granville, gave me away, in the absence of a father. I became tearful when I saw a gang of schoolgirls outside the church, my pupils from the Elephant and Castle. They showered me with confetti, sackfuls of the stuff, which only I knew would have been stolen. Other guests had demure sachets.

This particular group were the ones I had organized one weekend to visit a design exhibition off Trafalgar Square. They had never been out of the Elephant and Castle before. Now they had found their own way into Chelsea. I was as much thrilled by this show of initiative as anything else on my wedding day. They huddled together, as nervous as the sheep when they come down from our mountain and find themselves on the street. I knew that they were bursting to cheer and shout as they did in the school playground, but they were over-awed by the occasion, by my model gown, and the smart clothes of the guests. By so many men in top hats and tails, the grandness of The Boltons, and the upper-class accents of everyone around them.

I saw all this in their little pointed, pinched faces and I wanted to say to them that I understood how they were feeling, that I felt the same. I was inhibited too. I knew this was a mistake, that it was not how it was meant to be, that nobody should feel as uncomfortable as I did, least of all on their wedding day. I wanted to tell them how, even at the very last minute, as late as yesterday I had tried to pull out. Even though all my aunties had arrived from Paddington and were having tea at that very minute with my sister and my mother at the house of Mrs James from Porthcawl, off Sussex Gardens.

I don't know why I felt so keenly that I was not doing the right thing in marrying Michael, for when Sarah, our

179

first baby, was born, and subsequently Sophie, our second daughter, I couldn't imagine ever being happier. It seemed I had everything I'd ever wanted. And looking back now I still see those years as amongst the most idyllic of my life.

We had an uneasy start in Germany, where we lived in a large house, which went with the job, in a street of similar dwellings inhabited by high-ranking military staff. It seemed to me that we were surrounded by generals and their ghastly wives, all of whom kept inviting me to their morning, afternoon and early evening cocktail parties. Their cards lay unanswered on the hall table.

I don't think Michael quite realized just how socially uncivilized his young bride was until then. The truth was that these sort of women and the whole situation terrified me. I took to my bed and lay there all morning until Michael came home for a non-existent lunch. I serviced other appetites instead, then went back to sleep until he returned at the end of the day, when I'd offer another sex session instead of dinner. He was soon a shadow of his former self and I was happily pregnant.

But it couldn't continue. I started writing home saying how unhappy I was. I returned to Wales for my first married Christmas to be with my mother and help her through the first anniversary of my father's death. Michael's mother flew out to be with him in Germany. She suggested that what I was doing was not very fair, putting my mother before my husband. I was outraged. How dare she!

My mother was desolate this Christmas without my father and without me living in England. She referred to it as her 'double-loss', the cross she'd been called upon to bear within one tragic year. She had Sal and the babies, but the fact that both my sister and I now had a husband, a man in our lives, emphasized for her the stark fact that she didn't. I would have done anything, anything at all, to make up to her for that. But I couldn't, it was beyond my powers.

I could, however, return to live in this country. I could coax my husband out of his fine job. So I did. I told him that I would return to Britain on my own, pregnant, even if he didn't come with me. And he could tell that I meant it. He handed in his resignation. He had done his national service as a commissioned officer in the Irish Fusiliers, and part of him very much enjoyed the company and privileges of military life, just as my father had enjoyed his time in the forces. His boss told him that it had been a disappointment on both sides, our time in Germany. But that was my fault, I knew it was. I hadn't pulled my weight, socially speaking, as a supportive executive wife. And I had no remorse about that, I was sure there were better times ahead for both of us back in London.

Now that I knew we were no longer staying I pulled myself together for the duration, until Michael had worked out his notice. I took a job, teaching in a school for children of the armed forces. Though I was a qualified art teacher, there I had to teach everything: history, geography, English literature and language, games. I did it as I was shown, straight from the books. This appalled me, but I was assured that it was normal practice with the shortage of staff.

I peeped into the art room, where the class was being conducted by a person as ill-equipped to teach art as I was to teach the subjects I'd been given. A circle of bored children sat with pencils and small pieces of paper around an arranged still life of a chair and a broom. They were doing everything but draw, looking out of the window, whispering to each other, while the teacher read a book at her desk. The walls and corridors were empty except for one Constable print, *The Hay Wain*, outside the head-master's office.

I asked him if there was any chance for me to take some

art classes. But he said no, they were being perfectly adequately supervised. I offered to hold classes in my own time, after school. He looked astounded and asked why on earth I would want to do that. Art was the least important subject on the curriculum. And since these children all stemmed from military families, and the boys would undoubtedly follow the same profession as their fathers, and the girls would end up as forces wives, like their mothers, what point did art have in their lives?

I was speechless. I stared at the smear of moustache on his upper lip, his expression of disdain, the watery coldness of his blue eyes. He regarded me as 'arty-farty'. I unnerved him, I knew that. He hated his profession, he'd long since lost his calling, his vocational idealism. So he disliked it in me. He had the self-satisfied smugness of the English Philistine. I recognized him as the enemy. The bile rose in my throat.

'I'm giving you extra games, you'll be taking the fifth-form girls for hockey. Better for them than any amount of art – team spirit, and all that.'

'I'm pregnant,' I said mulishly.

'Splendid! Just what you need, spot of regular exercise.'

'But there's snow on the ground, and ice. It could be dangerous in my first three months.'

'Nonsense. Run along now. Good to have you aboard. We need young blood like you, pregnant or not.'

I got caught in a scrum between two hefty fifth-formers and sustained a fall on the hockey pitch. Pain ripped through my body and I started bleeding immediately. I was medically advised to stop teaching and take to my bed: it was my only chance of saving the baby.

Knowing that now I had only a month left in that hell-hole, I started painting dementedly with the intention of holding an exhibition on my return to London. Michael was astonished each time he came home from work to find yet more pictures spinning from my brush; they filled the dining room, the lounge, the corridor, the entrance hall. All the same: dark angry landscapes blooded with sunsets and stark menacing München-Gladbach trees. I was painting my hatred, that's what it was. My hatred of the military situation in which I found myself, and the bleakness of the surrounding terrain. I had transferred my resentment to all things German. And English. My racism was becoming absolute.

There was only one relief, one escape – the cinema. We went to the cinema as often as we could. Michael's passion for film equalled my own. It bound us together as closely as sex. When the cinema lights lowered and the film was about to start, with his fingers entwined in mine and mutual desire coursing through both our bodies, a bag of toffees at the ready, I felt as sublimely content as I would ever feel with any man.

I was the only female in the audience, the rest was made up of national servicemen all aged between eighteen and twenty. My pregnancy made me prone to nausea and the minutes before the lowering of the lights were a true test of endurance. Even Michael's stomach heaved at the regular exposure to adolescent acne on the necks of the boys in the rows in front. Poor things.

It was like surveying the craters of the moon. Boils as big and as white as tennis balls chafed against coarse khaki clothing, and burst before our eyes. The eruptions seeped stickily beneath short-back-and-sides, clotting under their collars. Some had been prematurely squeezed, so the ensuing inflammation was even more of a disaster zone. We nudged each other, Michael and I, drawing maliciously amused attention to those puckered, blood-splattered pus-tules. It drew us even closer together, this cruel pastime, setting ourselves apart, elevating ourselves to a superior position.

It reminded me of my father's sense of humour and how we, as a family, all joined in to jolly the atmosphere and help keep him sweet. How the big treat on Sundays, when he got hold of his old car, was to drive to Hyde Park and stop by the Serpentine to watch the oddities walk past. We couldn't open the windows in case they heard our critical comments and the hoots of mirth that followed.

'Here's one, here's a right one!' my father would shout. 'One leg shorter than the other, is that the trouble?' Or, 'Look at her, quick, look – Mrs Jimmy Durante! Don't blow that hooter, missus – wipe Britain clean off the map!'

Of course we loved it as children, even more when we were in the grip of puberty and our own attendant glandular uncertainties. What better fun than to transfer our anxieties by ridiculing the shortcomings of others? The fact that Barbara, with her own physical setbacks, would be in the car with us if she'd come to stay, made not a jot of difference to my father. Or to her, for that matter. She could be as wittily cutting in her comments as the rest of us, more so if anything. She found it the greatest fun.

I'd told Michael about Barbara, but he hadn't met her yet. I told him the full story of her birth and disability one night when we were still in Germany, driving twenty-odd miles in a tempestuous snowstorm to see Norman Wisdom in *Trouble in Store* – that's how desperate we were for social diversions.

I told him about the family rift caused by my father, which still lingered even after his death, which is why Auntie May and Barbara were not at our wedding when all the rest of the Pontycymmer aunties were. Michael had been astonished by these at the Lowndes Square reception, especially Auntie Eunice who screamed that the cham-pagne 'have gone straight to my elbows!' She, who could hardly cope with an annual egg-nog at Christmas. So he was prepared to accept that my family was eccentric, and a cousin with no neck was but another oddity.

I introduced him to her on our return to Britain. I took

him down to Wales to show him my beloved Pontycymmer, and then we drove on to meet Barbara. Both were a total shock to him.

'What's this terrible *smell*, Moll?' He wrinkled his fine patrician nose in Pontycymmer, an expression of disbelief and revulsion on his face. We were in my Auntie Eunice's and Emily's house. I didn't know what he was talking about. Then it dawned, and defensive fury boiled in me.

'It's the smell of urine, spilled urine, combined with floor polish. Since they've only got an outside lavatory and they drink a lot of tea and their step is not as steady as it once was, they spill a lot of slops from their bedroom potties when they carry them through the house in the morning. The lino is drenched with the stuff. Satisfied now?' I hissed with heavy sarcasm.

Though I had explained Barbara as having no neck, Michael was quite unprepared and taken aback at the sight of her. He averted his eyes and blushed with embarrassment, which now threw me off-balance, though I didn't show it.

It wouldn't have mattered to Barbara even if I had. She was used to this reaction; it didn't seem to bother her. As children when we walked along streets with other kids mimicking her, shouting 'Hunchback of Notre Dame!', it would be me throwing stones back at them, never her. And when grown women, who should have known better, pointed and stared and shook their heads, I'd be the one delivering the sharp kick to their surprised shins. She would just smile and walk on, unaffected. Or, more to the point, above it all. Perhaps she was unaware that she was different in any way to the rest of us. It was certainly never mentioned in the family in front of her.

The only time in her forty-odd years on this earth that she said anything remotely relating to it was when we looked at ourselves in front of her bedroom mirror as teenagers.

'Here,' she handed me a scarlet polo-necked sweater. 'This would look better on you than me. You've got a long neck, it will cover it up.' As though the swan-like look was a distinct disadvantage.

Michael was as angry with me as I was disappointed with him. Years later I could accept that it was insensitive and unrealistic of me to expect him to embrace Pontycymmer and Barbara without reservations. But not at the time. Though my second husband never had the chance to meet Barbara, his response to Pontycymmer was one of astonishment, too.

'This street, Albany Road, that you were born in,' he remarked, 'makes Coronation Street look like Park Lane.' This from a man who'd lived in a Bradford 'back-to-back'.

Now we were back in London, back in the bosom of family and friends, I really took to married life. Everything was as I imagined it would be after the honeymoon. It was as if we'd never endured the nightmare of Germany at all, as if we were starting our marriage here and now with the birth of our first baby almost upon us.

We were both looking forward to this. I couldn't wait. My body had ballooned out of all proportion to the event. Everyone was astonished by the startling physical change but I chose to view my pregnancy as a blossoming. I'd been wearing maternity clothes almost from the very first week, and wacking into the food now I had the excuse of eating for two. I put on about four stone with no trouble at all. I went from under eight stone, which I'd had to be in order to get into my wedding dress, to twelve.

That wasn't normal, according to the disapproving gynaecologist, nor was it necessary. He probed around in the flesh, trying to locate the foetus, inviting the medical students of St Mary's Hospital to do the same, when I went for my ante-natal sessions. They couldn't find anything, but I didn't mind; I knew my baby was snug and warm in there somewhere. I had never felt so sumptuously female, never so alluring as now, with child. I smiled at everyone in the street and they smiled back. Shopkeepers asked when the baby was due. We were living in Paddington in a tiny mews cottage that we'd found from an advert in the *Evening Standard*. I had the use of the garage beneath, in which to paint. There was enough space for Michael to make my frames. But for the moment he was too busy. He was now employed by a market research company just outside Oxford, where he drove each day. But to make more money, he also worked nights at a milk factory on the Harrow Road.

I took a job as a supply teacher for a few weeks, which involved stepping into the breach at any London school where a teacher might be off sick. I was nearly eight months pregnant and uncomfortably aware that my waters could break at any moment, if this baby so chose, in front of forty pairs of astonished schoolchildren's eyes.

I had no time to form attachments with any of those kids, the duration of each job was never long enough. Michael drove me from school to school in the mornings and picked me up after work. I asked him to wait around the corner, just as I used to beg James, and for the same reason: I was self-conscious about the grandeur of our car in those surroundings. I dreaded antagonizing the rest of the staff, however brief my stay. I was as emotional and prone to sudden tears as any other pregnant woman. It only needed a hostile stare to set me off.

Five days before the expected birth I was strongly advised to stop teaching. My blood pressure had risen alarmingly, bolstered by my burgeoning girth and the sweltering fact that London was in the thrall of a record heat-wave. I was relieved to stay at home, washing and rewashing my baby's tiny layette, counting the nappies, polishing the pram, trying out names for size, humming and smiling, staring into space, with my hands over my swollen belly, understanding that in a matter of days now this child would be in my arms.

I favoured Sarah for a girl, and Simon or Rupert for a boy. Sarah was my granny's name, and my sister's, although she was always known as Sally. Michael was in total agreement, we never quarrelled about names. We never quarrelled about anything, ever. Which was just as well because my hormones were playing havoc and above all I needed his total support. Some days, despite his continuing reassurance and the glorious vision of realized fertility that I found in my mirror and other people's eyes, I saw myself only as an obscenely swollen, palpitating gland.

To add to the confusion, my feelings for my young husband had shifted profoundly too, into an almost juvenile form of adoration. I trusted him implicitly, knowing he was mine. I could barely believe my luck. Every morning, when I woke to see him there beside me, a rush of pleasure heralded the day and thrilled me to the core. I was unable to get enough of him. I listened to his cultured voice and the ease with which he conducted himself in conversation, how charmingly he coped with social situations and I marvelled, as I used to with Judy.

I gazed at him all the time, when he was reading, or driving, or eating a meal. When he didn't know that I was looking, I devoured him with hungry eyes. His boyish countenance, his smooth hairless body, his straight nose, his delectable lower lip, his lean belly, his long thighs, his tapering fingertips. And I was filled with pride. This was the father of my child. Together we had made another person. We had the strongest bond that two humans can have. However life treated us and whatever happened, that would always remain. Our child.

Marriage was everything that I had hoped it would be.

Those other times were over forever. Nothing and nobody could tarnish this idyllic intimacy. There wasn't anything that could come between us, ever.

I went into labour at a horror movie on the Edgware Road. I was enjoying the film, despite my agony, so refused to leave until the pains were only five minutes apart. All the people in the surrounding seats were screaming at each fresh assault on the screen so my own guttural grunts passed unnoticed. Michael was white with anxiety, urging that we go straight to the hospital, but something told me that this baby would arrive when it was ready. The journey had only just begun.

I was right. The birth was arduous and long, involving a forceps delivery some twelve hours later. I'd been torn, and then been stitched as tightly as a spinster's sampler. But, when they lay the bloodied baby on my sweating breasts for the first time, the tenderness was as fierce and terrible as any pain.

So this was Mother Love, the force that sweeps all before it. The wrath and joy that knows no equal. The unconditional devotion that defends to the end.

I lay with my baby girl hoovering the sweet sticky milk from my breasts in a hospital ward full of other young mothers similarly engaged. There was no sound save for the sucking and the mewling discontent when newborn gums failed to grip. We gazed down on the soft fontanelles of our babies' heads. We counted yet again the number of minuscule nails on fingers and toes. We buried our noses in the crumpled crevices of our babies' bodies. We marvelled, every one of us, at what we now had. Each of our babies was the most beautiful, to us. Motherhood had come along to alter our lives. Now, for the very first time, I felt I had everything.

There was only one distressing experience in the events

surrounding my first daughter's birth, and that concerned my mother. She had come up from Wales with the intention of helping out when I emerged from St Mary's with the baby. This was customary in Wales when there was a birth in the family, probably customary all over the world.

She arrived the day after I went into hospital. And the day after that she departed in high dudgeon, mortally offended, claiming it was obvious that Michael did not want her around. The night of the birth, the evening of her arrival, he had left her alone in the house to go off and celebrate with pals, left her alone for hours and hours! When I accused him later he appeared astonished and answered mildly that he'd invited her too, but she'd refused. I explained that it was customary in Wales to celebrate first with members of the family; friends came later, when the mother and child were back home.

How could I also explain to someone English and normal, with no childhood experience of parental neurosis, that Welsh grandmothers were the most honoured members of the family, that nobody went out and left them alone in the house? Especially not when that grandmother happened to be my mother, a person to be treated with kid gloves all the time, to be deferred to first and last. That she was a damaged creature, requiring constant cosseting in order to avoid moods and silences of appalling intensity, and raging ructions like this one.

'She's extremely sensitive. She always has been. It's her nerves.' I lapsed into valley talk, where they refer to a psychiatrist as a nerve doctor and an asylum as a nerve home.

'She polished off a bottle of sherry on her own. She was hardly alone. Anyway it's nicer on our own. You won't need that much help, will you, when you come home?' Michael had already had a few celebratory ones himself. He strolled around the ward handing out cigars and a swig from his open champagne bottle to the other young fathers. He simply didn't understand what the fuss was about.

I was profoundly disturbed, despite the thrill of the baby. I literally found it unbearable when my mother was in this state. I knew what Michael didn't, that it would take months leading into years now for him to redeem himself in her eyes. She even nursed grudges against people who were dead. We would sit, Barbara, Sally and I, throughout our childhood in countless back kitchens, enduring the sagas of slights and insults, dating back to before our births. It was as if her adrenalin was fuelled by the negative memories of who and what and where. As if she couldn't enjoy life without these continually festering open wounds.

She bristled into the hospital on her way to catch the train back to Wales from nearby Paddington Station. She barely looked at the baby, hardly acknowledged that I was naming her Sarah after her own mother. I stared up at her eyes from my pillow; her eyes were always the clue. They were hooded and dull, the only dead thing in her face. The mouth was clamped hard in a rigid line, but the surrounding muscles of the jaw were working furiously. God only knows what pills she was on, but whatever they were they weren't calming her down.

My mother was still a beauty, a stylish and lovely woman. She was dressed from head to toe in her favourite fuchsia. Her hair had been specially cut and curled for the visit, I could tell. But there was no escaping the terrible turmoil in her lovely little face, the internal demons that were out to destroy her. My heart started pounding in sympathy with hers, but for once I could do little to ease her distress. I was too exhausted myself.

'I have always known when I'm not wanted, Molly.' My heart slowed down and sank. I wanted this to be the loveliest moment of my life, watching my mother become acquainted with my daughter, the three generations together. The mother whom I understood and loved with such a passion, and the child who was already receiving the same from me. But I had so recently come through a tough labour and hadn't the strength to coax and cajole my mother from the appalling depression which I knew would follow this incident, the pain of this imagined rejection.

I lay, numb with misery, my baby sleeping alongside my bed.

'Don't you want to hold the baby?' I pleaded.

She glanced over. 'This baby's half English, not a true Celt. A cold race, the English. Let's hope she doesn't take after her father, Molly. Let's hope you haven't made a terrible mistake, marrying him. I'll never forgive myself if it proves to be so, after all my encouragement to go ahead.'

Silent tears slid down my face as I watched her gather her belongings and stride out of the ward. She disappeared down the long corridor and out of the hospital to catch her homebound train, without so much as a goodbye or backward glance.

So, now war had been declared; it was out in the open. Michael, the cold and heartless Englishman, was not good enough for my mother's daughter. And I was dedicated to proving her wrong, to defending him against every innuendo, every veiled verbal attack, until the day of the divorce when she was triumphantly vindicated.

But at that time there were no clouds whatsoever on the domestic horizon, apart from this dark foreboding from my mother. I returned with Sarah in her Moses basket to London Mews, opposite Paddington Station, to congratulations from the sheet-metal factory workers on our right and the Australian doctor and his wife the nurse on our left. And a welcome home card with flowers from the prostitute and her butler, next door but one.

The butler was a new addition to the prostitute's ménage in the mews, which had housed as many as four girls on the game at one time. But they'd been working the streets then, a stretch of Hyde Park off the Bayswater Road. That was before the Clean Up The Streets of London Campaign had been launched. Now they distributed their favours via the local newsagents' windows, which carried millions of small-ads plus telephone numbers inviting calls from 'pussy-loving punters', or those requiring 'harsh disciplinary measures', or 'French instruction'. Those missives made enthralling reading, soon appearing on Paddington telegraph poles, in phone booths, on the walls of the laundry, the greengrocer, the Welsh dairy, the proliferation of public houses. They perked up daily shopping trips no end.

We had the dubious pleasure of sharing a party-line with this brothel, so that whenever the phone rang in their place it rang in ours too, day and night. It was with a certain reluctance that, when the baby arrived, we had to apply for our own telephone line in order to get some sleep. Now that the girls had built up a regular clientele, the pace was fast and furious and the phone rang incessantly. Business had never been better.

Michael and I would invite pals around, and we'd sit by the phone taking it in turns to pick up at the same time as one of the girls, and listen in to the haggling on prices. One pound for a blow job to a fiver for the full treatment. Whips and tie-ups were optional extras. We'd rush to our window to watch the clients arrive; sometimes they had rung from around the corner and were there within minutes. So we knew just what service it was they'd come for.

I was taken aback at how very respectable these men appeared to be. They could have been the fathers of any of our friends. Indeed one evening when I was painting down in the garage, next door to the brothel, and Michael was busily framing, a friend's father did come knocking at our door. He was covered in confusion, meeting Michael face to face.

'I seem to have lost my way,' he floundered.

'You need upstairs, sir,' Michael responded, impeccably suave.

I was shocked. Was this how it was between men, accepting infidelity as if it were the norm?

'The rising cock hath no conscience!' Michael quoted an aged clerk of court explaining the numbers of married men summoned for importuning before breakfast. Michael had been a young law student at the time, and not yet wise to the ways of the wicked world.

I didn't laugh. I didn't find it amusing. I recalled the hours that my own father spent roaming the West End by himself, telling my mother and us that he was just window shopping. Window shopping for what? I thought savagely.

But the days of the brothel were numbered, it seemed. The police had been tipped the wink by the greengrocer at the mouth of the mews, we thought. It had been his habit, when business was slack in potatoes and veg, to make a note of the lust-driven hordes beating their way down our alley. He claimed that having what he called a whorehouse in our midst was bad for his business.

'Not to mention fuckin' fornicators from the pub spunkin' it in broad daylight with that ancient old crone, Nellie!'

Nellie was a bag-lady, a toothless vagrant, eighty, if she was a day. She drank in the pub on the other corner of London Mews, and it was true – I had caught her more than once with her knickers down, shafting away under our kitchen window. It was usually sailors, very young ones, who pinioned her to the wall. They spreadeagled her tattered rags like passionate starfish, and Nellie wore them like a brooch, responding with a grin of wild and wicked

194

delight. To me there was something actually poetic about her mad couplings. I was sorry when she didn't appear any more.

I was sorry, too, when the gadabout girls went from next door but one. The sultry voluptuary (Welsh it seems!) who offered Michael 'home comforts on the house', whilst I was on my bed of pain delivering his daughter, was now doing a stint in Holloway. She apparently accepted some electrical goods in lieu of payment from a punter and the police had rapped her on a charge of receiving stolen goods. Shame!

Now there was only one prostitute plying her trade, but she had a butler to screen would-be trouble-makers, an ex-convict who could suss out any policeman who might be trying to trick his way on to the premises. She had a beautiful body, that girl. Michael said she couldn't be much older than me, but it was difficult to believe when you saw her face. It reminded me of the first lizard that I saw in Italy, exotic and ancient, with dark, tragic eyes and tough, wizened skin.

'She's a drinker,' the Australian doctor, next door, explained. 'D'you see how many bottles that poor bastard butler dumps into the dustbin each day? She'd have to drink to put up with the life she's chosen to lead, Christ almighty – wouldn't you?'

I pondered on this, but not for long. My own drinking gave me as much pleasure as ever, now that I was able to do it again, now that I was no longer pregnant. I didn't drink to make up for anything in my life, so I couldn't understand why anyone else would want to for reasons other than fun.

Then I visited my mother and tripped over a gaggle of guiltily hidden bottles behind the bath. The stench of stale sherry suggested they had been there for some time. There was a half-full cider flask under the bed, and a miniature whisky bottle lodged in the thumb of some silky Sunday-best gloves. I said nothing to anybody, certainly not to her, and preferred to suppose that it was not serious. But when I caught her lifting a bottle to her lips in secrecy at the back of the scullery on a visit to my Auntie Maggie's, I knew that I'd lost her, that her drinking was no longer a social thing, but was snatched at any time of the day. Now it was out of a deeper need.

She had expressed a longing to see her new grandchild but refused to visit us – ever again, she said. So I boarded the train to show little Sarah off to the family in Wales, to introduce her to all her cousins and aunties, especially my sister. I was looking forward to being in Pontycymmer as much as ever. I couldn't wait to see Barbara, who was also married, now, to Herman; they'd adopted a little girl, Hannah, and were hoping to adopt another one soon.

Michael had a wonderful new job now, had given up night work. This position was more suited to his Oxbridge background, and yet raffish enough to delight me. So when my Aunties Eunice and Emily demanded to know, 'How's the Oxford boy, Moll?' I was able to swank that he was working in television now, for the first of the ITV companies, Associated Rediffusion.

Their eyes brightened. 'Telly! He works for the telly! Fancy that, well, well! That's a nice bit of gossip for down the Co-op! Thanks, Moll – anything else?' They persisted from then on in saying 'Goodnight, Michael' to Derek Hart, on the 'Tonight' programme, even though this was on BBC, believing the two to be the same.

'We're going in for our own house. Buying it.'

'Never! Already! You only been married five minutes, haven't had time to save yet even!'

'In Kensington,' I added.

'Well indeed – Kensington! Near the Palace, is it then?'

'Very near, in fact.'

They nudged each other like little girls, over-excited in their wrap-around pinafores. I looked at their shining faces, at the undisguised love in their eyes, the dusters in their hands, the mops in their pails, and the spotless infants' schoolroom in which we stood. Beyond the cobweb hairnets on their heads I saw the familiar heap of the wimberry mountain, my mountain, the one I learned to know with my Tadci Noyle. The air smelled of coal and oncoming rain. London seemed a million miles away, as remote from me as another planet. Why, when I had the warmth and richness of this Welsh cocoon, did I strive for those alien English things? The answer sprang from Auntie Emily's lips. 'Your Granny would be so proud of you now, wouldn't she, Eunice? Wouldn't Auntie Sarah have been proud?'

'Yes indeed, yes indeed, that she would. We're all proud of you, Moll. Married, not only English, but with a car and a swanky house by Kensington Palace. We look to you. We missed our chance, see. But there you are now with your glamorous new life – doing it all for us! That's our girl!'

We were a popular couple. We drank socially, but I regularly passed out at the end of the evening, or was sick and had to be assisted to the car. I could never remember anything of the night before – I suffered total alcoholic amnesia after a party, or if we'd had people round to our lovely new little house. But that was normal enough, wasn't it? Besides, Michael enjoyed reliving my disgraces for me the following morning. He found my behaviour highly amusing – as did everyone else, he told me.

So my excesses were tolerated right from the start. Knowing this, that my husband wouldn't leave me however atrociously I behaved, that I could always count on him being there, may have planted the idea that I could get away with near-murder, socially speaking. If everybody thought me funny why not really give them something to laugh about? I started drinking with reckless abandon now. Neat whisky was what I liked best; it's a drink with no hanging about involved. The effects were instant and in my case catastrophic.

The photographer Johnny Timbers, a colleague and close friend from those years, still remembers the ritzy dinner party in Hampstead which transferred to the dancing area after dinner. I went missing; no one could see me on the dance floor. A tremendous crash sounded from the drinking and dining area.

'That will be darling Mollikins,' Michael drawled in sanguine fashion, 'just searching for a wee whisky.'

I had wrecked the antique dining table, split it in two. They found me, collapsed amidst the food on the floor. Scenes like that became more or less expected of me, I could be relied upon to provide the unpaid cabaret. I was young and beautiful enough to get away with it then.

But my industrious creativity took over during the day. How could I possibly enjoy myself in the evenings if I hadn't been a good girl, the best pupil, beforehand? I painted all day and every day, even at the weekends. I shared a nanny with the mother of the two toddlers next door. We couldn't afford one of our own at this stage, and the arrangement worked perfectly. Everyone was happy.

Why then did I look forward so much to blasting my senses to kingdom-come with alcohol? I couldn't explain it. And at this point it didn't appear to be a problem. In any case, I was cutting back drastically now because I was pregnant again. A fact that filled my heart with delirious happiness.

'I would like to have six children in all, that should be enough.' I snuggled into Michael's warm body, adjusting my swollen belly into the hollow of his back.

'You don't mean that, you're not serious, Moll!'

I was serious, absolutely. It is what I had always wanted, a home full of babies. Sarah would be two and a half by the time this new baby was born. She was a daddy's girl and had been from the very beginning. She could twist Michael around her tiny finger. She was a flaxen-haired goddess and he adored her, but only now that they could talk together, carry on a conversation. He had been uneasy with her when she was still in nappies. He found coping with a small baby actually terrifying.

Our second daughter, Sophie, was born in St Mary Abbots Hospital in Kensington. I was transported by this enchanting scrap of humanity sucking my milk, just as I was the first time. She was a beautiful baby, too, and as easy to rear, with the same placid nature as Sarah. Other young mothers envied me their sunny natures, the effortless ease of their teething times and their sleeping habits, but motherhood seemed so natural to me that I couldn't imagine it could be any other way. I was happy, so why should my babies be otherwise? My sister said that if I'd had boys as well as girls (she had two of each sex now), then I'd really know what living with small children was all about. I smiled an infuriating smile. I trusted otherwise.

My friend Mary Holland, at whose party I'd met Michael, lived next door to us now. I helped her get her little house. She then suggested two television director friends as neighbours for the cottage on the other side of us. We were becoming rather an artistic enclave there behind the newly opened Ark Restaurant in Palace Gardens Terrace.

Mary wrote for *Vogue*, and it was in her secluded cottage that Penelope Gilliatt, her editorial boss on the magazine, and John Osborne conducted their illicit affair in the afternoons, before they divorced their respective spouses to marry each other. She was married to Dr Roger Gilliatt, who had been Antony Armstrong-Jones's best man at his wedding to Princess Margaret. John Osborne was still ostensibly married to the actress Mary Ure. He was *the* theatrical name of the moment, since *Look Back in Anger* had triumphed at the Royal Court.

I watched these satiated lovers stagger forth after their sweaty sessions, with post-coital smiles pasted on, while I played in our sand-pit with my babies. I envied them their erotic assignations. It made me question my own domestic idyll. I was drawn by Osborne's dandified elegance and her glossy ultra-fashionable *Vogue* style. Her flaming red hair sang against the emerald green she was wearing. She had the appearance of knowing exactly what she wanted and where she was going. For the very first time since my marriage I felt that something might be passing me by. I wanted to enchant a man as raffish and celebrated as Osborne behind drawn curtains in the afternoon, instead of breast-feeding in my own backyard.

Mary's other friends, David Jones and Robin Midgeley, were both directors. Since we all lived alongside each other, we spent much time in and out of each other's homes, and the pool of our joint friends and acquaintances widened. David, the son of a Welsh preacher, worked on the television arts programme 'Monitor', which we all watched in holy reverence. He directed there alongside the young Ken Russell. I began to feel good about being a Celt again, especially since Mary was Irish and her mother, who reminded me of my own, was a regular visitor. David was going out with Judi Dench, and Robin was seeing Prunella Scales, both considered up and coming young actresses. This was a rare breed that I had never encountered before, and certainly not over a cosy garden wall as I was now doing.

I met Philip Saville who had just split up with his wife, the playwright Jane Arden. Philip was considered the sexiest television drama director and squired the most desirable girls around town; pouting Nyree Dawn Porter with her cloud of blonde hair, star of *The Forsyte Saga*, was succeeded by the cool brunette in Courrèges boots, Diana Rigg, later dominatrix from *The Avengers*.

Round at Mary's, too, I met Alun Owen, the Welsh-speaking Irish-Liverpudlian playwright, whose television dramas on 'Armchair Theatre' were winning him awards.

Johnny Johnson, the millionaire television jingles king, whose catchy tunes for commercials were driving the nation mad, had begun to collect my paintings. Through him we met Shirley Bassey and her husband Kenny Hume.

At one party we met Jeremy Sandford who was writing *Cathy Come Home*, which showed me that old Etonians didn't all sit on horses braying at hounds. His wife, Nell Dunn, had just finished *Up the Junction*, which was being made into a film. She didn't need the money, her father was Sir Philip Dunn, the tobacco millionaire, but she wrote because she loved it, she explained to me. Michael and I went to their house just over Putney Bridge and met John Bratby, who had recently completed their painting. Their neighbour, Edna O'Brien, popped in to meet us and that was also where we met the writer Wayland Young (Lord Kennet) and his wife, Liz – further examples of creatively motivated aristocrats with left-wing affiliations. John Michell, another example, was a painter we met at David Hockney's twenty-first birthday party. John was writing *A View from Atlantis*, which would sweep the boards and make publishing history. They were all friends. They all came round to our house. I was beginning to feel more secure in my own skin as I surrounded myself with deliberately chosen kindred spirits. We were all around the same age, going places, most of us coming from much the same background.

We were all consumed with our careers, me included. On our return from Germany, while I was still breast-feeding Sarah, I had an exhibition of my paintings, landscapes and portraits in oils on canvas and board, at the Studio Club in Swallow Street. That was the artists' club where I'd had my first memorable drink with Judy, the club where such painting luminaries as Johnny Minton drank. The exhibition was well received and I sold most of the paintings too.

Then a few years later I had enough work for another exhibition and was approached by the Comedy Gallery off Leicester Square. I got a lot of coverage with write-ups and photographs in *Tatler* and *Vogue*, and a favourable review in *Art News and Review*. The exhibition was a sell-out. I was on my way.

Our little cottage in Kensington was beginning to feel very cramped with two children and all my paintings and we decided we would have to move. I was now supplying the art department at Liberty's in Regent Street with larger and larger landscapes which often sold within a day of being displayed in their windows. I could sell as many as ten a week through the store which is why we could afford to look for a larger house in affluent Chelsea, an area we both liked.

I had been introduced to Mr Liberty himself, who worked from his wheelchair at the top of the building, and he congratulated me on so swiftly becoming his bestselling artist and proposed a major exhibition of my work within the store. This would be my fifth successful one-woman show and I was making a name for myself as a young artist of promise. I met Pauline Vogelpole of the Contemporary Arts Society and she encouraged me to exhibit in serious group exhibitions instead of merely 'selling my stuff through a shop', as she put it. I did as she suggested which resulted in my favourite canvas, the five-foot by five-foot *Spring in New York*, being bought by Eric Newton, the art critic of the *Guardian*. It was a lyrical piece painted entirely in cadmium lemons and yellows, housed in the bowels of the Tate, and later donated to the Brighton Pavilion Gallery as part of their permanent collection, by the Contemporary Arts Society.

We settled into a beautiful four-storey house in Old Church Street, but it was here that the difficulties, and suspicions of infidelity, in our marriage surfaced and the emotional separation between us began. I found it heart-breaking but I didn't know what to do. So I drank more which certainly exacerbated the situation. I changed now, when I had a drink, from a pleasant partner into a screaming virago. I could feel it happening, I could feel that 'click', and the personality switch was as bewildering to me as it was to those around me. I would lash out with my tongue and yet afterwards I couldn't even remember what I had said. Now apologies were required the following morning. Michael no longer recounted my exploits with amused pleasure, but rather with the weary resignation that I was increasingly feeling towards myself. I began to hate what I was becoming.

There were various reasons for our drifting apart. Politically we were poles apart. My father's deplorable support of Fascism in the thirties, his adoration of Oswald Mosley, was a source of great fun to Michael and his pals. Pontycymmer he found 'too depressing for words'. He never visited it again after the first time.

Although I didn't realize the full extent of his infidelities, I was made aware of them inadvertently towards the end of our marriage. I actually ordered him from the house because of a proven infidelity, proven with the Carlton Hotel bill, which I discovered in his dressing room upstairs and which secured me my divorce because it represented hard evidence.

Our physical fights were the result of my alcohol abuse, meaning to say that none of them took place when I was sober. An American psychiatrist claimed that I had been conditioned by my father into expecting violence to precede passion and a tender show of love.

'Did you always have sex after these appalling fights, no matter how badly you were hurt?'

'Marvellous sex. The best.'

'Point proved!'

I hadn't liked hearing this, nor the notion that I had deliberately chosen to marry a man who might supply me with what I was searching for.

My marriage to Michael lasted just seven years. In 1964 I was granted a divorce on the evidence of my husband's infidelity, and I was given custody of my two daughters, Sarah and Sophie, aged six and three. The three of us continued to live in the family house in Old Church Street off the King's Road. I had the front of the house painted a sunshine yellow to celebrate my freedom. I had a house-keeper to clean, shop and see to the laundry and an au pair to see to the children. Outside, on the kerb, I had two matching yellow cars, both collectors' items. One was an open four-seater Morgan Sports model, and the other a vintage Rolls-Royce. They were my cars, *mine*, nobody else's. I had a mink coat that I insisted on buying for myself, as a mark of pride, although there were numerous lovers who would have bought it for me. I had everything in material terms that I had ever wanted. I also had a chronically bruised, not to say badly broken heart, and what felt like a pebble permanently lodged in my throat.

I was wild then, hard and witty – a bitch. But it seemed that no amount of champagne could put a bubble into the soul of what I had become. I was withering inside, but who could I tell? I remembered the prostitute in the Paddington mews. For the first time I understood why she drank. The bond between my mother and myself deepened into a mutual dependence. We drank together.

I threw myself into affairs with all manner of men. I didn't know what I was looking for. One of my lovers was an American psychiatrist, who was over here from the West Coast, involved with the celebratedly controversial R. D. Laing. He treated many stars in LA and wanted me to move back there with him, taking Sarah and Sophie.

He told me that any man who got into a relationship with me over the next five years was in for a rough ride, and that whether I understood my own motives or not, I was punishing the male race for the breakdown of my marriage. He claimed that since he understood the female psyche so well, he was probably the only man qualified for the job of taking care of me.

He proposed marriage. I declined. He accepted this, but before he left he told me it was just as well for me to know — that I was multi-orgasmic. He beamed, expecting me to do likewise. I asked what did this mean, that I was prone to cancer, or what? I was fearful, I had two daughters to rear. He laughed and laughed, shaking his head. Multi-orgasmic was great, apparently. It meant that my sex-life would always be super-satisfactory, since I could enjoy orgasms so easily, and during love-making with him I have 'come' up to five or eight times a session. I smiled dubiously. This sounded like West-Coast jargon to me. It was the first time that I had ever heard of an 'orgasm', let alone up to eight on the trot.

Another lover was 'Loony', my dotty, doting aristocrat. It was he who had bought me the Rolls. He had combed the country for this car, dispatching countless minions to find one which was the exact year of my birth, 1932. I believe he tracked it down in Norfolk and paid the owner handsomely to persuade him to part with it.

Ours was an unlikely but supremely successful match, this aristocrat and me, based on camp and chortling sado-masochism. We represented either end of the social scale, the fatal attraction of opposites. When the Rolls was delivered to my door, awaiting my delight, I cast a cursory glance in its gleaming direction and curled a cruel lip.

'And what's that supposed to be, may I ask?'

'It's your new motor, m'dear.'

'A *black* car! You don't expect *me* to drive around in a *black* car, for God's sake, you infuriating fool!'

'I'll get it sprayed yellow – immediately, darling. How could I have been so thoughtless?' He was trembling in excited agitation at my displeasure.

I turned on my heel, tossing my Vidal Sassoon bob. 'Do what you bloody like with it – I don't care. Just remove the fucking atrocity from the front of my house, and yourself with it! Now!'

The next morning a case of champagne awaited me on the doorstep, and a diamond ring had been pushed through the letter-box. Every morning from now on, for the following five years, right up until I got married again (to somebody else), I could expect to find these offerings at my altar. The champagne came in handy for non-stop, open-house entertaining. The rings I passed on to my mother, or lost, or gave to the kids to play with. My mother's collection was subsequently stolen by a shifty window-cleaner down in Barry, who specialized in ripping off old-age pensioners.

'Easy come, easy go, Mama,' I comforted her when she told me of the theft.

'Let's drink to the rings,' she slyly suggested. I opened a fresh bottle of Glenfiddich. Any excuse.

My dotty aristo and my mother had a lot in common. They shared a love of antiques, beautiful gardens, historic houses and alcohol. He was exerting pressure on me, through her, to marry him, to live in his 'seat' in Cambridgeshire and, most crucially of all, to give him an heir.

My mother's love of laxatives provided yet another source of animated conversation between them. I said that since they were closer in age to each other than me, they'd make a good pair and why didn't they marry? But that didn't solve his need for an heir, since my mother had long since passed her child-bearing years.

I had slept with him once and didn't fancy a return run. It was cold and uncomfortable and involved spending the night between rubber sheets, wearing a mackintosh. He

206

was a rubber fetishist and told me that the most pleasurable thing I could do for him was to give him an enema. He introduced the hose-piping into the boudoir. I was chronically hungover, and this was the last thing I wanted to do. It was bad enough having to cope with my own vomit at that moment.

I spent many weekends at his country estate with my mother and the children, often inviting friends down with us. Sylvia and John got on well with my admirer and they stayed there too. Sylvia found it amusing since it reminded her of the way she had lived in Brazil. My mother took me on walks in the woods, suggesting that it might not be a bad idea to marry into all this, to become mistress of all I surveyed.

'The children would enjoy it,' she coaxed. 'He wants to buy them their very own horses, and you wouldn't have to worry about money for the rest of your life. Be sensible now, Moll. You're not getting any younger. You're thirty-two already, the choices will begin to narrow from now on.'

I stopped short in my tracks and took her face in my hands. 'I'd be dead in a year. Suffocated to death, you know I would. I need to be free now, to do what I want.'

She nodded miserably. 'I only want what's best for you. But don't listen to me – who am I to advise you? Look at what happened with Michael. I shall never forgive myself for that marriage, but how was anybody to know what a womanizer he'd turn out to be. And with a lovely face like that, as if butter wouldn't melt in his mouth.'

The trouble was, although I was free I had come to a crossroads in my life. I was no longer painting. That part of my life was over and done with, along with my marriage. I declared I would never paint again. The truth was that my painting Muse had departed. The morning after I threw Michael out of the house, the evidence of his betrayal in my hand, I found I simply could not paint any more. I went up to my studio at the top of the house, expecting to complete the abstract on the easel and nothing came, nothing at all. I was devastated. I had a drink on it. I had a drink and didn't stop.

I was suffering a most profound artistic block, which I was doomed to endure for the next twenty-five years. That was the length of time it took me to reach an alcoholic rock-bottom, to stop drinking, in order to resume a life of creativity again. To restore myself to myself.

The fearless face of fashion. (*Karl Stoecker*)

Above Fashion Editor of the Year, *Sunday Times*, 1972.
(*Kelvin Brodie*)

Below King's Road nuptials. Chelsea registry office.
Sophie, me, Patrick and Sarah.

Life is just
a bowl of
cherries.
(*Men Only*)

Manhattan highlife.
Total alienation.

Right Ariel
and me.
(*John Timbers*)

Below Out on
the town with
Andrew Logan.

Above right I fill my
life with friends.
L to r: Jill Bennett,
me and George Melly.
(*Richard Young/Rex*)

Below right Quentin
Crisp, my first male
nude, onstage at
Ronnie Scott's.
(*John Timbers*)

High jinks at the Alternative Miss World. Sarah as Marilyn, Divine and me.

My mother at eighty – still a beauty. (*Lawrence Lawry*)

Relative values: my darling daughters had had enough of me, 1984. (*John Timbers*)

'A prematurely aged woman in her fifties' – hitting alcoholic rock bottom. (*John Timbers*)

Above 'I spent many hours up the mountain, trying to make some sense of my existence.' (*John Timbers*)

Below Happy days are here again. L to r: Sophie with daughter Carson, Sylvia, me, Sarah, Sophie's son Paris and Sarah's daughter Jessie.

PART FOUR

Fashion and Frenzy

The further I distanced myself from my marriage, the more dramatically my life started to change. This was the early sixties and the social values, the snobbery which had held me in thrall and terror of opening my mouth, were being swept out of existence. Now it was fashionable to speak with an accent, whether regional like that of the Beatles, David Hockney, Albert Finney, Rita Tushingham, or cockney like Michael Caine, Vidal Sassoon, Twiggy and those three larky lads of the lens – the top fashion photographers, Bailey, Duffy and Donovan. Either way, wherever you came from, it was acceptable to be as working class as you liked. At long last I could relax, remove the plum from my mouth and talk naturally.

It may have been this easing of the social strictures that helped to highlight the basic differences between Michael and myself and hastened the end of our marriage. I turned like the worm, the underdog snarling and baring its fangs, particularly in drink, questioning everything he stood for and held sacred.

Feminism was already in the air, though as yet intangible, and sensing it I started to question what my role was and if, along the line, I'd been selling myself short. Alcohol helped; it gave me the confidence to take bold steps. It numbed my fears for the future, it enabled me to approach everything, even a new career, with insouciance. I started to live for the moment.

When I stopped painting, I was momentarily stumped as to what to do. It was clear that I must earn some money to be able to stay in Chelsea, living at my present level.

Michael agreed to pay a fiver a week for each child and he covered the mortgage, but I refused any maintenance for myself. A fierce (false) pride prevented me from accepting anything. I was capable of earning my own, I declared, when my lawyer beseeched me to change my mind.

'I don't need money from any man!'

I welcomed the challenge, though I lamented the loss of the easy money that I'd earned from my art. I left it to the Fates to decide what to offer me. I may have fleetingly said a prayer, but I doubt it very much. I had long since stopped talking to God. I didn't think he'd want to listen to the likes of me, a divorced harlot who had broken her marriage vows.

My divorce had been received with horror in my family. Pontycymmer was agog with the news. Overnight I had lost my status and become a scarlet woman. The chapel was offering a prayer up for my soul. Two of my aunties stopped talking to me again. They had only just forgiven me for painting people with no clothes on at art school.

I didn't know anyone else who was divorced. When I went for my interview at *Nova*, the editor Dennis Hackett viewed me warily. He was a Catholic. There were no other divorcées on the magazine. Yet *Nova* was aimed above all at the enlightened woman of the sixties.

How did I actually become a top-ranking fashion editor since those jobs were like gold-dust and surely demanded experience of fashion? I could say that like everything else that is meant to be, it happened without a struggle, an effortless channelling of creative energy. And this may be true despite the fact that I was in no apparent way qualified for the job. I stormed into the fashion arena with none of the necessary armour. Fools rush in where angels fear to tread. And it worked splendidly. It seemed that within five minutes, having come from nowhere, my name as fashion editor of *Nova* was now familiar in that tight hallowed circle which comprises Fashion with a capital F.

My fashion pages were making waves from London to Paris to New York.

I had received the offer of the job in a roundabout route. It was actually at a dinner party of Len Deighton's after I split up with Michael that I met Clive Irving, a key figure at IPC, the publishers of *Nova*. I had gone with Peter Dinely, a wealthy young friend of my batty aristo. Peter owned Bapstys, which had hired out the firearms for the film of *The Ipcress File*, based on Len Deighton's first novel.

I'd known Len, a fellow Aquarian (an astrological fact we would celebrate each year with a party for others born under our sign), for a long time. He'd been at St Martin's Art School with Malcolm, that ill-fated fiancé of mine. As it happened, Jean Hart, Malcolm's ex-wife, was also at the party. Later she married Bill Oddie, one of the Goodies, a hugely successful television trio.

The room was full of famous faces, but I knew most of them already. David Frost was there, and Paulene Stone, the gorgeous flame-haired model, still in love with Duffy, but later to wed Laurence Harvey.

Clive Irving was sitting next to me. 'What do you do?' he asked.

I told him about the boutique I'd just opened off the King's Road; how I was trained as a painter and knew all about colour, but my painting Muse had departed, and now I was applying my colour know-how to clothes and design instead of canvas. I said that the idea for the boutique had come from working for Biba, the only boutique of its kind in London, so far.

'How did that come about?'

I explained that I'd been to see an old pal of mine, Sheila Allen, who was playing Lady Macbeth at the Royal Court. Backstage in her dressing room I'd met Maurice, from wardrobe, who had run me up a couple of hats to match my Liberty print furnishing-fabric frocks. My style was my own and I could never find, even at Biba, things which were entirely to my liking. Before I knew it Maurice and I had set up business in the front room of my house in Old Church Street, at first making hats and bags for Biba, but then selling our own stuff straight from the house. The word spread fast, until my front garden, and more to the point, my neighbours, saw a steady stream of clients. I was worried that I might lose my lease on the house since trading was strictly forbidden in that oh-so-residential street. There was a High Court Judge living opposite which meant that a policeman was on point duty day and night outside our house. It had been a brothel in another century, and I was scared he might think that I'd set up business again, even though many of the faces coming in and out were well known. His jaw dropped when he spotted Julie Christie, unaware that she shared a little house just up the road with Warren Beatty. She actually was taking a look over our house with a view to buying it for them both. We used to drink with her and a former boyfriend up in the Queen's Elm at the corner of Fulham Road and our street.

The chairman of Christie's lived next door, and Ernestine Carter, fashion editor of the *Sunday Times*, was on the opposite corner. None of this quite went with what I'd taken to doing in my front room, tainting it with cheap commerce, so I looked for premises in the area to start my own shop. And that's what we called it, The Shop in Radnor Walk, in the same street as my Welsh chapel, off the King's Road.

I chose to look the other way when I passed the chapel. It made me feel so bad, as if my granny was there on the step beckoning me, with my Tadci there with her, both knowing that I had lost my way.

The Easter weekend that we started trading, we were the only place open in the area where it was possible to spend money on clothes. If we had employed staff we wouldn't have been permitted to do so, but since Maurice and I were the owners there was no problem. We sold every single garment in the place – there was a queue all the way to the King's Road at one point. My first customer was an eighty-year-old, who bought a complete matching set: an orange mini skirt, long jacket, handbag on chains and matching hat. She said she hadn't had such fun in years, and walked out wearing it all. It was this outfit that *Newsweek* photographed to illustrate their famous piece on 'Swinging London'. Practically every girl on the King's Road was wearing the same style but in one of the four different colourways. We never looked back. I was still coining it in with Maurice, I told Clive Irving, with pride.

He asked me if I had seen *Nova*, the latest glossy magazine for women. I laughed. 'Why on earth would I do that? I never look at those magazines. Does anyone, any more?'

He said that *Nova* was breaking new ground in women's magazines and the first few issues had been well received, except for the fashion pages which were rather uninspired.

'Old hat, I expect!' I said, nodding. 'Fashion's different these days, it's younger. It comes from the street. It's fun now, not formal. I haven't seen that on any fashion pages. The models have still got their noses in the air as if everything is about couture still, instead of ready to wear. You only have to look at Biba, or our little place, to see where it's at.'

He looked intrigued and asked for my number, quietly so that his wife couldn't hear. I gave it to him readily. We got on well. He was attractive and listened attentively. Who cared if he was married, certainly not me. I'd been married too, hadn't I? That hadn't stopped my husband being unfaithful. It hadn't stopped the girls going to bed with him.

Mary Holland rang in the morning. 'Be prepared for a shock, kid,' she chuckled. '*Nova* magazine is going to offer you the job of fashion editor. They've been in touch with me, asking about you. You met Clive Irving at a party, didn't you, and impressed him with your ideas. Go for it, it could be fun. They'll pay you a lot of money. Could see to you until you start painting again.'

Within a month I was the new fashion editor of *Nova*, and within two, I had become the lover of my boss, Clive Irving.

Clive was the only one of all my lovers whom I became involved with in a working situation. Before and since I have always made it a rule that the personal and professional shouldn't overlap. Which is not to say that I didn't find it fun, because I did. There is something deeply erotic about sitting in an editorial meeting, exchanging cool glances and differing opinions, knowing that the whole issue will really be worked out later between hot sheets and heady bouts of passion.

Since Clive was married, and immensely involved in his work, lunchtimes were when we consummated our mutual lust. We skipped food at first, meeting back home in my bed, snatching a shared bowl of cornflakes to keep our strength up, then going back to our separate offices when it was over. Having prided myself on my culinary expertise and hostess efficiency during my marriage, I worried about only offering cornflakes. But these were his favourite food, taken with top of the milk. My children were outraged, once, to find a fresh packet opened and the plastic toy on special offer removed before they'd even seen it. So I bought us our very own packet, placing it high in the food cupboard, our private supply. Kellogg's cornflakes could have used us in their advertising, promoting their product as a sexual stimulant, or at the very least as a source of enduring stamina.

I liked Clive's enthusiasm in the sack, he never left without going for 'seconds', in those early days. But as the years went by and his ambitions started paying off, and we replaced the cornflakes with picnic hampers from Fortnum's, including the finest claret, the sex took on a heightened sensuality. It was the drink that did it for me, emboldened me to talk filth with this sweet and familiar lover. Though it wasn't only the claret that encouraged us both to treat everything about our affair with humour and understanding.

We liked each other a lot. We talked of my children, our mothers, and our careers. When I eventually left *Nova* to become fashion editor on *Harpers & Queen* magazine, it was Clive who suggested my appointment. My first and only pillow appointment. Since I *was* actually the best person for the job at the time, there seemed nothing irregular about it to either of us. It didn't feel like pulling strings. It was simply how it happened, a leisurely post-coital editorial decision. We, neither of us, then, envisaged our affair coming to an end.

It lasted five years, the same length of time as my other two constant lovers. It amazed my female friends how I could juggle these three lovers (and whoever caught my fancy in the meantime) for as long as I did. None of them was ever aware of the existence of the others, though they understood that I went out with other escorts. But all three of them were in committed relationships of their own. I had chosen it so, each on the face of it unavailable, since I didn't wish to commit myself to a one-to-one with any man at that time.

Anthony Shaffer was married, but would call in after dropping his child off at school and we would have a drop of my aristo's champagne and pop into bed for a quickie. But this only worked for a while, then it became too complicated and too rushed, as pressure of work mounted. Also I might only just have got rid of whoever had been spending the night with me, namely Cedric Price, the third and perhaps my favourite of the three.

I first met Tony Shaffer with Mary Holland, and a

217

mutual pal called Rex Berry, at a theatrical club in a basement off Leicester Square. Tony was with his latest bride, a beautiful creature, pick of the Dior models, slim to the point of emaciation. I had never actually met a fashion model at that time. I was still painting and the only models we'd been taught to appreciate were those built on Rubenesque lines; the more to paint, the better.

His twin-brother, Peter Shaffer, had been hailed for his first play, *Five Finger Exercise*, which Tony says the family sat through in horror on the opening night, recognizing the characters on stage as themselves. Tony himself was yearning to write for the theatre too, but was tied up in his own production company, making lucrative television commercials. 'Go to Work on an Egg', for the Egg Marketing Board with the Fay Weldon slogan, was one of them. He'd qualified as a barrister, but hadn't enjoyed that either.

'If you want to write, then write!' I couldn't see what the problem was. If a person wasn't happy doing what they were doing then they must stop doing it, that's what I'd always believed: that's what my granny told me. Tony seemed astonished that I should approach it as simply as that. I said that I didn't want to see him any more unless he stopped whining and did something about his predicament.

He left the world of advertising and started writing *Sleuth*. He used to bring it around and read it to me in bed. Audience reaction, is what he termed it. Unfortunately we had usually already been out to dinner and I'd have had a skinful, on top of which we would have sated our carnal passions. Every single time he read it to me, though propped up on pillows and his manly chest, I'd fall asleep in five minutes flat. In later years, when *Sleuth* had become an international success on stage and as a film, garnering all kinds of rave reviews and awards, Tony claimed that I had helped immensely: 'If I couldn't keep you awake after five minutes, what chance had an audience?' He rewrote and rewrote, until finally I did stay awake. Enthralled, in fact. That was the final version.

I met Cedric Price, the visionary architect, when researching an article on avant-garde architecture. He had a hip-flask full of brandy, a white starched collar, a striped shirt, suede brothel-creepers and a demoniacally roguish twinkle in his eye. My heart responded like a pancake being tossed in a frying pan. A kindred spirit. For the next five years we never looked back.

He was living with somebody, too, though they weren't married. I always blame myself, my drinking, for the fact that we didn't move in with each other, get married, make the whole thing more permanent. The incident is burned in my brain, calling him Clive instead of Cedric. If I could go back and change any one thing it would be that.

I was sitting in a New York hotel room, gazing idly at a telegram from Clive saying how much he missed me, MISS YOU, CLIVE, while Cedric was on the telephone telling me the same thing. I was drunk, confused and sleepy. I put my hand over the receiver to yawn and then replied, 'I miss you too, Clive!' There was silence at the other end, and an ominous click.

With one slip of the tongue, the game was up!

On my return to London, I tried to lie my way out of the situation. But it was no good. He couldn't trust me again. Though we continued as best we could because we couldn't stay away from each other, it was never the same. The commitment was no longer there.

Though I felt deeply for all three of these lovers, Cedric was the one I felt to be more of a soul-mate. He was universally admired for his ideas, for his humour and humanitarian view of life. He introduced me to Buckminster Fuller, and the memory of 'Bucky' sitting in my house with Sophie, my youngest daughter, on his knee, explaining the intricacies of life in his inimitably simple way, is one that I treasure always.

My girls, Sarah and Sophie, loved Cedric best too. Even my mother, who didn't rate any of my lovers, except the aristo, warmed to Cedric. When I finished with all three of them to marry Patrick Hughes, my second husband, she wailed, 'But what about Cedric?' It was her ultimate card, the one sure way to touch me to the quick, in her effort to make me change my mind.

Cedric was the one who understood my drinking the most, too. There was never a tinge of reproach. Far from it; with us the more we could imbibe together the better. But he differed from me, he seemed never to suffer from the hangovers which were now absolutely crucifying my every waking day.

I spent ten years in the world of fashion, from 1964 to 1974, collecting some of the most covetable awards along the way, but apart from my business ventures with Maurice, until I joined *Nova*, my only other brush with this world had been with the fashion students at Brighton Art School.

I'd had great fun with Maurice, making the hats and bags for Biba, and fun with Barbara Hulanicki and her husband Fitz, delivering them, and trying to extort my money on the spot. Both became and remain amongst my closest friends, although Barbara still tells how Fitz used to climb out of the window at my approach, knowing I always demanded cash in hand for work completed. I didn't care. I would pick up the kids from school and invite several of their pals on the jaunt, buying ice-cream on the way, then let the lot loose amongst the crushed velvets and chiffons. I only had to do that twice: from then on Fitz would greet me at the door. Accounts were settled right there on the pavement, before Sarah and Sophie and their howling mob could even pass the portals.

He'd give me so much work to get on with that Maurice and I had to employ extra help. I got a taciturn, twenty-stone African mama, who only came to life and started work when certain music was playing. We'd just bought Tom Jones singing, 'It's Not Unusual', and fixed the record-player so that it played non-stop. This was her favourite listening. The amount of work the three of us got through was phenomenal, but Biba sold our stuff as fast as we could make it.

Then I went on to open my own boutique which I also greatly enjoyed. I took Terry Donovan on as a third partner, with Maurice and myself, and it all seemed so effortlessly successful. Compared to the soul-searching required in painting, the enforced isolation, the sense of being wrenched and scoured by the demands of the quest, fashion was pretty superficial – wasn't it?

And yet, when I started my first job on *Nova*, I could see that this world was not as it had appeared all along to me, that, in fact, it took itself *seriously*. This was the first shock, one that turned me against it from the start. It was clear to all that I was a maverick, one who would do things her way. But the hardest thing to forgive in me, this upstart from nowhere, was the irreverence that I brought to my professional position. Nevertheless, I was so completely confident, proving subsequently to be ahead of the times, that whatever I chose to do on my fashion pages was acclaimed and copied elsewhere. I became, in spite of myself and my scorn of what I was doing, a total law unto myself. A name to be reckoned with. From being placed right at the back at my very first season in the Paris couture collections, working on this new magazine *Nova* which nobody had heard of, I graduated to the best seat in the front row, the most prized position of all, later representing *Harpers*, and then the *Sunday Times*.

I thought it was all bullshit and was bored to distraction. I loathed my colleagues, especially the Americans. I took delight in dressing myself up in the most inappropriate clothes to scandalize them and amuse *Women's Wear Daily*. And however sycophantic they became as my fame spread and my accolades increased, I would remember just which of them had even bothered to talk to me in those early days when I had been banished to the back of beyond. There were only three, two of them dead now. The late Jean Rook of the *Express*, the late Prudence Glynn, the best fashion editor *The Times* has ever had, and Jane Reed, who was then on *Woman*.

I had good reasons to remember the very first time I covered the couture collections in Paris, romantic reasons. As soon as the unmistakable mixture of Gauloises, coffee and brandy filled my nostrils, I was reminded of the Paris I became acquainted with when Judy and I arrived here as fledglings. A curdling excitement started in my stomach, the same excitement that had overwhelmed me on my honeymoon when I'd stayed here with Michael en route to the South of France.

I remembered our first night and how we'd booked into a tiny back-street hotel in St Germain and gone off to the Existential Club to hear the singer Juliette Greco. Michael had had to leave me there to go back to the hotel for more money to pay the exorbitant bill for our drinks. Then, much later, when we returned to the hotel, the concierge had shaken his finger at me, as if I was some kind of tart, and forbidden me entry with Michael, claiming that this was not that kind of hotel. His parents had to be roused to search for the passports we had deposited with them earlier which confirmed we were man and wife, before we were allowed to go up to our room and get on with the honeymoon. It must have been the only hotel with such moral scruples this side of the Left Bank.

I forget the exact name of the sumptuous hotel I was

booked into in my new role as fashion editor of *Nova*. I believe it was the Plaza Athenée. I know it was not the George V, which I would have recognized from my days slinking past the desk there with Robert. But this hotel was in the same smart quarter of Paris. The staff treated me reverentially, as well as they might. I had dressed the part of fashion editor to the extreme, having seen enough Bette Davis and Joan Crawford movies to acquaint me with high style. I was clearly something to do with the exalted world of haute couture, which was so beloved of the French.

I looked simply splendid in shiny patent-leather high heels, matching handbag in a long envelope shape, and a sequined pillbox hat with a veil which totally covered my face. I was wearing a black tightly fitted pony-skin suit, with a very short skirt. I had imitation diamonds – or were they real? I can't be sure, because my aristo was already in my life. They were glittering stones anyway, on my ears and on my fingers. My mouth was a pale beige-pink, but outlined in brown pencil. I had so much lip-gloss on that it looked as if I had fallen lips-first into a tub of glycerine. My face was very pale and matt. I was wearing false black lashes, top and bottom, and loads of mascara. I was thin. I looked slightly ill, as if I was running a fever. My eyes were enormous, like the eyes of a starveling or Dracula's daughter.

I felt insolent, decadent, like a million dollars. I looked the more extraordinary since sixties casual chic was considered *de rigueur* now, not the sexy pastiche of the world of high fashion that I was wearing. I was delightfully out of kilter.

This would be the third issue of *Nova* I had worked on. My first was a total triumph, my second a disaster. Everyone would be looking to see how I would fare in the daunting world of haute couture. I didn't know what the hell I was supposed to be doing, but my inner voice would see to things. I could only be guided by my own instincts, having learned already not to listen to anyone else.

I had not been very well on my first day at *Nova*, but I could hardly explain why. People weren't talking freely about abortions then; it wasn't considered a suitable topic for casual conversation. And mine was an abortion which I hadn't wanted to have. I only resorted to it because my lawyer had advised me to do so. He said that I might lose custody of my daughters if I appeared pregnant in court for the divorce proceedings. That's how it was in those days.

I didn't want to think about the baby, so I drank instead. To my pleasurable surprise drinking was a popular pastime in this new magazine world of mine. People drank at lunchtime, sometimes all through the afternoon from wine and whisky bottles at their desks. They rallied into the bars as soon as work was over. There was champagne on offer at every fashion event. If I hadn't had the taste for it already, I sure as hell would have developed it now. Perhaps this paltry fashion job wasn't going to be so bad after all. I might manage to keep myself afloat on a sea of champagne corks at least.

Dennis Hackett, my editor, gave me instructions for my first issue.

'Furs and jewels,' he announced.

I'd stared at him blankly.

'Furs and jewels.' He waved me irritably away.

'Yes?'

'For God's sake, woman! Furs and jewels, just get on with it. I want twelve pages, six spreads on furs and jewels. It's that time of year, the advertisers expect to see furs and jewels. We work three months in advance, like all the glossies, so by the time this issue comes out women will be thinking about buying their new furs for the winter. And their husbands will be choosing the jewels to go with them.'

'Will they?' I was astonished. Did this world really exist?

Dennis picked up the telephone, dismissing me with his fingers. 'Peccinotti's shooting the pictures. I don't want any tales about the two of you not getting on. He's a difficult bugger, but then so am I. And it's your job to fit in and not cause any trouble. Got that?'

I was seven years old again, staring back at this abrasive bully as I'd stared back at my father, the resentment rising like bile in my belly.

'Fucking bastard!' I swore quietly as I turned to go.

'What was that?' His hearing was quicker than I had imagined.

'Fucking bastard!' I faced him with it, why the hell not? Who wanted his poxy job anyway?

He burst out laughing. 'That's more like it! We'll get on fine, you and me. Now we know where we both stand. I can't abide arse-lickers.'

And so it was, until the bill came in for the insurance on that first issue of mine on furs and jewels. They could hear his cursing in the cocktail bar on the Savoy, the other side of the Strand from IPC.

I had taken him at his word, furs and jewels. It was not a world then with which I was over-familiar. Nobody told me how to go about things. I had four assistants and two secretaries, none of whom apparently knew that I had no idea of what was expected of me. How could they know that all I'd ever been was a hat and belt maker and a painter, and before that a schoolteacher, and before that a helper in my mother's B and B, or behind the counter in my dad's sweetshop, or selling candy-floss at the end of Brighton Pier. The sum total of my job experience.

'We'll divide everything into colour zones,' I announced importantly. I knew where I was with colour at least.

They looked at me blankly, my staff. My *staff*!

'Five colour zones,' I continued briskly. 'You have two days to get all the stuff in.'

'Two days!' they gasped. 'We usually have weeks.'

'Weeks! Bollocks! Two days to get it all into this office so that I can sort out what I like. The five colour zones will be red, black, white, brown and patterned. Each of you can take whichever colour zone you prefer, fight it out between yourselves. Whoever chooses red will visit the leading jewellers and bring me garnets and rubies, pink diamonds, etc. I want earrings and bangles and bracelets and rings and brooches and beads. And to match up with these I'd like the same in red furs. Red Fox, dyed rabbit. The same applies to the other colours. White diamonds with white mink. Brown beaver, fox and sable with amber, for instance. Leopard skin, zebra and lynx and all the other patterned furs to match up with patterned stones like onyx, and tiger-eyes.

I shudder now at how thoughtlessly I was promoting the slaughter of innocents in the pursuit of mere fashion. But I had no such conscience then, I didn't even consider what I was doing. I could only feel relief that inspiration had rescued me from my immediate predicament.

'We don't usually work this way,' one of the fashion assistants ventured. I looked at her supercilious expression, at her groomed hair and immaculately plucked eyebrows. I sacked her the same afternoon to keep the others on their toes.

We used a vast roof-top studio at the *Sunday Times'* building for what I quickly learned to refer to as the 'shoot'. Harri Peccinotti, *Nova*'s art director, who was taking the photos, was irked by the number of security men on patrol. They were there to guard their precious gems and furs, some of which individually cost over a million pounds. I had no idea there would be such a fuss. My assistants were white and shaking with tension. I couldn't imagine why. This was only make-believe wasn't it? It was just a fantasy that anybody actually read what fashion editors wrote, nobody in their right mind then went out and bought their winter or summer, or autumn or spring wardrobe – did they, for Christ's sake? These people obviously thought that they did. Their livelihood depended on them believing so!

Harri did a beautiful job. They were extraordinary photos, although he balked at so much stuff at first.

'How the hell am I meant to photograph all these rings?'

'Two on each finger, fingers linked together. Three models, ten fingers, twenty rings each, equals sixty rings in one shot,' I snapped. 'In close-up, of course – any problem?'

In one afternoon I'd become a first-class bitch. I was fast learning the art of survival. When one of the young models fainted away because she hadn't eaten since the day before yesterday, I rang the agency to complain. It cost money, I said, waiting for her to resume work. That's what Peccinotti had said to me. I was only offloading the shit.

I passed the assistant I'd fired in the corridor when she came back to clear out her desk. She was crying. I looked at her coldly. Afterwards I learned that she had recently split with her husband and had a small child to support.

'Tough titty,' I replied. 'I have two.'

Everybody applauded that first effort of mine. Dennis Hackett was particularly pleased. But the next month's was a disaster. Sun and ski clothes. Winter sports and winter cruising, that's what the advertisers were expecting that month. Who were these mysterious advertisers, these people that we had to keep happy at all costs? I allowed my assistants and everybody to give me advice. Good taste was what was needed for this assignment, apparently. Winter swimwear from places like Fortnum & Mason and Harrods. I put my foot down there.

'I'm sorry, but I'm never using Harrods as a stockist.

Never, do you understand?' I couldn't explain why; that the Harrods assistants had sneered at my mother. My poor little mother. And all she'd done was try on their fucking finery! How could I tell that to these girls?

The model was hopeless, I thought so from the start. She looked as though she'd been head girl at Cheltenham Ladies' College. I was assured that this was the look we were after. An air of refinement, that's what the advertisers went for when it came to winter wear on the Riviera. Those bastard advertisers again!

When this issue came out, I got the blame for the hackneyed set of photographs which could have graced *Woman's Own*, according to Dennis. I knew from then on only to trust myself, whatever everybody else said. In the end I was the one who'd take the stick anyway.

So, here I was in Paris for my very first shot at the couture collections. My job hung on this one; if I came back with as pedestrian a set of photographs as last month's I was for the chop, Dennis told me. My jolly assistant Jane Wood was with me. She was my only assistant now. I had got rid of all the others. I preferred to work with a tight team, I said. Harri Peccinotti was here too. Since time was so tight before the magazine went to press he would plan and do the layout with our chosen photographer here in Paris.

We had just signed into the hotel, having arrived straight from the airport, and were awaiting the celebrated French photographer, Jeanloup Sieff, one of the best fashion photographers in the world.

Vidal Sassoon had flown in from London to do the hair of our model for the twelve-page fashion spread. The girl we had chosen was Kelly, a stunning black model from New York. This was the first time that a black girl had been chosen to model the collections in any magazine. The advertisers found the use of colour in this sense to be too controversial. Though this was the sixties, the publishers, the management, could not believe that the readers of a glossy magazine would identify with a black model. But Dennis Hackett, my editor, was as open-minded about this as I could have hoped, and was supportive over us using Kelly. Harri backed me up on this one, too.

Those photographs, that fashion assignment, subsequently won us, as a team, as a magazine, the coveted Design and Art Directors Award, the Gold Medal. But we were not to know that then and everybody (but me) was still apprehensive, I could tell.

We were late. The Dior show, for which we all had tickets, refused to allow anybody entry after it had started, even the great Jeanloup Sieff. Where was he? Jane and Harri walked out to the entrance, while I, unperturbed, sat in the vestibule leafing through a magazine. Who cared if we missed the Dior show anyway? It was all rather dated, surely. I wouldn't want to have anything photographed from there. I didn't say that though; let them find out for themselves. I was more interested in following up a lead that I'd been given in London by some architects that I knew, pals of Cedric's. They said to look up the work of someone called Paco Rabanne, an architect who was currently working with plastic discs, adapting them to clothing. He was a young Spanish man, whose family had always worked in fashion with the great Balenciaga. That afternoon, I planned to slip away and visit this Paco Rabanne with the hope of getting Jeanloup to photograph his clothes on Kelly, instead of the traditional haute couture. This is what following my instincts meant. I might also feature something by the modernist Courrèges, who preferred to work with the latest technological advances in fabric, such as plastic-coated material, PVC, so that his clothes looked like interplanetary designs. That was what I was interested in. And I was the Fashion

Editor, after all. They would have to abide by my decisions, no one else's!

There was a commotion at the entrance of the hotel. I looked up. It couldn't be Jeanloup arriving, could it? What else could explain this flurry of excitement? I stood in preparation, eager to see what was going on.

An avalanche of young males poured into the space before my eyes. I had never before seen such beautiful young men: dark, flashing eyes; sweet, sculpted lips; strong, muscled bodies. Superb specimens. I stared at them. They stopped in their energetic path and stared at me. The air was electric. I could feel every pore of my body exploding in animal excitement. I sensed the same response in them. Tumult broke out. They were crowding around me, laughing, touching, bunching their fingers in the air, exploding kisses of appreciation. I was overcome, caught up in their enthusiasm. I couldn't stop laughing either. I would have liked to remain there forever. Who were these boys, these beautiful creatures, who singly could cause chaos in any girl's heart let alone a whole group of them?

I was not allowed to find out, I couldn't exchange anything other than a shrug of regret. Jeanloup had arrived. We were due at the House of Dior. Jane and Harri were calling. I had to go.

I left the boys deploring my departure, howling like deprived dogs. Their misery was a mirror of my own, I could assure them. I stared with regret from the back window of our cab. They had crowded on to the pavement outside the hotel, waving, beseeching me to come back. I caught my breath.

'You made a hit there,' Harri said drily. 'That was the entire team, the whole entourage of Real Madrid. The match is on here in Paris. A major world event in international football terms.'

We returned to the hotel that night after midnight, at

two in the morning, to be exact. The fashion pages had already been shot, using Paco Rabanne's plastic-disc clothing on Kelly with Vidal Sassoon's geometric-cut wigs. The Spanish football team had awaited my return. The first of them entered my room at two-thirty a.m. I eventually got rid of the final one at seven in the morning.

I would like to boast that I had pleasured the lot. Several decades later, when presented with the opportunity to sample this much beauty in one single night, I agreed eagerly. An entire rugby team of Welsh valley boys fared more favourably than the prize of Spain.

But I had literally to fight for my honour as they knocked on my door in turn, never taking no for an answer and, in the end, I was forced to call on the management to cool their ardour. Other occupants, I believe, were also complaining.

Harri, who was trying to sleep in the room beneath mine, refused to believe that I hadn't taken my pleasure but had actually been fending them off.

'Half the girls in the world would have given their eye-teeth,' he remarked, viewing the string of livid love-bites around my neck.

I had to spend the next week in turtle-necks back home in London, tricky times with my team of regular lovers there.

I remained on *Nova* from 1964 until 1967, when Dennis Hackett gave me the sack. I like to put it as bluntly as that, though the circumstances were rather different. Either way I engineered my going. I'd had enough of it on *Nova*; I felt I was repeating myself and it was time for a change.

Dennis called me into his office. 'What have you planned for April?' he asked, mildly enough but with just a touch of exasperation. The advertising department must have been on his back. My pages had become so unfathomable, so obscure, so utterly 'way-out' according to them that they could never be certain of getting any fashion advertising at all. I was informed that the wives of management had long since ceased to look at my fashion pages: there was nothing on them, such as dainty cocktail gowns or spring suits with white cuffs and collars, that they would ever wish to wear.

What had I planned for April? What indeed! We were now in December; we always worked this far ahead. But I could never tell when inspiration would strike, it was usually at the very last minute, usually over a drink. This morning I was suffering a chronic hangover, even worse than usual. But my editor was awaiting an answer, drumming irritably with his fingertips on the top of his telephone.

I gazed past his head, over the rooftops of Covent Garden, narrowing my eyes like some end-of-pier soothsayer.

'White on white!' I murmured dreamily.

'What's white on bloody white?' His tone was harsh and sarcastic.

'White on white – white-skinned models with bleached blonde hair, flown in from Scandinavia, preferably albinos, wearing all-white clothes. White linen suits, white cotton frocks, white satin chemises, white chiffon dance-dresses, white maribou mufflers. We'll fly them to the Alps and photograph them against the snow, just before dawn when the light is pure white . . .' I was waxing lyrical now. Nothing could stop me. I could see it all.

Clearly Dennis was having difficulty. I'd lost him along the way.

'Will we see anything at all if everything is white, or would that be asking too much?'

I thought for a moment. 'Distinguishing one white from another was not uppermost on my mind. The stunning *effect* is the thing, surely to God!'

He exploded. He ranted on and on about how he'd been carrying me for months, that my pages were incomprehensible to anyone other than the most effete, that it was time to regularize, to come down to earth, to offer a 'service' to our readers. I looked at him, knowing that the end had come. He was asking me to compromise.

'You'll see their eyes and their mouths. Black mascara and scarlet lipstick in amongst the white.' I was sticking doggedly to my guns. There wasn't an editor on earth who could tear me away now from my April team of snow maidens.

'You've gone over the top this time, Parkin. Either you come down to earth and join the rest of the mortals, or . . .'

'I'll take the or,' I said without hesitation, emboldened by hangover. 'I'll fuck off today. No sweat!'

Before I'd even passed through his secretary's outer office, and walked the length of the corridor to the ladies' lavatory, the rest of the staff had been informed of my sacking. Alma Birk rushed out of her office to offer condolences.

'On what?' I said, surprised.

'Dennis has just phoned me that he's sacked you.'

'Has he – bastard!'

'You'll get another job.' Her concern moved me. But I felt something was wrong here. Hadn't I walked out? Wasn't it my choice?

By midday, the whole of Fleet Street was humming with the gossip. A plum fashion editor appointment up for grabs.

I had never been dismissed from any position before, had never forced or been forced into a showdown. I stood in front of the mirror in the ladies', looking at my lower lip trembling, my eyes swimming in tears. Suddenly I was terrified. What would the girls and I do for money now? Was I mad, could I afford this kind of arrogance? My ego

233

said yes, stand up and show them. But I felt sick; sick and shaky. I needed a drink, that's what I needed. With luck I could track Cedric down and get out on the piss, or persuade my friend Irma Kurtz, the literary editor on *Nova*, to get round the pub with me, or take my team for a boozy lunch opposite at Boulestin's. I'd be all right. Something would turn up. Who needed poxy *Nova* and this crap job anyway? With luck, God would take pity – if he still remembered me.

I didn't know where I would be going. However, as soon as the news of my leaving broke, there were plenty of offers. Bea Miller, chic editor of *Vogue*, asked me in for an interview, but I couldn't imagine myself working there. At least I had been allowed, indeed encouraged, at *Nova* to approach fashion with some degree of humour. I didn't feel *Vogue* had its tongue sufficiently in its cheek. I said airily that I was thinking of becoming a photographer. Bea said to be sure and tell her when I'd care to shoot some pages for them.

I had a call from Jocelyn Stevens on *Queen*. I felt wary of going there before we'd even met each other. This was the man who had fired Claire Rendlesham, in my opinion the best fashion editor this country ever had. She'd been too difficult to work with, too neurotic, though admittedly brilliant, he said to me at the interview. I looked at his cold blue eyes and patrician good looks. He'd be saying the same about me, I knew he would, and I'd end up a nervous wreck. We shook hands over guarded farewells.

The world of advertising held out lucrative offers. But all the people I met seemed such self-important and mercenary little shits that whenever I did jobs, such as styling the clothes for television commercials, I would come away feeling depressed for some unaccountable reason. I refused further offers, although it was money for old rope.

While still on *Nova* I was given time off to play a film

role in an underground movie to be shot in Connecticut, by the American film director Lionel Rogosin. They paid for us all, me, the children, and my mother (to look after the kids) to sail off to America on the SS *France*. We had a wonderful time.

I had already acted, if you could call it that, in a documentary-style drama that Lionel had shot in London a few years previously. An anti-war film called *Good Times, Wonderful Times*, which had won various awards around the world in film festivals, including Cannes.

This new film was to be a comedy and I was playing the lead. On our arrival in New York, *Good Times* was playing to full houses at the Carnegie Cinema. It was strange seeing my face on the huge poster outside. We bought the *New York Times* for the newsvendor, because their photographer had snapped Sarah and Sophie, then only aged four and seven, gazing up at the Statue of Liberty on our arrival. They were wearing cute little mini dresses from Carnaby Street. Their hair was down to their small bottoms, their fringes long in their eyes. Sarah's hair was flaxen, Sophie's a rich chestnut. They turned heads wherever they went, these beautiful little daughters of mine. Now they were on the front of the *New York Times*. We stood there with the paper in our hands staring up at my poster. We really felt that we'd arrived in style. America was extending its welcome.

Part of the reason for my visit was to promote *Good Times, Wonderful Times*, as well as make the new movie. An evening reception had been organized at the United Nations building, presided over by U Thant, to honour film-makers of particular humanitarian distinction. De Sica had come from Italy for it, and I was there with Lionel as the star of his film.

The evening is burned in my brain as being one of almost total humiliation connected with menstruation. My menstruation had always been a nightmare to me, from the time of my first period at the age of eleven. It happened within an hour of our cat giving birth to four kittens beneath the blankets in my bed. My mother was livid at having to change my sheets twice. Since cash was so short at home, both my sister and I were required to sit and tear up old sheets and towels and look forward to wearing these monstrous napkins, like bulky bolster pillows, between our legs every month for as long as it took. My mother told us that we were lucky, that most of the people in Pontycymmer were required to *wash out* these bloodied rags and *use them again*! She said that's what she and her mother had to do, pennies and old sheets were so scarce. That always managed to silence me. The mere thought of boiling up such tasty morsels on our gas stove, doubtless in a saucepan which would later be used for our food, made me heave. I was noted for the delicacy of my stomach.

My periods had always been particulary heavy. And on that evening of solemn ceremony at the United Nations, honouring our anti-war film, it started unexpectedly. I had no one to tell. I was surrounded by men. My mother's words of warning, that periods are a private thing and men in particular are never to know when you are menstruating, rang in my ears. I slipped into the ladies' room and stuffed lavatory paper into my crotch; there were no other female provisions. I tried tearing the roller towel from its moorings. I wrenched the entire contraption from the wall. The noise was horrendous. The procession was awaiting me on the other side of the same wall, out in the august corridors of power.

I emerged with a brave smile on my face and squirmed my way through the interminable length of the building, with De Sica and U Thant on either side of me. I walked primly, thighs locked, so as not to dislodge the wedge of lavatory paper in my pants. I was wearing a figure-skimming black linen sheath, any bulge back or front would become immediately apparent. I could have said to these courteous gallants, these men of distinction. 'Hey, d'you happen to have the odd Tampax or two on your person – I'd be ever so grateful if you could see your way clear to loaning me a couple . . .' They must have intimate knowledge of women, especially De Sica, being Italian. He'd acted with Sophia Loren, and she must have bled on a monthly basis too, mustn't she?

I said nothing. We arrived at the enormous conference hall where they were screening our film. There was an international audience of thousands, who stood and clapped, at our entry. I sat in misery at the front of the multi-tiered seating, blood seeping from my body. I couldn't wait to get away. I discreetly stuffed a flimsy paper handkerchief into my gusset to reinforce what was there already.

The film seemed interminable, wracked as I was with menstrual cramp. I wondered how the Queen managed in these circumstances. But then she had a couple of ladies-in-waiting handy to slip her a change of tissue. She'd never get caught short in full flood. I watched my face on the screen and marvelled at my posh accent. Did I really talk in that affected manner when I was with Michael, at the time I was making the film? I must have done. My mind departed from my immediate problem, pondering on how much my life has changed since then. I started to need a drink badly. Really badly.

Further horror was in store. The film ended and amidst the tumultuous applause I was being wrenched from my seat and urged on to the stage as the star of the show. They wanted to present me with vast bouquets of blossoms. I couldn't believe this. Why was God doing it . . .

I stood on the vast stage, a fixed smile on my face, feeling the blood trickling from the confines of my knickers. If I was lucky someone would shoot me now and there'd be an explanation for this scarlet gout, which at any moment must reach my knees.

'Please, please,' I murmured through clenched teeth, 'let there be an assassin in the audience. Make this an international incident of tragic proportions, don't humiliate me any further. Let this nightmare end.'

No such luck. I hobbled off the stage, legs together, like a cripple. I was besieged with well-wishers, congratulated on my performance by women in sumptuous gowns with jewelled handbags. I didn't feel I could whisper to any of them that I was in desperate need of a Tampax or a torn-up strip of old towelling.

I excused myself and limped to the ladies'. I spent hours mopping myself up, and when I emerged insisted on being driven straight back to the hotel, to my mother and children. I refused to go to the party.

'It's been an emotional evening for her,' I heard someone say.

'Artistic temperament,' another added. 'You find it in all the great artistes.'

My mother had the time of her life on this trip. She insisted that we visit Niagara Falls, despite the fact there was an airline strike and we had to travel all night by train. The train was full of young soldiers, preparing to fight for their country in Vietnam. I was shocked. The war had not seemed a reality to me until then. Those kids couldn't have been more than eighteen, if that.

We stood on the boat that circles the waters at the base of Niagara. They had given us oilskins to keep us dry. The noise of the cascading water was deafening. The excitement, enthralling. My mother clutched my arm. Her face looked like a little girl's.

'Thank you, Moll, for bringing me. This is a dream come true. I used to sit on my father's knee at the kitchen table in Pontycymmer and point to the Kellogg's cornflake packet with the scene of Niagara on the back. "I'm going

238

there one day," I'd say to him. "Aye, aye, *bach*, and pigs can fly!" he'd say back. But here I am after all. I wish he could see me now.'

'He can, Mama,' I told her. 'He's up there looking down.'

She just laughed.

On my return to London, I was offered a scandalously lucrative job advising the direction of a fashion photography session for a big budget movie starring Herman's Hermits, who at that time in the mid-sixties were even more successful in the States than the Beatles. Hard to believe but true!

The sequence was being shot in Rome and I wangled a trip out of it for my mother and the children, all on expenses. We filmed a lot at night, the daytimes were simply too torrid. Afterwards we'd be joined by Sergio Leone, a friend of the director, who was busy making spaghetti westerns in the hills outside Rome. The meals and the drinking went on almost until dawn.

One night I returned to the luxury hotel where we were staying to check on my mother and the kids. They seemed to be sleeping soundly enough. I didn't learn until months later that there had been a hullabaloo in the hotel that evening. Sarah and Sophie had been untraceable and the alarm went out for them until they were found in the grounds with some American children, whose parents were in a frenzy. My mother had got paralytically drunk in the hotel bar with the barman, a Welshman who'd earlier worked at the Ritz in London. Sarah and Sophie had seized the opportunity to escape and go swimming in the floodlit hotel pool on their own, where they'd been led astray by the American children, who'd also given their cocktail-partying parents the slip.

My mother had made them promise not to tell me this

exciting news in case I should accuse her of not being a responsible grandmother. All three had only just taken to their beds when I was checking on them. The kids said afterwards that it was the very best night of their entire lives.

When I came back I opened a restaurant just off Sloane Square in Chelsea, with Maurice as my partner again, as we'd had such a great time together with the boutique. It seemed like a good idea; it wasn't far from the house and it would give me somewhere to welcome all my pals, I thought, instead of interminably cooking for them at home. It would get me out of the house.

Plenty of people opened and closed small businesses in the sixties, just like that. Just for fun. And everybody ate out then, around the King's Road. It had the feeling of Greenwich Village to it that summer.

The bistro was known as the Red Brick when I took it over. But some wag, some pal, took a ladder and knocked the bottom off the B, so that now it read as the Red Prick, aptly named. I never for a moment envisaged that this bistro would take off as it did, become quite as popular. It played absolute havoc with my love-life since there was no exit at the back, no way to escape other than through the front door past my team of accumulated admirers.

The air was thick with hurled brandies and bitter insults after a certain point in the evening, when the alcoholic consumption had passed an unprecedented high. Donald Baverstock would be bawling at John Mortimer. Mortimer would be insulting John Calder. Nicol Williamson would be baiting Johnny Thaw. Robert Brownjohn would be belching in everybody's face and food. Little Millie, the teenager currently in the charts with 'My Boy Lollipop', would break into song at the pudding stage.

My pal Irma Kurtz, still a commissioning editor at *Nova*

then, was my pony-tailed cashier. Jane Wood and her lover Peter Murray, a young architectural student, ex-lover of Janet Street-Porter, now a respected publisher, were my waitress and waiter. Maurice was downstairs in the kitchen cajoling our recalcitrant chef.

We went through six chefs in the six weeks that the restaurant was open. For that memorable six weeks it was *the* place to eat. Everybody came, all the actors from the Royal Court around the corner, half of Fleet Street and the publishing world. John Mortimer, an ex-lover, brought increasingly snooty girlfriends around there for the evening. It was their idea of horror, this Bacchanalian meeting place. The food was horrendous. We never closed until four in the morning. The local constabulary used to pop in to lend dignity and colour to the place, when the neighbours complained. They stayed for hours. It felt just like Pontycymmer.

I screwed a sanitary inspector at the back of the filthy kitchen, when he expressed doubts about renewing our licence. We got the licence, but he came back for more. I gave him a discreet hand-job every time he happened to be in the area, which for some reason was quite often. A nice man. I don't believe his other clients were so obliging. He seemed in need of sexual attention, I thought.

'I've had enough of this lark, haven't you, love?' I said to Maurice one day, after about the sixth week. Tony Shaffer had wined and dined me around the corner in the ritzy Le Gavroche earlier that week. 'This is where you belong, Moll,' he'd said in his lordly way, signing the bill which would have kept my staff in wages for a month. 'Instead of sweating your guts out like some kitchen slattern in that hell-hole you actually expect humans to eat in!'

I was the first to admit that the organization was not all it might have been, nor the standard of fare. We'd run out of bread the evening before and I'd had to offer sliced

Mother's Pride, all I could get, to my sophisticated clientele, which had not been to their liking. Sliced Mother's Pride.

I'd had to suggest that an early diner take his poxy prick elsewhere, a grandiose fart who'd spoken to my staff in a coarse way as if they were servants, just to impress the daft girl he was with – twenty years his junior and not his daughter, either. He'd tried to give me an Old Etonian mouthful back. But my loony aristo had shown me how to get the better of such swank. I threw his velvet-collared coat out on to the pavement after him. I thought he might sustain his first coronary judging by the colour of his face. I wouldn't have cared, the publicity would have been good for business. But now I'd had enough.

'Shall we put SHUT on the door and piss off to the pictures?'

'What about the washing up from last night, Moll?' Maurice was game for anything but he did have this responsible streak, still.

'We'll sell it as part of a thriving business.'

'Fifty-fifty?'

'Nah, dope, you can have it all. Something else will turn up for me. It always does.'

And it did. Within a fortnight I was the new fashion editor for the newly launched *Harpers & Queen*. Clive Irving had already mentioned it to me so the seed was sown before I'd actually dumped the restaurant. A friend, Donald Baverstock, had been begging me to give up the restaurant as being a waste of my creative talents. I respected Donald, the whiz-kid of television's 'Tonight' programme, which launched Alan Whicker's career amongst others. Donald, being Welsh, was a friend close to my heart. He cared about my future, he claimed. I believed him. But I disagreed with his suggestion that I might like a career in television. I was already being asked to appear on various chat programmes, but the thought of having my own show never actually appealed.

It was the same with acting, performing in films. I had enjoyed making the films with Lionel Rogosin, because I liked him. He was a kindred spirit. But when it was suggested in the States that I should make a serious career of acting and get an agent, something in me withdrew. It simply was not what I wanted to do, however much of a success I could make of it. I have been fortunate throughout my life, that whatever I've been involved in professionally has always been fun. My Tadci Thomas influenced me there.

It was very different on *Harpers* where the firm grasp of the Establishment, of conservative values, was too deeply entrenched for me to make much of a mark. But it was here that I succeeded in introducing the magical Sarah Moon's photographs to the world. Sarah Moon was one of those originals who surface now and again; her combination of fey artistry and female mystique was to influence fashion photography for the following decade.

Indeed, I made an immediate impact on *Harpers*, although it almost cost me my job straight away, when I called a bunch of prospective advertisers, whom the entire staff were trying to woo at a special lunch, a bunch of Philistine turds whose ads didn't deserve to be in our magazine anyway. I further compounded my felony by telling Marcus Morris, my managing director and acting editor, who was attempting to curb my tongue, that his face reminded me of a stained sanitary towel. When he sternly asked me to remain after the guests had gone, I invited him to show me his member. Whilst he was still obviously in shock, I managed to fumble with his flies and yank the flabby contents out, the sight of which sent me into an unflattering paroxysm of uncontrollable laughter. Then I fled, feeling that even I had gone too far.

I rang Cedric and asked him to pick me up in a taxi. I

was slumped, in full fashion finery, outside the National Magazine Building in Vauxhall Bridge Road, actually in the gutter with the contents of my expensive handbag scattered around me. Passers-by were giving me a wide berth. As his taxi approached, the driver pointed me out. 'Disgusting at this time of day. Look at it.'

'That,' replied Cedric, with offended dignity, 'is the lady we have come to collect.'

To everyone's surprise the ads started flooding into *Harpers*, that very afternoon, in the wake of that memorable lunch. It was rumoured that the magazine, under the flagship of certain fresh members of staff, at last had new life breathed into it. An invitation to the subsequent weekly advertising lunches became a hot ticket in the business, historic events, but after the first débâcle, I kept a cautious distance from the champagne. People complained these lunches were never quite as much fun as the first.

I lasted for three issues and then got 'the sack' – again! The circumstances were very similar to my dismissal from *Nova*. Marcus Morris summoned me to his office and greeted me as brusquely as my previous editor.

'What exactly are these meant to represent?' He indicated a sheaf of fashion photographs which I'd shot earlier in the week. I looked at them proudly. They were black and white, harsh, dramatic images of dark-eyed brunettes with angular cheekbones and passionate mouths. They were photographed against racing clouds and a crescent moon, with a stormy sea in the background and the slope of deserted sand-dunes. Each goddess clutched a crucifix which hung on silvered chains from her neck. The gowns were shaped like ecclesiastical robes. Floor-length capes flared in the wind, their hoods in some shots completely covering most of the faces except for the lewd lower lips, each pressed to a silvered cross.

'Brilliant, eh?' I smiled with satisfaction. These photographs were exactly as I'd envisaged them, precisely as I'd discussed them with the photographer. We had set off for Camber Sands late at night and worked right through until dawn to get this eerie feel. I had organized the session well in advance so that carefully chosen dress designers and jewellers had been working for weeks to produce exactly what I wanted. We all had good reason to feel proud of the results. Six pages of utter perfection.

There was a strange, strangled sound, emanating from Marcus. His face was even more mottled than usual, his hands even shakier. I'd been cruel to him only the previous day, when he'd hobbled in on crutches wallowing in everyone's sympathy.

'I fell over at the weekend,' he said to me by way of explanation, even though I hadn't asked. 'I fell from the scaffolding on my new house.'

'Who pushed you?' I said coldly, barely bothering to look up. 'Johnnie Walker?' I thought he probably hadn't forgiven me.

'These are – these are – *witches*!' He was trembling with rage!

I looked at the photographs again. I nodded. 'They could be seen as witches, yes,' I agreed, pleasantly enough.

'These are witches! And I will not have them in my magazine. Do you understand? The whole thing is blasphemy and nothing to do with fashion at all. Tell me who on earth is going to be traipsing around town done up like this?'

As it happened, six months later Yves Saint Laurent showed his Vietnamese monks collection and everyone was sporting crosses and cloaks. If Marcus had allowed me to run our feature we could have scooped old Saint Laurent by several months, but alas he was in no mood to see reason then. He didn't trust me to know what was in the air, which is what I was being paid for, presumably. Silly boy!

I waited for it and it came. 'It has been suggested to me by my own good wife that it would be pleasant to actually see some nice spring suits that our readers might like to go out and buy.'

'With white cuffs and collars,' I responded sweetly.

His face relaxed. 'Precisely.' He hadn't thought it would be this easy. It wasn't.

'Or else?'

'These photographs are unusable. They'll have to be reshot and that's my final word.'

I rose from my chair. 'I'll take the alternative, Marcus. It's been horrible working with you. I can't pretend otherwise.'

I was back in front of the lavatory mirror again. Different ladies', same expression, lower lip trembling, eyes swimming. This felt like rejection. This was the sack, wasn't it? But why hadn't I hung in there for some kind of remuneration? It was just as bad as when I'd left *Nova*. I'd been drinking the night before, that was the trouble. The drink gave me Dutch courage, it urged me to shoot my mouth off when caution might have been better. I'd been planning to take my mother and the kids off to the sun. There was no job in the offing now. No point asking God. He'd surely had enough of me. But a drink would help matters. Cedric would come to the rescue with a large Bloody Mary or a bottle of champagne. Yeah, that felt better already – a bottle of champagne to celebrate my freedom, with Cedric. What could be nicer!

It was Mark Boxer who was instrumental in luring me to the *Sunday Times*. He'd assiduously supported and encouraged me over the years, always sent word of congratulation to whatever editor I'd been working for when one or other of my spreads had caught his eye. Even while I was doing my brief stint at *Harpers* he had invited me on a freelance basis to contribute a major piece on furs and jewellery for the 'Look' pages. He gave me so much space to expand that it couldn't fail to catch everyone's eye, an entire page, in fact, mostly visual since I couldn't really write then.

When I left *Harpers*, the *Sunday Times* rang. The editor, Harry Evans, asked me to go for an interview, and invited me to become fashion editor on the 'Look' pages. Since I thought I'd be working for Mark, who understood me so well and admired how I worked, I accepted. Little did I know that now I would actually be required to write!

I said to Harry that it wasn't really my forte, that I couldn't write. He laughed and said he liked my modesty; no bugger could write on his paper but few had the honesty to admit it! Nobody could accuse me of not having told him.

On my very first week at the *Sunday Times*, Hunter Davies, renowned for having written the definitive, hugely successful biography of the Beatles and for being married to Margaret Forster, of *Georgie Girl* fame, replaced Mark Boxer as editor of the 'Look' pages.

I was in trouble again. He asked for my copy and I explained that I didn't type. He told me to write it in longhand, or dictate it to my secretary. I explained that I couldn't write.

'What the hell did Harry Evans give you this job for then?' His exasperation knew no bounds.

'My flair?' I stood my ground.

'You're not bloody flairing on my time! Next week you go up north and interview a working girl on how much of her money she spends on clothes and what she buys. Then you come back and interview a girl in the south, pinpointing the difference – if there is any. Got it! I'll get you bloody writing, if it's the last thing I do.'

'Fucking bastard!' I swore into the mirror of my powder compact.

I'd had a similar confrontation over writing my own fashion copy on *Nova*, with Dennis Hackett. He'd forced me into it one evening after hearing me entertaining friends over a drink in the pub.

'You've got the Celt's way with words, you lazy bitch. None of this "I can't write" stuff – it won't wash with me. From now on you write your own words.'

And I'd managed very well, he'd said. Even so, now I would do anything to get out of it, because the thought of writing for the *Sunday Times*, then regarded as one of the finest newspapers in the world, scared me rigid.

I travelled up to Bradford with my old mate Johnny Timbers, who was to do the photographs. I got completely plastered on the way up, dreading the next morning and my first interview. I tried to pick up a fellow traveller, according to Johnny. Embarrassment all round as the appalled commuter pretended it wasn't happening. Johnny got me off the train and steered me safely into the chauffeur-driven car the *Sunday Times* had laid on for us. The following morning I was so crucified by a hangover that I could barely focus on my interviewee.

'I've never done this before. I don't really know what to ask you,' I apologized.

'Sorry. I can't help you. I've never done it before either.'

'Shall we start at the bottom and work up? How many pairs of knickers do you have?'

She answered without hesitation. 'Thirty-five. I buy a pair of knickers every week, it's about all I can afford on my wages. I wear two pairs at a time, with tights in between. White cotton next to my skin for health reasons, nylon tights, then a pretty floral pair on top of the tights for when men look up my skirts. I wear a mini, you see, and have to walk up and down stairs all the time in our typing pool.'

Suddenly I was a statistician with riveting facts to report! I became known and valued for my interviews. I was a natural, they said. Another career had fallen into my lap. I combined my fashion knowledge with interviews. It was now that I met and made friends with Jill Bennett, when I talked to her and her then husband John Osborne about their wardrobes as part of a series called 'Me and My Clothes'.

I devised all my work around interviewing, if I could, since I found it (and still do) so fascinating. Just talking to people and listening, that's all it was. But that was how I learned to write – by listening to the differences in speech patterns, in basic sentence constructions, noting how certain words and phrases could elicit a humorous response and others disturb or move the reader. And then, once I began to understand what an extraordinary world the written word could open up for me, I became dissatisfied with merely writing for a newspaper. I wanted to spend my entire time writing fiction. I would not be able to do this for a few years, not until I was married again and we decided to leave London to make a fresh start.

I met Patrick Hughes down in Barry in 1969, not long after I joined the *Sunday Times*. I was there for two reasons: my mother's latest suicide attempt – the third now, since my father's death – and because I'd enrolled at the summer school to study photography. Patrick was one of the lecturers on the painting course. He was already recognized as a distinctive Surrealist artist, had been critically hailed as such since the age of twenty-one. Now he was twenty-nine, seven years younger than me, a married man with three sons, a lecturer at Bradford and then at Leeds College of Art.

We were married in 1970, the day after his divorce came through. Our wedding at Chelsea Register Office saw the union of his world and mine. The reception was held around the corner in my house, in Old Church Street. The Surrealists – Tony Earnshaw, Paul Hammond, Conroy Maddox – were there in full force. Jeff Nuttall, artist, performer and author of the cult classic *Bomb Culture*, had come dressed as a Teddy boy, in a two-tone drape jacket and bovver-boy boots, with his hair licked into a duck's arse. Angela Flowers, Patrick's art dealer, was with her partner–lover, Bob Heller, editor of *Management Today*. David Sylvester, the art critic, a colleague of mine on the *Sunday Times*, voiced the astonishment that we all felt at the beauty of the latest hot-gossip lovers, who were making their first public appearance here today. Namely, blond Eric Boman, the brilliant fashion illustrator, and Peter Schlesinger, until now the apple of David Hockney's eye. The romance coincided with the film about Hockney and his work, called *A Bigger Splash* – renamed wickedly by Barry Fantoni in *Private Eye* as *The Bugger's Pash*.

Thea Porter in a golden kaftan arrived with a consort of exotic eastern men. She had designed my wedding dress as a wedding present. I would have liked black this time, since I married in white the time before, but Thea refused to dress a bride in black. She claimed it would be bad luck, and insisted on violet. She had kitted me out with a sumptuous beaded face-mask which meant I was unable to eat anything at all, and could only drink through a straw. That didn't stop me.

At one point the champagne seemed to dry up altogether, to everyone's distress. It was locked in one of the bathrooms, chilling in a bathful of ice. For years I spread the scurrilous tale that it was Wayne Sleep and Jeff Banks who had locked themselves in, having it off together, until it got back to their ears and Wayne confronted me with it. It wasn't sex at all, but a surreptitious puff on a shared joint that had drawn them together. I apologized.

My mother was holding court down in the kitchen, wailing a lament in the arms of Edna O'Brien.

'This marriage will be the ruination of my Moll,' she moaned. 'I know it will, I know it will. I feel it in my bones that she's going to lose everything. He's a bigger bastard, this husband, than the first!'

Edna whispered to me on her way out that she found my mother 'marvellously fey'. That maybe I should listen to her words of warning, that she was a mystic and probably knew what she was talking about.

These were not the words, especially coming from Edna, a fellow Celt, that I would have chosen to have ringing in my ears on the eve of my honeymoon. Not when I'd married 'English', again!

When we reached the remote Irish cottage which Angela Flowers had lent us as a wedding present, I broke down and howled. It was freezing cold and damp. I was coming down with the flu. All the erotic underwear that I'd purchased from the tart's shop in Shaftesbury Avenue, which sells to the strippers of Soho, I'd readily swop for a thick, knitted cardigan.

I tottered, sneezing, up the stairs in my seven-inch stilettos, bearing the first breakfast tray, wearing open-crotch net tights and a nipple-baring lace bra. I'd assumed there would be a long mirror before which to cavort in this get-up, to turn myself on first of all. But all I found was a small shaving mirror in the bathroom. I could just about focus on a few goose-pimples.

We spent the honeymoon walking in the rain and reading erotic literature in bed. Everything was gentle and loving between us and yet there was a tempestuous undertow that felt all too familiar – the racing heart, a sense of impending explosion, a clash of wills – just like with my father. Patrick sensed a darkness in me, but neither of us realized how dangerous it would be to our marriage. Not then.

During the ten years I was a fashion editor, I was forever being hauled over the coals for straining the fashion budget. Why must I fly models in from Paris, Milan and Manhattan, simply because their faces fit a feature, or their legs happened to be longer, or their smiles that much wider? There were girls in *Debrett* who would model for free. Photographer sons of the peerage who'd shoot six pages of fashion for nothing. Sixth-formers from Roedean who'd give their eye-teeth to be fashion assistants, whose parents would actually pay for the privilege . . . penny-pinching, poverty thinking, leading to a dearth of creativity and dull, dull, dull magazines!

And yet, it was all those extraordinary flights of fancy, for which I had to fight every inch of the way, that put the ailing circulation of *Harpers* back on its feet and won for it the D and AD awards; which won for me in 1972, when I was at the *Sunday Times*, the prestigious Fashion Editor of the Year award for 'outstanding contributions and achievements in the world of fashion'.

It was on *Nova*, the magazine above all others which is nearest my heart, that Dennis Hackett and Harri Peccinotti encouraged me to follow my instincts. And, because the combined hostility from those two proved an equal match to my own when it came to fighting for what we believed in, I have never known such creative conflict before or since – nor seen a better women's magazine than *Nova* was at the height of that tempestuous period. But it didn't come cheap.

I had never had an expense account before I started work at *Nova*, and I couldn't really be bothered to use it. I had too much going on in my life to footle about with petty professional housekeeping, for God's sake. But the rest of the staff berated me, since it was being suggested to them from executive level that if Molly could manage without claiming expenses so could they. I was letting the side down, but I hadn't looked at it that way until a union militant pointed out that management was there to be screwed, since they sure as hell were screwing the workers. Me included. You only had to look at their profits and ask where they were going.

This sank in; it made sense. I thought of my grandfather and the paltry gold watch he was given after years spent toiling in the pits to put fat on other people's stomachs, and I thought of my own hunger as a child. I changed my mind over the expenses business. If others could screw management, then so could I. Only I would do it better, with more panache!

I started in a small way, but when I joined the *Sunday Times*, I cracked open a bottle of champagne and really got stuck in. I was taught to fiddle expenses by old hands on the newspaper who'd been at it for years. The perks of the job, they called it. The more imaginative the excuse I gave for my lavish spending, the more unquestioning would be the payout.

I saved all the bills I could find from the bottom of my handbag: bills from when Sally, her husband and children came to stay; bills from the Trattoria Terrazza for evenings and Sunday lunches with my two daughters and Patrick's three sons. I took taxis to the cinema in the West End and shoved in those receipts along with theatre tickets, ice-creams, day trips to Brighton for the entire family and any visiting aunties. Piddling stuff really to start with, but I got better at it as I went on. I could have been done for extortion, but it didn't feel evil.

On one occasion I put down fur research for a feature on couture furriers to cover a day trip to London Zoo for all our kids and their cousins. I can't actually remember inventing the excuse for a massive Christmas blow-out at the Terrazza until Jimmy, the sardonic wit in charge of passing expenses on the *Sunday Times*, summoned me up to his office one morning. His room was perilously close to Harry Evans's, the editor, on the sixth floor.

Whenever I landed on that corridor I began to palpitate for all my past misdemeanours, never mind my present ones. On my very second day at the paper I had arrived at seven a.m., just to look willing, and was disastrously joined in the lift by Harry Evans, who entered unexpectedly at the second floor to find me swigging my breakfast from a half-empty bottle of champagne. I was nervous. This job was more than I could cope with. Once again I had conned my way into something for which I was under-qualified. I couldn't write, how could I work for a newspaper of this standard? I sure as hell needed this drink to get me started on the day.

I offered Harry a gulp, too, pressing the bottle to his lips with the usual enthusiasm of early inebriation. He politely demurred, claiming it to be a shade too soon in the day. I winked and leered at him and struck a pose of studied seduction. I can't remember whose bed I'd just left but I know for certain I wasn't fully satisfied. There was just one more poke left in me. I can't be sure but I think I told him this. I still blush at the memory. The poor soul left the lift a couple of stops earlier than originally intended, I'm sure. Within hours I was bundled back home in a taxi, hilariously intoxicated, incapable of speech even. All I could manage was a raucous chortle and a line or two of song. The contents of my handbag were still being returned to me from various departments on various floors of the building as long as a month after the escapade. Apparently I'd taken it into my head to give the place a bit of a going over, have a little cruise around.

I never quite felt that I managed to live down that first startling impression, not with Harry Evans or the entire staff of the *Sunday Times*, for all the years of excellent service I put in there. Even when I won the Fashion Journalist of the Year Award, I felt my professionalism had been superseded by this sex-crazed, piss-pot image I seemed to have acquired along Fleet Street. The first time I entered El Vino's the entire roomful of male journalists craned around to look. I was wearing violet lipstick and a crushed-velvet cloche with a lavender feather that caressed the clouds. My companion was astonished at the reaction. He said that he had brought many female colleagues, far more beautiful than me, into this male bastion and never a brow had been raised before. I surely didn't look that spectacular. I said nothing. I knew the reason: the word had spread.

Either way there are enough journalists still employed at the *Sunday Times* to remind me that the whole business has gone down in the annals as probably the least auspicious start to a journalistic career on that prestigious organ of any employee before or since.

I have yet to learn how many men I jolly-rogered on that spectacular walk-about. The state of my underwear when I arrived home left me in no doubt that not all the Thomson employees practised Harry's fastidious and commendable restraint. Either that or the taxi-driver got lucky.

So it was understandable that I got shaky around the sixth floor and anything to do with the hierarchy of the *Sunday Times*. When Jimmy bid me enter, my heart was in my Manolo Blahnik boots. I adjusted my cream satin Biba cleavage to distract him. Nothing doing. He was a Scot, was Jimmy, and not to be messed with.

'I'd like you to take a look at that framed document on the wall, lassie.' He smiled pleasantly enough. The smile of a cobra.

I stared at the typewritten paper. I saw it had my name at the top and my scrawled signature at the bottom. I could tell by the loops and curves that I was well-gone when I wrote it.

'Worthy of framing wouldn't you say, lassie? I've had everybody in to see it, including the editor. Harry agrees with me that this is a one-off. We both think that anyone who displays this degree of imagination is wasted on this newspaper. They should be away writing fiction.' He leant forward, his eyes like twin icicles. 'Twenty-four lunches for twenty-four Father Christmases is not on, lassie. It simply won't wash with me, pull the other one. I read the interview, very good, too. *One* Father Christmas who happened to work in Pontings. You can't kid me that you researched twenty-four of those poor blighters, let alone fed them a slap-up meal at the Trattoria Terrazza. Get your act together, Molly. You're a popular girl around here and a damn good journalist, but don't push your luck or take me for a fool, that's all I ask. I've been sorting through expense claims for the past thirty years, and I've seen some rum 'uns but this takes the bloody biscuit! The only one worth framing. Now get out of this room, and turn over a new leaf. You're a bright lass, you understand professional integrity. Try practising it in regard to your expenses from now on. It will get you a whole heap further.' He waved his hand at my framed missive. 'You're worthy of better things – all this is second-rate piddling stuff.'

In 1974, after five years, I left the *Sunday Times*, the place that I had come to regard as my home, my womb. The circumstances were marginally the same as my other two sackings, from *Nova* and *Harpers*, with the crucial difference that this time I was given a sweet financial settlement.

Harry summoned me to his office. I sat my side of his desk, while he asked me if I had lost my interest in fashion. This was a difficult question because I had never, in truth, been very interested in the first place. I only ever saw clothes in terms of shape and colour, not as status symbols and evidence of social standing. But he had perceived that I was becoming more and more engrossed in the art of writing, that my interviews with people about their clothes were driven from a curiosity to do with their speech patterns and vernacular rather than any sartorial information that I might impart to our dear readers. This was not what I'd been employed for – I was not fulfilling my obligations.

Within an hour I was back in the ladies' in front of the mirror, but no tears this time, no trembling lower lip, just the need to get home to tell Patrick and the kids – and open the bottle, bottles, of champagne. Yippee! Now I could do what I wanted, which was to sit at home all day and not have to go to the office. Just sit at home at the typewriter making things up and never having to report another fashion show as long as I lived. It could not have come at a more opportune moment. I'd recently been approached by a publisher with a view to writing a novel for them and Patrick and I were keen to leave London, particularly now that the kids were growing up.

The *Sunday Times* money kept us comfortably until the rewards started to flow in from other sources, from my novel, which did extremely well, and from all my free-lance journalism, radio and television work.

Patrick and I moved to Cornwall because we had visited it to stay with the Canadian artist Bill Featherston and his wife Natalie, and met various local painters. It was just too seductive a package to ignore. Especially since I had never encountered a landscape as ravishing as West Penwith, a light so luminous, a sense of Celtic mystery as strong as my Welsh mountain. It felt like a home from home.

There was another reason for the move: a financial one. The mortgage on our large house near the Portobello Road and the high life-style which I had easily managed on a fashion editor's salary was much harder to cope with now. But it was bumping into Terry Frost at a private view at the Mall Galleries that finally made up our minds for us. He told us how his son Anthony, a painter like himself, now rented a coastal retreat in Cornwall for a mere pittance and that there was a converted barn on the other side of the road, between St Ives and Pendeen, which was up for grabs at twelve pounds a week.

'That's ours,' I said to Patrick. 'We'll take the midnight sleeper down to Penzance tonight and secure it with the agent, won't we?' We did, and a month later we moved in.

Now I became a writer of comic-erotica and continued to be so for the next decade. I had chosen this genre because it was what I enjoyed reading the most. I read every book, verse, article, by every humorist from Evelyn Waugh to Joe Orton to study and discover my own style. I perused the eroticists from de Sade, through Bataille, to Terry Southern's *Candy*, then I combined everything into what I wanted to say.

My books were romps in the same tradition as the seaside postcards of Donald McGill and the paintings of Beryl Cook. Indeed, it was always these paintings I imagined as my covers. The sexist covers that I was landed with broke my heart. But who was I, the mere author, to understand what sold? That's what my publishers said. And the books did sell, and even got good reviews, so I turned my face in the other direction when it came to the covers, and concentrated on just sitting down and writing.

I left the world of fashion with no regrets whatsoever. My greatest fear was that I might cop my load on the motorway, driving my car, and be hauled up to the Pearly Gates and asked by St Peter what I did for a living before being allowed entry.

'Fashion editor for the *Sunday Times*,' I would have to answer, ashamed. I knew that this was not what my granny had intended for me, this ambience of snobbery, of materialism and false vanity. I could tell at a glance the cost of what anyone had on, I could guess where they'd had their hair cut, what plastic surgery they'd undergone, whether their tan was applied or the real thing, which perfume house they patronized, what shape their bra was, or even if they were wearing one. I could recognize the line of a Dior, a Saint Laurent, a Cardin, a Marks & Spencer. I had supported the careers of Michael Roberts, Zandra Rhodes, Manolo Blahnik, Ossie Clarke, Andrew Logan, Barbara Hulanicki and countless others, all of whom would have made it to the top without me. So what!

I was a familiar face in the street from the amount of television I was doing, such as 'Three After Six', with Jeremy Thorpe and Lord Hailsham – as unlikely a television mix as you could wish for. 'Late Night Line Up' on BBC 2 had filmed my 'One Woman's Week'. I had startled evening viewers of 'The Frost Programme' by saying the word poke, which got confused with Kenneth Tynan saying the word fuck, so I got branded publicly as a foulmouth. So what!

The truth is I was now getting tired of my own persona, of having myself rammed down my own throat, of being wheeled on by the media for any controversial quote. I needed time to be indoors, away from the hullabaloo. My body and spirit required a slowing down period. I had to turn my back on the cocktails and take stock of my life, before I disappeared up my own alcohol-drenched arsehole.

The barn that Patrick and I lived in was in a remote area on the edge of a cliff-top, between Pendeen and St Ives. I loved standing at the window, staring out at the cows, listening to the wind tearing at the windmill generating our electricity. Patrick was away painting in his studio and our children, his boys and one of my girls, were amusing themselves in the granite barn, where they slept, on the other side of the road.

We had no children living permanently with us now, and I missed my daughters. Sarah was sixteen and living and working in London. She had a job as an assistant stage manager at the Orange Tree Theatre in Richmond. This was what she wanted, what she had always wanted, my first-born. She had been obsessed with the theatre since the age of five. Whenever there were more than one or two children in our house, Sarah would start organizing them to perform. When she was thirteen I relented and allowed her to change schools. She left Holland Park to go to the Arts Educational Stage School in the Barbican. They did lessons in the mornings and stage work all afternoon. By the time she was fourteen she'd passed her 'O'-levels. At sixteen her 'A'-levels were already behind her. When we decided to move to Cornwall, her reaction was one of horror. She needed the metropolis, she claimed. Nothing would persuade her to move down with us. We arranged for her to live with my good friend Martha Hill, above Martha's eccentric clothes emporium on Marylebone High Street, next door but one to David Shilling's very first millinery establishment; David who was to become my favourite milliner.

Sophie, at thirteen, was away at boarding school, at Frensham Heights. Her progress away from home had been the same as Sarah's, a phone-call of homesickness every day at the beginning, tailing off to once a week and then once a month, when she'd settled in.

Patrick's sons missed Sarah too. John, the eldest, was the same age as her, but was still at school in London where they lived with their mother. James was three days older than Sophie, both Geminis; it was like having twins around. And brighter-than-a-button Solomon was two years younger again. They were all, the boys, besotted with Sarah. She was their Queen Bee. But they appeared to have made the transition – not too painfully – of transferring their adoration to Sophie now. All four arrived together to spend their school holidays with us. Within a week they were transformed, their pallor replaced by berry-brown skin and high energy. We tramped over the moors and climbed the cliffs and took them swimming to work off their excess energy, otherwise their sheer exuberance would be unliveable with. Nobody had any trouble sleeping at night.

I was dictating my third novel, which my publishers expected to do as well as my first two. My secretary blushed with excitement when I dictated a passage of extreme erotica. Then she started chuckling as I relieved the sexual tension with a joke. I'd maybe have my hero pass wind in the act of coition. It only took something as basic as that to set her off. I had come to judge my reader's reaction by hers. But I had to be careful; I'd already had to sack one secretary when her blushes inhibited me into cooling my stuff for fear of embarrassment. Comic erotica was tricky material to write, requiring a delicate balance if it was not to tip over into the banal, or earn the criticism which had been levied at it already, that of outright pornography.

I was enjoying my work, I was having fun. I looked forward to the family returning. The evening meal was already prepared, the time was nearly upon us when we would sit around the big table and get together for the evening, the time of day that I liked best.

My second marriage was a joy to me. When I woke in the morning it was with the same delight that I knew in the early years of my first marriage. I gave myself utterly to this relationship. I wanted it to work more than anything in the world. And yet, looking back, I suppose the move to Cornwall actually represented the first nail in the coffin. To me, anyway, it pretty soon became apparent that my drinking, which I had come to associate with our way of life in the London fast lane, had simply accompanied us.

We were locked, this man and I, in physical combat. The sex was urgent, insatiable. This was a sexual union,

261

with every possible permutation. I enjoyed the sex, I couldn't get enough of it, it was like living on the edge of an abyss. We set ourselves impossible targets such as intercourse twelve times a day on high days and holidays. It was my job to dress up, to titillate, to be imaginative, to do everything and anything to induce, maintain and prolong my husband's erection. It was my responsibility to wrench each ejaculation from him. He complained, he whimpered, he bellowed that it was like having his scrotum scraped with a rusty razor, the final few orgasms of the twelve. Certainly in terms of volume they were scarcely worth receiving.

'More like sparrows' farts than anything else!' I would say derisively.

Nothing satisfied me: as with my drinking, I was always pushing for more and I was increasingly drawn to anything that would heighten my excitement and sense of danger. Those years in Cornwall, five in all, alternated between scenes of total tranquillity and a deepening sense of dis-ease on my part. Something was wrong, but what could it be? I had everything I could wish for. I was living in a part of the world which had always drawn me, on a dramatic coastline of description-defying grandeur. I walked on a stretch of moorland protected by the National Trust, fringed with storming seas and secret coves. Overhead, high daytime skies raced with clouds and the blinding clarity of the sun.

The landscape touched something raw and unhealed in me, leaving me at even more of a loss. I appeared to have a perfect life. I was a successful novelist, able to produce a book a year with no problem at all. I had a young husband whom I adored and who adored me. Our children were everything that we hoped they would be. We lived in a cosy flat over the Wimpy Bar in the middle of Fore Street, St Ives, and worked together in a massive studio which used to belong to Francis Bacon, on Porthmeor Beach.

We were surrounded by our pals, other artists such as Patrick Heron and Delia, Terry and Kath Frost, Tony and Jane O'Malley, Karl Weschke, Rose Hilton, John and Judi Emanuel, and Dr Roger Slack and his dear wife, Janet. No shortage of kindred spirits there.

I initiated the Swimmers Club which braved the icy seas all through summer and winter, every day, even with snow on the ground. Sometimes as I swam, laughing with my fellow swimmers, embracing those of our children who chose to brave the elements with us, I thought of turning swiftly in the water and striking out for the horizon, leaving all of it behind. A perverse and danger-ously destructive voice was calling me to abandon all that I held so dear, to choose a death by drowning. Had I done so it would have been inexplicable to everyone, myself included. Yet at times the urge to obliterate myself was barely resistible. I told no one. Who could I tell? Instead I breast-stroked it to the end of the swim, the darkness churning inside me waiting to take over, held at bay – but only just these days – by another drink.

My mother's serious suicide attempts had abated, but she was on stronger medication now, strictly supervised by the consultant at the mental hospital.

'What do you think about having a mother in the asylum?' she asked cheerfully.

'You're not in an asylum, you're in your own front room at home.' I evaded the question.

'I'm an out-patient,' she snapped back. 'Don't talk to me as if I'm not all there.'

I laughed out loud. It eased the tension. She played these tricks with my sister, trying to upset her. But she couldn't upset me, and she knew it.

'What do you think of having a lunatic for a mother? You haven't answered my question,' she persisted.

'I'll have to ponder on it.' I looked out of the window over to Barry Island and the fun-fair, where people were having a simple and normal time, instead of having to answer questions like this.

'That's long enough!' She clapped her hands. 'What are the results of your pondering?'

'What do I think?' I answered slowly, trying to be honest. She deserved that. 'I think it's fine. It means you're special. Not on the same wavelength as other people. The worst part about it is that you can't express yourself by writing or painting. You don't play your piano any more. So all the rage in you gets turned inwards. That's what I think. But I need to ponder some more. The right answer is somewhere, but I haven't found it yet.'

Her eyes filled with tears. She held out her hands. 'What would I do without you, my Moll?'

The Cornish idyll ended in 1979 when Patrick and I packed up and headed for New York City. Friends placed the blame for our separation a year later, and subsequent divorce, on our horrendously hectic New York life-style, but those who had seen so many marriages flounder in the social claustrophobia of St Ives knew better. I now regard New York as simply having given us an extra year; we clung together there as if in a hellish fever, but the fire, the loving flame between us, was already flickering and needed a kill-or-cure blast of excitement and fresh air if it was to survive at all. It didn't.

My drinking had taken an ominous turn though I didn't recognize it then. I thought I had it under control and took all measures to prove it. Every so often I'd announce to everyone that I'd given it up for good – well, for at least three months. And I'd last that long, drinking lemonade in the pub on darts night at the Gurnard's Head. But I always went back in the end, by which time, inexplicably, it was worse. The tolerance wasn't there, it took less to make me drunk.

This didn't affect the sex, which was just the same; as urgent and exciting as it had ever been. We made love three times a day, as we always had. Once in the morning on waking. Once during the day, usually after lunch, standing up in the studio where we worked together. And always last thing at night before falling asleep in each other's arms. But if we were out and drinking, I could just as easily find myself kissing someone else by the end of the evening, never quite knowing how the situation had arisen. The frightening alcoholic blackouts were encroaching.

We chose New York because Patrick had a wealthy patron who had been buying his work through the Angela Flowers Gallery. This man, Marty, a lawyer, lived in Manhattan and invited us over for a brief trip. Patrick loved New York and when Marty suggested that we give it a try for a year, we both jumped at it. Why not?

Sarah was happily settled in London now. Sophie was leaving us to start as an art student at St Martin's School of Art in the Charing Cross Road. Patrick's eldest son, John, was at university. His second son, James, was starting art college, too. Solomon, the youngest, had still to sit his 'O'-levels at school. But before leaving we organized for the children to pay us a visit. Something for all of us to look forward to.

'Better than trolling down to measly old St Ives every holiday,' they claimed. 'Time we became world travellers!'

Patrick and I strolled over the cliffs on the night before we left. This was the same walk that we'd taken for the five years that we'd lived in St Ives. I felt closer to him then than any time before or since. We stood entwined together, buffeted by the wind, our ears filled with the screaming seagulls and the sea sucking on the rocks below.

'Advancing into the unknown,' I said lightly, meaning America.

We turned to kiss each other; I could taste the salt air on

his soft mouth, and another taste – one of mutual fear, the mutual fear of inevitable separation.

So where best to live in New York but that ship in the night with the siren call that has lured so many other free spirits before me and will continue to long after I am gone, God willing. The legendary Chelsea Hotel. Many have perished within these portals. The plaque on the front pillar proclaims this is where Thomas Wolfe wrote *Look Homeward, Angel*. It is where my fellow-countryman Dylan Thomas drifted into his final poetic coma, and where George Kleinsinger died, he who wrote the imperishable 'Tubby the Tuba' tune. Aaron Copland still lived here on one of the upper floors. Marilyn Monroe slept here with Arthur Miller. Several of the 'superstars' who featured in Andy Warhol's most famous film, the eponymous *Chelsea Girls*, lived here at some time or another. Jack Nicholson and Anjelica Huston stayed here, Elliott Gould took an apartment here after his divorce from Streisand. Brendan Behan blathered his way up these stairs. Quentin Crisp took up residence, only removing himself after a murder and on overhearing the following discussion in the downstairs foyer:

Aged Female Resident: 'What's happened? Why're the cops here?'

Cop: 'Come for the corpse.'

Resident: 'Corpse? What corpse?'

Cop: 'Someone got stabbed, lady. Now move along, please.'

Resident: 'Stabbed! Gee, stabbed! Wow! How many times?'

Quentin found this curiosity indelicate under the circumstances, and didn't care to continue living in a place where people treated the loss of life on such a casual basis.

We saw a lot of Quentin. I was as comfortable with him

as anyone I had ever known. When I reminded him that he was my first male nude at art school, not to say life itself, he sighed.

'I was so beautiful then. People rarely admit to lamenting the loss of their looks as they grow older, but it is the one thing I do regret.'

On arrival, Patrick and I occupied the very room where Sid Vicious knifed Nancy some months before, though hers was not the aforementioned stabbed corpse. I found it unbearably ghoulish and asked to be moved. I am not normally squeamish but I did take against the blood-stained carpet, and the psychic side of me was deeply disturbed by the sense of hovering trauma over the bed.

I made the first of many trips to sort out the most congenial living space for Patrick and myself with the manager, Stanley Bard, son of the owner of the Chelsea – a man who holds deep feelings of respect and admiration for artists, inherited from his father. His Jewishness, his beautiful brown hooded eyes reminded me of Malcolm, of a Ben Shan painting, or an El Greco Christ. I told him this and it pleased him. We set off on the right foot. We understood each other. He very much wanted me to live at the Chelsea for the year that we planned to be in the States, and agreed to accept and hang one of Patrick's rainbow paintings in the vestibule, in part exchange for rent on two apartments which would be converted into a self-contained unit with its own small corridor on the seventh floor. In addition, he would paint it white throughout and lay white canvas over the existing carpets to make it modern and pristine. One of these apartments would be for Patrick to paint in and for me to write in. The other would be our living quarters.

When people expressed surprise at what I had achieved with a man not known for putting himself out in this way, Patrick shrugged. 'Moll's a witch. She can do anything.'

I was reminded of James.

It did seem to others that life was continuing to hand me everything on a plate. Only I had the growing premonition that this move to Gotham, especially the Chelsea, marked the start of the downhill slide. I was reaching the end of the line. I was gradually losing control. The fear was the worst, the fear on a daily basis. The ever-tightening and paralysing grip of paranoia. But this didn't incapacitate me until the end of the year. At the start of it I could still cope.

I went across the road from the Chelsea to have my hair done. The camp hairdresser, on learning that I was living there, asked if I knew Sid and Nancy, because he used to do her hair. It gave him great satisfaction to know, he confided, that she went to her maker with her roots freshly blonded, since he'd only done them the day before. Others might have viewed it as a waste of money. Stanley Bard's view of the case was that it wasn't murder at all. He saw it as a love-pact, an act of passion, that went sadly wrong somehow. Stanley wouldn't hear anything bad about his guests.

We settled down in Manhattan with no trouble at all. On the night of our arrival we walked into the hotel's downstairs restaurant to find some old pals propping up the bar, and we drank with them until five in the morning. These were two of the three Liverpool poets, Roger McGough and Brian Patten. We got totally out of it on Harvey Wallbangers, the speciality of the house. And from then on that was all we ever drank there. We ate out every single night, the rate of exchange was so favourable, well over two dollars to the pound at the time. We liked eating at Elaine's best and she gave us preferential treatment, not only because I had interviewed her for the *Sunday Times*, on an earlier visit to New York, as being *the* theatrical Manhattan restaurateur, but because she was an old pal of Muriel Belcher of Soho's Colony Room, of which I had been an habitué for many years. Muriel Belcher, indeed, was one of my earliest role models, when I knew I would be a person of the *demi-monde*.

It was at Elaine's that I got to know Woody Allen, another of her firm favourites. He always occupied his own table, just there by the ladies' lavatory, so that he could check out what was going in and out in the way of interesting girls, I imagine. He almost always ate by himself, and everyone respected this and left him alone. Except me, who was unaware of the rules. Well, how would I know? I was a new girl in town.

I introduced myself first before I sat down. I said, 'Hi, Woody,' and held out my hand. The entire restaurant took a sharp intake of breath. This was sacrilege. Everyone knew that Woody hated to be disturbed while he was eating. Who the hell was this interloper, this insensitive freak!? Forks were poised in the air. Spoons were still halfway to mouths. Not a sound could be heard.

But I was a witch. I fixed Woody with my glistening eyes. I smiled at him slowly and watched his lips until he was forced to respond. He was mesmerized. Of course! He beckoned to a chair and I slid into it slowly. The bond was forged. The audience breathed again. Normal restaurant noise resumed. From then on any evening that we both happened to be dining at Elaine's, I would pass his table on my way to the loo and he would invite me to sit down and exchange words with him. To the envious curiosity of all. Acceptance at the very highest level! No sweat!

Now we were on chatting terms, Woody and me, I went to see him play jazz over at Michael's Pub every week. I one night bumped into Charlotte Rampling in the powder room. We hadn't seen each other since John Mortimer's wedding in London. The reception had been packed with exquisite creatures like Charlotte, and Shirley Ann Field. Since I knew that Shirley was an ex-girlfriend of John's, and I certainly was, I would have loved to dig the dirt with Charlotte and ask if she was too. But there was something magnificently glacial about her, the kind of distance that Garbo must have projected and, even though the booze had loosened my tongue sufficiently, courage failed me at the last minute. Though I was highly regarded as an intuitive interviewer and few subjects, if any, daunted me, I knew that Charlotte would be a hard nut to crack, not giving an inch unless it was on her terms. If I were still painting what wouldn't I give to do that particular portrait. I discreetly analysed the heart-stopping structure of the head and shoulders in the mirror.

Though I rarely thought about my painting, it was still there buried deep inside me like a cancer eating away at my vitals. I was unsettled by my encounter with Charlotte Rampling. She had unnerved me, somehow. She seemed so 'on course', so centred. I started meeting females in New York, with this same air about them, of actually knowing who they were, of being true to themselves in a way that I seemed to have lost. Though no one would have guessed it from my exterior.

I interviewed Grace Jones, for the *Sun* newspaper back home. They splashed it across the centre-spread along with other items of show-biz gossip which I picked up easily from pals and our all-night, every night, club life. Grace was at the height of her cabaret and concert success. She and her raw music ruled Manhattan. She was with her lover, her French Svengali. She was pregnant, expecting his child, and although transported with wild delight she asked me not to print this because she had a new album coming out. I was a responsible interviewer, with a trustworthy reputation, and could therefore get interviews with female stars who wouldn't talk to anyone else. This interview was a scoop, but it had come via a mutual friend, the high-flying fashion photographer Eric Boman.

I had used Eric's drawings to illustrate fashion articles of mine on the *Sunday Times*, a couple of years before I left. He was an art student at the Royal College then and had been discovered by Mark Boxer, when he was art director at *Queen* magazine.

Eric now lived in Manhattan, sharing a ritzy loft with Peter Schlesinger, the stunning beauty he stole from David Hockney. All three were friends again, everything had been forgiven and David stayed with Eric and Peter every time he was in New York. We regularly went round for dinner. The ex-pats stuck together in New York. We were family to each other, in place of the real thing on the other side of the Atlantic. We celebrated our birthdays and Christmases and bank holidays together. We allowed Americans into these hallowed circles with caution, but when we did we embraced them wholeheartedly. This was their country, after all. If any friends from our London set popped over, like Manolo Blahnik, we would gather together to catch up on the gossip. What Bianca was up to, or Michael Roberts, or Ossie . . . the social structure was as delicate as a duchess's, as impossible for an outsider to enter as that. Ours was an international network.

We met Divine when Andrew Logan and Michael, his boyfriend, came to stay at the Chelsea. Stanley Bard, not realizing that Andrew was a close and long-standing friend of ours, put him into a cockroach-infested hovel off a corridor that was rarely inhabited except by ghosts. They ran, white-faced, to me for rescue and I had to intervene in getting them properly settled.

I was thrilled to meet Divine, Diana Dors look-alike and drag star of John Waters' kitsch movies. His name was currently on everyone's lips, a *cause célèbre* for eating poodle shit on-screen in John's latest cult hit. I was emboldened to ask Divvi if he actually did eat the stuff, soft and steaming, straight out of the dog's arse as it was deposited on the pavement. He laughed and said, sure, they'd fed the little pooch with caviare all day and it tasted no different, 'cept for being hot and tastier. I asked why he had done it and he said that it was a straight choice: whether to be an unknown transvestite performer for the rest of his days, or to break through a taboo for a few seconds and become instantly and endlessly famous.

We were friends until his death just a few years ago, meeting up all over the world with mutual pals like Zandra Rhodes, and of course, Andrew and Michael. Divine was the epitome of the 'exuberantly tacky extravagance' ethic to which I clung so tenaciously.

The *Sunday Times* got in touch to see if I could secure an interview with Bette Midler. Years before, when I'd approached them proposing an interview with Bette at the time of her London appearance at the Palladium, they'd turned it down in a particularly snotty way, asking who the hell she was. But now her smash film *The Rose*, based on the life of rock star Janis Joplin, had come out and was storming the world.

I had managed to interest *Men Only* in the original interview. They were the only ones who would run it, but that suited Bette and me, anyway, because we could talk about the raunchier stuff, which a more establishment paper might have vetoed.

We got on like a house on fire, kindred spirits for sure, and started giggling together right away. She saw by my appearance that I wasn't the average run-of-the-mill journalist. She fell in love with my David Shilling hat and almost succeeded in seducing it off my head. But it was my favourite, a shiny straw bowl of scarlet cherries, à la Carmen Miranda. Carmen turned out to be a mutual idol. In fact we shared many things, me and Bette, including a deep distaste for sand in the snatch which we'd both experienced while having sex on the beach. She actually lost her virginity in this manner, a gritty initiation which neither of us would wish on any young virgin. After the Palladium she was going straight down to Brighton to do her show there, and tried to persuade me to come with her. But Patrick was waiting for me; we planned to take the midnight sleeper back to Cornwall. I promised to look her up in New York if I ever went there. I organized a duplicate chapeau for her from David Shilling before Patrick and I left, on the off-chance that Bette and I would get together again. David was thrilled to think of Bette wearing one of his creations. I dropped her a line to tell her this, but after *The Rose* she became totally incommunicado. Bad things were happening in her life, and she chose to isolate herself, I learned later. I, of all people, understood that, though my bad things hadn't started to happen yet. Only inklings that they might be on the way.

Miraculously, in spite of our racy lifestyle, Patrick and I both managed to get our work done. Like Dracula, we turned the twenty-four hours around to suit ourselves and the nocturnal life we had chosen to lead. We went to bed at 8 a.m., having breakfasted around 6.30 a.m. at the Empire Diner, after an exhilarating night of excess. We rose at around 11 a.m. and started work immediately.

At 1 p.m. we went swimming on the other side of the road at the YMCA pool. We swam twenty lengths, no more, never less. We stood for lunch in the Vitamin Bar, next door to the Y. It took no time at all to swallow a vegetable vitamin draught, with a fruit one to follow. We returned to work until 6 p.m., when we went to bed, sleeping until 11 p.m. We woke, showered and took a snack to fortify us for the hours ahead. We might dine later with friends in a restaurant, who knows? We went with the flow, wherever it took us.

We needed a full hour to prepare ourselves for the night. On some occasions there was make-up for us both, mine more lurid than Patrick's. His was a subtle job, which took me longer than my own, involving soft brushes and shades of pale greys and browns around his eyes. Mascara on his lashes. A delineation of the cheekbones. Nobody would know unless they had the eyes of a hawk or were one of the maquillage artists who ran with the fashion crowd. We were both heavily perfumed, usually with the same scent, Shalimar by Guerlain. By midnight, we were ready to hit the town.

Not all our friends actually worked every day for a living, though most were high profile personalities. But we were still imbued with the work ethic, and couldn't enjoy ourselves until we had completed the job in hand. Patrick was painting for an exhibition to be shown back in London with Angela Flowers. My publishers, W. H. Allen, were waiting for my eighth novel which I was writing with great difficulty. But I was managing to post a lot of journalism back to London newspapers and magazines. I was being paid £1,000 per 1,000 words by the *Sun* for everything I did. I wrote a monthly column for *Men Only*, and was on a hefty retainer there because I could be relied upon to supply them with what they wanted – sex and more sex.

A pal of mine, a past colleague from the *Sunday Times*, was passing through New York, and when I told him what I was earning, his nose rose in the air. 'Shame money!' I jeered back at him when he went on to say that I was prostituting my talents. But the phrase stayed with me. Shame money! For the first time in years I thought of my granny and something painful shifted in my chest. But there was no way I was prepared, or could afford, to give up this easy cash. The kind of recreation we were embroiled in was costly. It didn't occur to me there was any other way to enjoy Manhattan, except by riding this helter-skelter.

Our life careered crazily from day to day, from gig to gig. Studio 54 had been shut down, pending enquiries of a legal nature, so now we patronized the fashionable Mudd Club instead. This was the loud and lascivious haunt of

David Bowie and Brian Eno and others equally celebrated, well known for its theme evenings. We attended the *Mommie Dearest* party, the gathering of the season to promote Christina Crawford's book. At a certain point the event turned into a scene of sado-masochism as those guests who had come dressed as Joan Crawford began beating the others who had come as young children.

The line of sleek black limousines idled outside, waiting to whisk the rich and famous and legless back in the light of dawn; the same restrictions applied at the door, and entry was barred to those who didn't fit the required image. We had no difficulty getting in anywhere. We looked the part all right. Patrick, crew-cut, smoked-shades, suitably lean and laconic, with the prized northern accent, slightly Beatle-sounding to American ears. Me, an eccentric dresser *par excellence*, with the unmistakable air of the riff-raffish international set.

I described typical New York night life in the monthly diary that I wrote for *Men Only*. Everything in it was geared to sex:

Started off the month with an absolutely tremendous bang – or should I say gang-bang! I speak of the SPERMATHON recently staged at Plato's Retreat, in which the 24-year-old nymph TARA ALEXANDER proposed to produce at least seventy-five male orgasms. She ended up having fucked, sucked, and jerked off eighty-two strange men. And then had it off with her husband.

Speaking of it before the SPERMATHON was about to start, TARA confessed, 'I've been thinking about this for weeks. I hope all the guys have. I haven't been training but I've abstained from sex for four days to stay horny. For me that's a lot. I got plenty of rest. I suppose I do have exhibitionist tendencies.'

Over 1,200 responses had arrived after TARA's intention was announced in the press and on Midnight Blue, the Cable TV Show. And invitations to 750 hornies were sent out, but perhaps predictably far fewer turned up on the night. One publicity-shy man performed with a paper bag on his head, with two holes for the eyes to see what was happening. He came with no difficulty at all.

As for TARA, she delegated her body to four men at once, the anatomical accommodation being her vagina, her mouth, and two extremely capable hands. As a topless dancer at the Lucky Lounge in Queens, and having played two obscure roles on the silver porn screen, this is TARA's bid for fame. She had employed a nurse for assistance, a girl called DAN-IELLE, who wore a transparent leotard. She swabbed the queueing cocks with alcohol and fitted those who wished to enter TARA vaginally with French letters.

When it was all over, TARA, nipples swollen and hair dishevelled, claimed to have experienced twenty-four orgasms herself. What gave her so many was 'the feeling of so many guys coming inside me. It was a powerful experience but I'm still not satisfied. I want a hundred more now'.

If somebody had asked me then why precisely I was writing this bilge I would have been as astonished by the question as I am now when I look back on my year in Manhattan. When my daughters ask me why on earth I stayed if I found it all so depressing, why I continued in a marriage which was causing me so much pain, I can only answer that at the time there seemed to be no alternative! Extraordinary! I forget that much of the time I was so anaesthetized with chemicals of one description or another that my own feelings meant nothing to me, indeed I didn't allow myself to feel. I was moving through life in a haze.

We dressed up for the exclusive opening party for Mr Chow's New York restaurant. Sipping champagne with the alluring Paloma Picasso I found my gaze wandering, along with everybody else's, towards her pert nipples. The image of her with one firm breast bared had recently appeared in Helmut Newton's erotic coffee-table book, *White Women*. She told me how, at the Café Un Deux

Trois, where we had both been the night before with other people, at the end of her meal, the management had invited her to order anything she liked. That was how eager the restaurant was to engage the patronage of such celebrities.

'Anything? You offer me anything?' cried the daughter of wily old Picasso. 'In that case I shall accept what I have already had.'

She indicated the remains of the champagne and caviare supper that she had enjoyed with her chums. They swept out, all eight of them, without paying. We on our table were offered whatever liqueur we would care for. By this time, later in the evening, they were amending their generosity.

We didn't mind. We were too interested in the coke-snorting going on in the ladies' lavatory between bouts of high passion featuring two of New York's top models. On the next table was Philippe Junot, still married at the time to Princess Caroline of Monaco, canoodling with a ravishing countess of European extraction.

We drifted amongst this particular coterie and were therefore photographed wherever we went as being part of the scene. Wherever the action was, on any particular night, that's where we were, on all the best guest lists. My closest pal was Anita Pallenberg, common-law wife of Rolling Stone Keith Richards. We spent evenings in the company of Mick Jagger and Jerry Hall, partied with Andy Warhol, attended gatherings of Paul Simon's (thick with security men guarding the Renoir on the wall). Marisa Berenson's kid sister, Berry, took me round to Halston's for cocktails; she married Tony Perkins, who lived around the corner from the Empire Diner. I visited Diana Vreeland in her scarlet, scented apartment. She invited me to tea, after Zandra Rhodes had written to inform her of my arrival in Manhattan. We rubbed shoulders on a nightly basis with Blondie, the biggest star on the music scene. We racketed around town with Little Nell and Divine, eating regularly with Quentin Crisp. I was photographed with Erica Jong at the publishing launch of her latest novel. She told me her little girl was called Molly, too.

I recently heard an early recording of 'Walkin' the Dog', on the Jazz FM radio station. This is *the* Rufus Thomas! The *legendary* Rufus Thomas with his 'Walkin' the Dog'! I listened and laughed out loud, rising and dancing to the beat, remembering that lovable man and his infectious laugh.

Patrick and I had been in New York almost a year by the time I met Rufus. He'd been flown in to perform at a jazz club we visited on a nightly basis, one of our regular downtown port of calls. It was around one or maybe two in the morning, very early in the night, by our standards. I had a spritzer in my hand, and a line of good cocaine up each nostril. I was as slender as a pencil, my arse as tight as a drum-skin from my daily swim. A David Shilling sequinned beret on my boy's haircut was cocked over one eye. The other eye had false lashes as long as my fingertips. I was drenched in whatever perfume I had purchased that afternoon at Bergdorf's. My scarlet and black heels were by Manolo. My stretch-silk jersey was Missoni. I was looking good and I knew, as sure as day follows night, exactly how to get any man or woman I wanted.

Rufus was mesmerized. That was no surprise. What did surprise me was how excited I was by this charismatic, grey-haired, ugly-attractive, wide-mouthed man, who reminded me so much of Louis Armstrong. We made love, as soon as his gig was over, in his dressing room. We couldn't take long, because Patrick thought I was spending a penny and powdering my nose, but it was good enough for each of us to know we wanted more. We arranged another meeting, and so it went on.

It ended when Patrick and I left New York, more suddenly than we'd intended, and I couldn't contact Rufus before our departure. We never saw each other again. Perhaps our affair was meant to be as sweet and succulent as this, an indication to me that I hadn't yet withered away, that I was still capable of spontaneous sexual joy.

We were provided with a welcome respite from the frenzy by a trip to the Cannes Film Festival, all expenses paid, for the screening and subsequent publicity launch of *Andrew Logan's Alternative Miss World – The Film*. I had been, as a close friend of Andrew's, a judge of these almost annual kitsch-fantasy satires on the actual Miss World contests, since the first one in 1972. For the filmed version my fellow judges were Zandra Rhodes, Lionel Bart, Janet Street-Porter (who failed to appear through illness) and Joan Bakewell. Other pals like Jill Bennett and Diana Dors couldn't make the judges' panel because of prior commitments, which was a shame. It was above all a night that they'd have enjoyed, good for a laugh.

I had recorded the commentary for the film before leaving England. It was a project particularly close to my heart, because both Sarah and Sophie had appeared as contestants and I had been too drunk at the actual event to witness their triumph. Sarah was flown to Cannes, too. She'd shone as Marilyn Monroe, her chosen role, and many considered her the winner, but as usual the prize was awarded to a male. Their camp impersonations of high glamour could never be topped.

The undoubted star of the whole show, apart from Andrew, was Divine, dressed as half-man, half-woman. He had compèred the evening spectacularly gowned as a larger-than-life Diana Dors. Maybe it was just as well

Diana couldn't come. But when we were at Cannes, where we drew a major portion of press coverage because of our bizarre appearances, Divine hardly rated a paragraph or the attention of the photographers. Money had foolishly not been provided for his dresser and make-up artist, so he refused to get into drag at all. The high spot was of Sarah marooned in the waves, hemmed in by the paparazzi of the world as she posed topless in diamonds, the archetypal blonde starlet, an adored goddess, the spitting image of Monroe. We still tease her about the spectacular magazine spreads. I looked on, she says, like some proud and pushy stage-mother. Yes, that's exactly how I felt!

Cannes gave us a taste for the ocean, so when we got back to the States, we took time off and spent it at the summer retreat of Michael Menzies, an old pal of mine from London, who worked in the film business. He'd rented a plush estate on the beach at Fire Island for a month. This was the usual practice for wealthy male New Yorkers of a certain sexual persuasion in high summer. I had never before seen such beautiful clones. Young men in the very finest peak of physical perfection, all Adonises.

In the late afternoon everyone went to the all-male tea-dances, where beautiful couples smooched in baggy beach-shorts, with bare bronzed chests, to the tunes of Cole Porter. I had never felt so utterly undesirable, so excluded from anywhere in my life. The only female I encountered throughout our visit was the check-out girl at the un-believably expensive supermarket.

'She's giving you the eye, honey,' drawled one of our sophisticated house guests.

'So what you going to do about it, huh?' asked another in amusement.

'Sod all!' I stumped off. It was difficult enough not being the centre of lustful attention, but I wasn't about to sell myself short. I didn't fancy that woman.

My preference has always been for males, though it was

true that I had once entertained a fierce, female photography student whom we'd come across stripping in a topless downtown bar. I have to admit that she'd certainly known what she was doing: my orgasm was as intense as any I'd ever had. But when she tried to involve me further with a gang of militant feminist lesbians from her college, I declined; it wasn't a direction I cared to explore.

Whoever visited us from London thought we were having the most brilliant time. And we were, weren't we? What more could I want? New York was everything that I had ever hoped it would be. It lived up to all my expectations, the Big Apple. But increasingly I felt I was living in Hades.

One night, drinking with Anita Pallenberg, on the sidelines of yet another orgy, I glanced over at the writhing bodies and started hallucinating. What I was looking at was the full horror of a painting by Hieronymus Bosch. Bestial. Insane. Depraved. And unholy. It was the beginning of the end.

And yet when the end finally came, it was me who brought it about. Me who spotted a young rock star and became mesmerized, as only a middle-aged woman can, with a beautiful youth. There was nothing I could do about it. We met Ariel when we went to one of the many small dives and clubs around the Greenwich Village area. Patrick was at the bar ordering our spritzers. I sauntered through to claim front-row seats for the gig which was about to begin – then Ariel came on and started singing.

My heart leapt to my throat just as it had when I first saw Rupert, Malcolm, James Robertson Justice, and both my husbands. Why do these things happen? And, sitting there in the front row in my swooping violet hat, he could hardly have missed me. He didn't.

That's how it started.

It should have been more fun than it felt to me from the start. I still loved Patrick, but now I was torn by the

281

inexplicable tenderness I felt for Ariel. He represented innocence to me, and inexperience and youth. For a wonderful moment Ariel seemed to supply a return of magic.

He pleaded with me to leave Patrick and marry him. We lay in his bed talking incessantly about Patrick. He was with us more strongly in his absence than if he'd been lying there alongside us.

That night I lay awake marshalling my thoughts as best I could. I knew that I couldn't choose between these two men, but that neither was enough on their own. I would have to break away from both because the situation was no longer tenable. I needed time now to be completely on my own.

I returned to London with Patrick, leaving Ariel crying in Manhattan. My mother was becoming senile, and couldn't manage the journey to the States. I couldn't bear the thought of remaining this far away when she really needed me, and I knew that my marriage would not last much longer whichever continent I was on.

PART FIVE

Scraping the Barrel

We had spent exactly a year in New York, although to me it felt like a century. A century in which I had accumulated such shame, such guilt, such self-disgust that I could barely look at myself in the mirror. The only relief, the only joy I could find, was in the reunion with my family back in London.

We gave away most of the belongings we'd accrued in New York, and the rest we stored to be sent to us later. On our return we booked into the Chelsea Arts Club on Old Church Street, several doors away from the yellow house I had lived in for so many years with my children and, at different times, with each husband.

It was autumn, 1980. The rooms we occupied were on the first floor of the Club. If I leaned out far enough from the back-bedroom windows, I could glimpse the lawn and flower borders that Michael and I had planted in our garden when we'd moved there so long ago. The leaves had already changed colour, but hadn't yet fallen completely from the trees. To me they represented the state of my marriage, but I didn't realize then how close it was to the end. Within a week the back garden became a landscape of bare, skeletal branches. Within a week the separation, which both Patrick and I so dreaded, had become an actuality. I boarded the train at Paddington and left him for good, to go to St Ives.

The events that led up to this dramatic wrench were unendurable to us both, but for different reasons. I could see that if we remained together we would destroy each other. On our third evening back we got caught up with a suitably bizarre crowd at a club called the Blitz, run by Steve Strange and Rusty Egan. In the morning I woke up to a cocaine and spritzer hangover, just as I had on so many mornings in the past year. But back in London this chosen way of life seemed inappropriate, not to say grotesque. I was sick of it. I'd had enough.

During that week my family had come up for a few days to stay with us at the Chelsea Arts Club. My mother, Sal and Granville and their youngest daughter, Rachel. Their other three kids, Sian, John and Rob, were all away at various universities. My own youngest, Sophie, had started at Leeds College of Art where, amongst her painting tutors, were our pals Jeff Nuttall and Anthony Earnshaw. So she didn't attend the large Sunday lunch get-together, but Sarah did with Ike, her boyfriend.

It was the kind of function I enjoyed most, surrounded by family. Very Welsh. But after they had gone a bitter quarrel sprang up between Patrick and myself. We were in our bedroom.

'Is this how it's going to be, all over again, now?' he shouted, enraged.

'What?' I answered coldly, deliberately obtuse, guaranteed to infuriate.

'You and your fucking family, you and your fucking tribe!' Patrick was not a believer in families. He had chosen to see his own mother only once in all the eleven years of our marriage. I viewed this as the English way of treating one's parents. My mother was old, and confused. How could any of us know how much time she had left? No man, no husband, could alter how I felt for her, could dictate how often or not I should see her. When we'd gone to New York Patrick had breathed an exaggerated sigh of relief.

'That will be the end of the daily calls to your mother, I trust. Or does the umbilical cord span the Atlantic?'

It did. I rang my mother every morning when I was out

286

shopping from the telephone kiosk on the corner of West 23rd and Seventh. I'd done it every day of my life. Why should I deprive her of the comfort now? It was only a matter of having the right change, no big deal. But I never told Patrick, it wasn't worth the hassle.

It took just a few further short, sharp, vicious sentences to finish my second marriage. We were both, I believe, as sick as each other of what it had become. It was as if a glorious feast had simply come to an end, and to continue would have led to mutual destruction. It just needed one of us to make the final move. I made it.

I left the room and went into our study-cum-dressing-room, next door. I lay on the single bed there, the first and only time in eleven years that we hadn't slept together. I lay staring out of the window at the lamp-light shining on to the tree outside the window on Old Church Street.

There was one leaf left on the bare branch. I watched it all night, limp and dying. If this fell before dawn it would represent my marriage. I didn't close my eyes all night, contemplating a cold and cruel future, but one which I had to face all alone if either of us were to survive. I was frightened, terrified of what I was about to do. It would have been so easy to slip into the warm bed next door, to hold this man who had meant so much to me for so long. But my inner voice told me to be strong, to stay firm, to strike out on my own. For the first time in years I felt my granny was with me.

In the morning Patrick stumbled in, sleepy, and loving. I looked through the window and watched the leaf fall.

'I'm leaving you,' I said. 'The marriage is over.'

I took the train down to St Ives and stayed there, sleeping and eating and writing in the Porthmeor Beach studio all on my own until I'd finished my latest novel. My publishers had given me a fortnight's deadline. I had been trying to write the novel all year in New York, but what I'd written there was rubbish; confused and meandering, and quite clearly the reflection of my mental state. I'd never, until then, had the slightest difficulty with those novels of mine. I'd simply sit there and one sentence would tumble out after another. I didn't know exactly what plot or characters there would be, how the tale should start, or whether it had a suitable middle or end. The end came when I was about to reach 65,000 words, which I'd been informed was the minimum number of words acceptable as a novel by any publisher. I wrote spontaneously, from the top of my head, never rewriting a single word. And it had worked for seven novels with effortless ease, feeling like the greatest fun. But this wasn't true any longer. It wasn't fun any more, and if my work was an expression of me, the light-heartedness could no longer be there.

As fate would have it, I bumped into Terry Frost on the train down. If I hadn't, I would have sobbed all the way to Cornwall, maybe even got off at Devon and taken a train back. We didn't drink on the train, just talked warmly with great ease. I'd always felt close to Terry and Kath Frost and their family and still do. I kept trying to tell him that I'd left Patrick that morning, but I couldn't trust myself to do so without bursting into tears. As I left the train at St Erths, to catch a connection through to St Ives, I blurted out the words. He went white. He was shocked. His reaction brought home to me how many times I would have to go through this, telling people and accommodating their dismayed expressions.

I wanted to laugh, to make light of this latest drama in my life. But we knew each other too well, this old friend and me. I felt too raw to pretend. He held my fingers in farewell, and squeezed them until I thought they would break. I waved his train out of the station on its way to Penzance. I was the only one on the platform and the desolation and sense of aloneness was suddenly so unbear-able that I couldn't stand it a minute longer. Although the St Ives train was almost due, I took a taxi instead so that at least I'd have the driver to talk to, another human voice.

Letting myself into the studio, I dumped all my luggage and ran like a mad thing down to the deserted seashore where my screams could be drowned by the gulls. I daren't venture on to the cliffs in case my feet led me to the spot, high above the rocks, where my pal Jill Bennett and I used to joke that we'd throw ourselves over when the going got too tough. When our hangovers grew too terrible to bear, on her one visit to me in St Ives, we'd stagger over the cliffs to this place and, linking arms, dare each other to jump. We christened the spot the Niche, from which death would be inevitable, the drop was so sheer. When I saw a lot of her later on in London, we often spoke longingly of our need for the equivalent of a Niche closer to home. We felt that by the time we'd travelled all the way down to Cornwall the compulsion to hurl ourselves over might have abated. But now the compulsion for me was too overpowering to risk testing and, although I spent the next fortnight in St Ives, I still stayed well away from the cliffs because of this fear.

But, on my final afternoon, I did go. The Niche seemed to be calling me. Helicopters were circling above the cliff, trying to trace the body of a woman from Carbis Bay who had wandered off in the night a few days before. They had found one of her pyjama buttons in the heather near the spot where I chose to huddle. But there was no sign of her body, and the helicopters moved further along the jagged coastline to Zennor. One of them flew out to sea. I peered over the Niche and thought about my life and death. There was obviously no point in my leaping over now. The helicopters would get me before my blood had grown cold. They'd revive me and I'd live on as a maimed and dribbling vegetable, a burden to my children and friends.

And, anyway, perhaps things weren't that bad. OK, I was old and finished and what man would ever want me again, but I had a sense of achievement. I had finished my novel an hour ago, had managed to wrench it out of my very guts in just fourteen days, working non-stop, all through every day and every night.

It was called *A Bite of the Apple*, was a fictionalized account of New York life. There were enough laughs and sexual permutations in it to satisfy all my fans. George Melly gave it a glowing review in the *Sunday Times*, and its sales outstripped all my previous books.

There was another reason why I was temporarily feeling more hopeful. I hadn't had anything to drink that fortnight. If I was suffering from withdrawal symptoms, I hadn't had time to acknowledge them, I'd been so intent on finishing the book. I promised myself a binge at the end of this intense period of work, the carrot held in front of the donkey.

But there was another reason to stay sober. Sarah and Sophie were appalled by the turn of events, appalled by the emotional effect that the split with Patrick was having on me. Neither encouraged me to go back to him, however. They both clearly saw the destructive element in our relationship. They rang me every single evening. Sarah rang first, before the curtain went up in the Cottesloe at the National Theatre, where she was an assistant stage manager now. Sophie rang me from Leeds, between her afternoon and evening classes at the art college. I was pathetically grateful for their calls and needed to be sober when I received them. My children's opinion of me had now become of paramount importance. Since I was having to reconstruct a life on my own I had to know who was a hundred per cent on my side, this was what my growing sense of self-pity was telling me. Cut off in Cornwall, cocooned in self-imposed isolation, albeit for work reasons, my girls were my only link with human life and those who loved me, it seemed to me.

This wasn't strictly true. Patrick wrote every day too. He didn't ring; I asked him not to. If I heard his voice my resolve would weaken and, as each day passed, I knew that I had chosen the right course for both of us. He could have taken the train down, he could have lifted the telephone. But he didn't. We both loved each other still, and always would in the way long-married husbands and wives, no longer together, can. But it was time to attempt some kind of survival separately.

Although I didn't receive other calls because I needed to remain undisturbed, I did get in touch with warm and close friends such as Johnny Timbers, and Sylvia, those two fellow Aquarians who stuck with me through thick and thin. Sylvia was widowed now. Her adorable husband, John, had died some years before and she was living on her own. Although both the men in her life had been snatched from her in premature death, her wise words of consolation were balm to my troubled soul now. She had started writing her political memoirs and I could see that there was more to existence than just having a husband at one's side. But Sylvia had never understood the extent of my destructive behaviour. I had made great efforts to hide from her just what a part alcohol played in my life. She couldn't imagine anyone resorting to it, in any circumstances.

But my mother could. Her first words, when I broke the news that Patrick and I were splitting up, were, 'At last! Thank the Lord! Have you opened the champagne yet, because I will!'

I held a party in the studio the night I was leaving. I supplied the booze to make sure there was enough, and about thirty of my Cornish pals brought whichever dish they most excelled in making. There was just the right amount of sweet and savoury delectables. Since we drank from paper cups and ate from paper plates, there was little that needed clearing up except to put the empties and left-overs in rubbish bags for the bin-men. A gang of them saw me to the station where I caught the sleeper back to London. I had managed to become completely arse-holed at the party, but I clung on to the precious manuscript for my publisher in my leather shoulder-bag; the shoulder-bag that Patrick had bought me in Greenwich Village after a light-hearted lunch in One Five on Fifth Avenue months ago . . .

We had agreed that Patrick would have vacated our rooms at the Chelsea Arts Club by my return as I couldn't trust myself to see him yet. Sarah came and stayed with me on my first night. She slept in the bed that I'd lain awake in all night. I was in the one I'd shared before that with Patrick.

All divorced wives that I've ever spoken to lament that first night alone in the marital bed, however appalling their marriages may have been. I was no exception. Sarah wasn't due back from the theatre until very late. I went to bed about ten o'clock, but by half past I was driven by my desolation to find company in the bar downstairs. By the time Sarah came home I'd already picked up a stranger; anyone would have done. He was in my bed, to her surprise, disappointment and probably disgust. But her feelings were nothing compared to how I felt in the morning. Another hangover, another man. Was this how it was going to be? Apparently so. But now I had only myself to blame, no husband to shoulder his share.

Both my daughters were kind and loving creatures, sad to see their mother disintegrating before their eyes. I shuddered, in future years, to remember what I put them through then. But at the time I was so anaesthetized by my own misery that I thought little about anyone else's survival other than my own. I was even prepared to sacrifice the well-being of my own children, as if driven to emulate my mother and what she did, despite herself, to my sister and myself.

Sarah says that when Patrick and I separated she grew up overnight. She hadn't imagined that I would fall apart in the way I did. I doubt she realized how much this was due to drink and all the stuff I'd pumped into my body that year in America. If she didn't know it then, she would come to know it during the time we all lived together, Sarah, Sophie and me. In the end she moved out – she'd had enough.

We stayed at the club for a couple of weeks and then I moved into a mansion in Cheyne Walk. It had been Mick Jagger's, but it belonged to Keith Richards now, and Anita gave me free run of the place, since it was empty, anyway. The girls were going to join me in a few days. Sophie had left her college in Leeds after the Yorkshire Ripper had murdered a young student there.

'It'll be just like old times, before Patrick,' she said cheerfully.

Not quite. Further, much further down the line.

As I stood in bright sunlight on the doorstep of the house, the hairs on the back of my neck rose like fur on a cat who senses there is danger ahead. It was extraordinary, but I was inexplicably cold, icy cold.

The boy from the Rolling Stones' office who handed over the keys asked who would be staying in the house with me. I told him I'd be there on my own until my daughters joined me. He looked anxious and laughed strangely.

'You wouldn't catch me doing that – what, stay in that place alone! Whew – no thanks!'

It wasn't until Anita rang from New York to find out how I was getting on there, that I discovered the house was haunted.

'What can you hear?' Anita asked.

'Strange rustlings down the central stairwell, like the swishing of crinolines.'

She laughed laconically. 'Yeah.'

'And I wake at four in the morning and it's freezing cold, and there's a sweet, sickly smell—'

'Sure thing. But don't worry. You're strong. If anyone can calm those evil spirits it has to be you, Moll . . .'

My old pal, George Melly, suggested throwing a huge party every weekend to turn the spirits around, to let them know that I was in residence now and that it was fun, fun, fun, fun all the way. Barbara Hulanicki shuddered each time she entered. She brought her Catholic crosses to place on the mantlepiece. The evil was palpable, she said.

Marianne Faithfull, who lived at the Chelsea Arts Club alongside me, refused to step inside, even in the daytime for a cup of tea. The four poster bed in which I entertained and occasionally slept is where she attempted suicide when she was living in the house with Mick. Bianca wouldn't come in either. She said wild horses wouldn't drag her ever to step inside there again.

There was a shrine to Jimi Hendrix on the first floor. The crystal ball and the lights in the room operated under their own ghostly volition. The shafts of crystal light flickered over the ceilings, day and night, night and day, in eerie patterns. The floorboards creaked beneath the weight of unseen footsteps, and the sly slithering of what sounded like sumptuous silks brushed against the stairs leading down from the sixth floor.

I stood at the doorway of each empty room every dawn, screaming dementedly, 'Leave us alone, leave us alone. I am here now. I am here. I am here.'

I renewed my friendship with the actress Jill Bennett, who lived relatively close by in Chelsea. She was single too, now divorced from John Osborne. We paired up together, painting the town, and became inseparable, photographed wherever we went. When people asked about our friendship she referred to us as 'different sides of the same coin', she from the right side, me from the wrong side of the tracks, but kindred spirits for all that.

I first saw Jill when I had just arrived in London. I was dining with James Robertson Justice and she was with the revered Shakespearean actor Sir Godfrey Tearle. It was the same set up: older, larger-than-life characters with impressionable, big-breasted, adoring girls.

'It must have been at the Ivy; we ate there all the time,' Jill said when I first told her.

'So did James and I. You were wearing a cashmere twinset, with a string of pearls.'

'How predictably boring! My taste hasn't changed. Never mind, when we're out together people will think I'm your secretary. I'll be the drab at your side.' We both laughed, she with her magnificent nostrils flaring, her head thrown back in a suitably theatrical attitude.

We mirrored each other in many ways and were drawn together from the first time we actually met, when I interviewed her and Osborne for the *Sunday Times*. We had kept in touch and though I had moved to Cornwall with Patrick not long after, I made a point of seeing her when the news broke of her marriage split. I was shocked by her appearance. She wasn't eating, it seemed. I was never to see her this upset in the rest of the time I knew her.

Our living accommodation up above the Wimpy Bar in St Ives was too cramped for Jill to stay with us when she came down to Cornwall on a visit. The place was agog with excitement to have such a theatrical celebrity staying there. We put her in a tiny B and B on the opposite side of Fore Street, near us, overlooking the harbour. They placed fresh flowers in the room and were most apologetic that the bathroom and lavatory were not en-suite, but pointed out the hand basin and running water in her bedroom. At the end of the visit they asked her in awed terms whether she had enjoyed her stay.

'Marvellous, darlings, but I shall be pleased to get back to London and not have to cock my leg over your basin for a fucking pee in the middle of the night.'

Jill adored both my girls, but decided to pretend that Sophie was actually her daughter and not mine. We all fell in with the pretence. Word leaked out that Sophie was the daughter she had borne Gary Cooper, when they had their famous clandestine affair in Hollywood, and I had adopted the baby to spare the scandal and save Jill's career. Not to mention Gary Cooper's, of course. We only just managed to keep the item from leaking into the gossip columns, Jill whispered it with such conviction.

She asked me to write a play specially for her when I moved to Cheyne Walk, but nothing actually came of it and the whole thing petered out, although I was paid by the producer for my efforts. The play wasn't any good and wouldn't have enhanced her reputation or mine. I was relieved although I felt for her disappointment. Amazingly, I did manage to produce another novel, *Love Bites*, while I was living there, as before, by writing around the clock until it was finished, but I was finding it increasingly difficult to concentrate on any project which required sustained effort. I could just about manage magazine articles of 500 to 1,000 words; I could still crank those out like the rest of the hacks, even through my excruciating hangovers.

The house was getting me down, getting us all down. Both my girls decided to leave and they moved in with different sets of friends. I visited my mother down in Wales. Her senility was encroaching fast, though she had managed to come up for a visit over Christmas, when I took her to the Embassy nightclub in Bond Street to celebrate her eightieth birthday. She spent her time in her back bedroom, staring at the gas fire, smoking cigarette after cigarette and sipping sherry all day in her dressing gown.

The front door was open, so I stole up the stairs and crept into her room. There she was, smoke spiralling through her nicotine-stained fingers. I stood before her, smiling; she was not expecting me down from London. It was a surprise, one she would have responded to with delight at one time. Now she just stared up at me, blank and uncomprehending.

She didn't know who I was. My own mother didn't recognize me. My blood ran cold. I knelt down close, quietly, so as not to frighten her.

'Who are you?' she puzzled, smiling politely. She cupped my face in her hands. I was too choked to answer.

'Are you on the stage? You've got a lovely face, all made up like a film star. Do I know you?'

'I'm Moll. You know me, you silly old boot. You've known me all my life . . .' I managed the words. This was the first time it had happened, though I had been told to prepare myself for it. Comprehension, slow recognition struggled to the surface.

'*My Moll*? You are *my* Moll – oh, no! My Moll's in London.'

'She's here now. Let's get your coat over this dressing gown. I've got a taxi outside to take us for a run. I'm down for the day. It'll do you good to get out.'

She burst out crying, tears of joy. 'My Moll, my Moll.' She kept touching my face all day, like a child.

I drank all the way back to London. I didn't move from the bar in the buffet. When the train arrived at Paddington, I had just about managed to drown the agony and, duly numbed and floating, was free enough of pain to go on the toot with Jill and Ricci Burns, my hairdresser, another dear party friend. We ended up at Langans, as usual. Peter Langan was there, Peter my old comrade. He joined me, as usual. It was already dawn and I was the last to leave, the only one in the restaurant left there alone with Peter. He was performing cunnilingus under the table between my abandoned knees, as usual. Tears streamed down my cheeks, my mother's fingers were on my face.

Peter glanced up. 'Christ, whore,' he said affectionately, squeezing my hand, 'I'm not doing it that badly, am I!'

I spent the summer in Wales, with Diana and George Melly. They had a converted Norman tower down there, near Abergavenny. George didn't normally come until August, which he spent there every year, but he arrived before that this summer so that he could bid for a stretch of the River Usk that ran alongside their property.

It was a literary household that month: Bruce Chatwin was there completing his latest novel, *On the Black Hill*. The writer Edward Fox, whom I'd worked with on the *Sunday Times*, was in the middle of writing *White Mischief*, and Francis Wyndham had come down to work on the book which he and Diana were editing, of the collected letters of their close friend, the late Jean Rhys. I had met Jean through Diana and interviewed her for the *Sunday Times* shortly before her death.

I felt inadequate in the midst of all this creative industry, although Diana did her utmost to encourage my flow. I preferred to work in the extensive gardens, helping her plant and pick vegetables. Anything rather than get on with my new novel. The home-made wine didn't help. I couldn't wait for my first glass of elderberry before lunch, and then I'd wolf down as much as I could over lunch. I mowed the grass in the afternoon and picked raspberries and gooseberries, and then I lay under the trees waiting for inspiration to strike, or walked by the river watching the fish rise to the surface.

I lingered until the sun had set on this idyll, and then wandered back beside the cows which were being led home by the Welsh tenant farmer. I felt ashamed, being Welsh myself, to be living in this English residence, as if I was betraying my own. There was great resentment locally over the numbers of English who were buying up these country properties, thus forcing the prices up so that locals couldn't afford them.

In the evening we sat around the kitchen table eating the delicious dinners that Diana had prepared. I told her that I was thinking of leaving London and coming back to Wales to be near my mother in her final years. I drank a lot and got very maudlin, but Diana was used to people unburdening themselves on her warm shoulders.

I looked at her beauty and remembered her when we were both young and she was an exalted fashion model in the magazines. Her name was Diana Ashe then. We had her face around our house for months on end on a knitting pattern modelling a cardigan that my mother took it into her head to knit. She never finished it, but couldn't bring herself to throw the pattern away, just in case her enthusiasm returned. I thought I was truly blessed to have such friends as George and Diana at this my most difficult time. I helped Diana to make more and more home-made wine, hoping that my own consumption would go unnoticed. What I didn't reckon on was the effect it was having on me. I was gradually losing all control, and my behaviour was becoming increasingly unpredictable and inappropriate. A drunkenly unforgivable incident occurred one night. I alienated Diana, also George, and the friendship never survived this body-blow. It remains one of the regrets of my later sobriety.

I returned to Cheyne Walk, in deep depression and with awful remorse, for my belongings and moved down to Pontycymmer. Now I was comfortably close to my mother. I had marvellous friends in Pontycymmer, Wendy and David Phillips, and Ivy, and Dennis Mapstone, who all helped me come to terms with my mother's oncoming death. I managed to crank out a novel while I was there, my last – I never published another one. Called *Breast Stroke*, it was all about a group of swimmers. The genre was the same, comic erotica, but this one was pure – or impure – fiction. I had used up my life. It was no longer a fantasy, I was now down to the nitty-gritty.

I slept with anybody and everybody. I was the talk of each shift in the colliery, so my lovers told me. They said, the old-timers, who remembered John the Bump, that my grandfather must be turning in his grave. I was past caring.

My drinking changed drastically within a week of my arrival in Pontycymmer, however. Wendy Phillips, whom I wasn't particularly close to at that point, although later we were to become and remain good friends, called round to 'have a serious word' the morning after a gruesome night before. We had all, a gang of females, gone up to a club in Blaengarw where there were amateur entertainments. Wendy was singing – she is renowned for her rich contralto. I was now drinking spirits most of the time and when they asked me what I wanted, I answered vodka and tonic. They'd run out of tonic, there being little call for it, so I drank neat vodka instead, about twelve in one sitting.

Walking home, down the valley, the kerb rushed up and pounced at my nose. I broke it, not for the first time. When Wendy came round in the morning, the blood was still dry on my misshapen face.

'I'm going to tell you something now, that you are not going to like. I used to drink spirits like you, but one night I had seventeen Southern Comforts and the next morning my tongue was thick and hanging down to my nipples. I had alcoholic poisoning and was bad for a month. People like us, we can't take spirits. You are going to have to drink lager, or beer, like the rest of us. Otherwise you're going to be dead by the end of the year. You'll be gone before your mother, I'm telling you now!'

That was the first time that anybody had drawn such brutal attention to my drinking habits.

'I hate the taste of beer,' I muttered, not meeting her stern look.

'Then you are going to have to get to like it. You'll find that it will give you a longer night, instead of being the life and soul of the party for the first couple of hours, then puking up in the lav, and passing out in the boot of somebody's car. I know, love – I've done it too. Trust me. It's good advice.'

'Thank you, Wendy,' I whispered, chastened. This was true friendship.

I spent many hours up the mountain, trying to make some sense of my existence. Looking back now, I realize I spent almost eighteen months in Pontycymmer. But time held no meaning. My mother was slowly dying. I couldn't think further than that. When Sarah visited me she was appalled by what she saw as the squalor of my circumstances. She was patently distressed. I couldn't see what she meant, although I was having to go over to Wendy and David's for my baths and Wendy washed all my clothes in her machine because I had no hot water.

Sophie was more sanguine; her painter's eye picked up the colours and shapes of Pontycymmer. She brought a bunch of art students down who were enchanted by the place, seeing it as *Under Milk Wood*, complete with all the characters. They returned to London with haversacks full of the magic mushrooms which abounded on the mountain, and enthusiastic plans to export them all over the world. Nothing further happened except that they all got high on magic-mushroom omelettes back home in Soho and King's Cross and Hackney.

I had at last returned to the chapel. I went to the Tabernacle every Sunday to feel close to my granny and my Tadci. I understood that even though I might be sullying the fine reputation of my forebears by my drinking and general bad behaviour, I was being shown unconditional love by Wendy and David and their family, by Ivy, and by Dennis who drove me every few days to Penarth to visit my mother. I also had the staunch friendship of those such as Tom Hopkins from the farm and Jack in the café on Ffaldau Square, allies that I knew would always be there for me. But the urge to move on came back to me one morning up the mountain. It was time to go. My mother was floating in a no-man's-land now, and the nursing staff said she could go on for years like that, not really knowing who or where she was, or who I was when I went to see her. So I went back to London; I was desperately low in funds and at least there I would have the chance of picking up odd bits of work.

The months that followed are so hazy I have difficulty remembering events with any clarity. I started to hallucinate with terrifying regularity, so I couldn't distinguish what was real and what was not. But worse, I could go into amnesic blackouts without any warning. One moment I would be at the Chelsea Arts, where I had gone back to live, drinking downstairs with the adorable rascal old Ronnie, and the next I was in Soho exchanging barbed pleasantries with Jeffrey Bernard (if it's possible ever to exchange pleasantries of any kind, barbed or otherwise, with dear Jeffrey) at the Coach and Horses.

I was whooping it up every afternoon with Ian Board and Francis Bacon, and jazz pianists Kenny Clayton and Barney Bates, and the rest of the crowd at the Colony. As usual, I lamented the loss of the legendary Muriel Belcher with Ian, making the same old resolve to get down to writing the definitive book about her and the Colony Room. She had instantly become my role model when she had called me a 'dear little cunty' on my first visit there with Malcolm back in the mid-fifties. She made me a member on the spot, when I returned years later with the *Guardian* political journalist Peter Jenkins, an occasion on which I left legless with Frank Norman and Colin Mac-Innes of *Absolute Beginners* fame.

Although I introduced exciting and valuable new members to the Chelsea Arts Club, such as the jazz legend Slim Gaillard, whom I spent much time with, I knew my days there were numbered. I sensed it wouldn't be long before I'd have shat in that nest for good and all. My behaviour was becoming more and more unacceptable. I was screwing the staff, in particular the junior chef; he slept in my bed, next to the bathroom, where we had exuberant sex with loud music and lots of candles into the early hours.

I took over the bar, the dining room, the garden, with my bizarrely garbed cronies. My language was enough to straighten the posh perms of other stately lady members. There was a mass protest, a walk-out from the bar, when I made an entrance one evening with the great Divine, dragged-up as Elizabeth Taylor, and my own daughter Sarah in her Monroe get-up. We were waiting for the masses to descend from the cinema on the King's Road, known then as the Essoldo, where the British film prem-ière of *Andrew Logan's Alternative Miss World* was taking place. By now, all three of us were sick of seeing the film; we featured in it, and must have viewed it over a hundred times as part of the promotion, making personal appearances from here to Cannes.

The following week I received a letter from the committee of the Chelsea Arts Club, requesting that I 'kindly amend my language and behaviour', following complaints from fellow members.

I was so affronted that I moved out that very afternoon in a huff.

'Can you imagine!' I expostulated to the select crew at the Colony. 'In this club I'd be thrown out if I didn't behave badly!'

'That's right, you old tart! Have yer changed yer dirty knickers yet!' Ian rejoined warmly.

'Fuckin' wankers,' I seethed. 'That's the last they see of me. I thought that club was meant to be for *artists*, for bloody *bohemians*, not a bunch of suburban scrotum-suckers with halitosis, and blathering businessmen with their shitty bollocks in their back pockets! How's anybody with any spunk expected to socialize with these limp pricks without pissing in their soup and farting in their puerile faces!!'

'You tell them, darling,' crooned Francis. 'Here, have some more champagne.'

I loved the Colony; it was my home from home. I couldn't imagine my life without it. Especially now, after blotting my copy book at the Chelsea Fucking Farts Club. What on earth would I do if I didn't have the Colony to go to, and the Coach and Horses, the French and Ronnie Scott's? This had become the pattern of my evenings. When Scott's closed at about three, I would go on to the Greek dive in Earl's Court drinking retsina until five a.m., after which the proprietor, Amlett, would take us over to Smithfield Meat Market where the pubs were just open-ing. There, in spite of being a vegetarian, I would blithely wend my way between corridors of raw carcasses, the fresh blood of slaughtered pigs and cows and gentle sheep, probably from my own beloved mountain, staining the sawdust, acknowledging the cheers on arrival from all the meat porters: 'Moll's here!' The dazed meat porters whom I would demoniacally fuck the living daylights out of in the downstairs ladies' lavatory of whichever pub was nearest. Any number, who cared, s'all good fun!

The sister of the barman at the Chelsea Arts Club offered me her despised flat on the Pepys Estate. It was the most violent council estate in Deptford, and she was too scared to live there any more. I had difficulty reaching it since few taxi drivers would take me, as one of their number had been dragged at knife point from his cab the previous week. I was advised by the women on the estate to stay inside and lock my door at all times.

A local gangster took a shine to me and waited day and night outside my flat paring his nails with a flick-knife. His mother rang me up and advised me to leave. Her son was not to be trusted, she said. He was of sub-normal intelligence, couldn't read or write, and had only recently come out of prison on a hit-and-run, armed robbery job. She wouldn't like to see him back inside for my murder, but he was violent and jealously possessive over me. She couldn't think how this could have come about since I had only just moved in.

I didn't enlighten her. I didn't tell her that I had already slept with the poor lout. That I'd sleep with anything these days; her son was one of a cast of thousands.

But immediate escape was at hand, a legitimate and urgent reason to flee. Sally rang from Wales to say that our mother had developed pneumonia. Her voice suggested to me that the end was very near. I sat on the train to Cardiff, a journey that I had travelled so many times before, and all I could see from the window was my mother. I couldn't bear to believe that this force, this fragile presence, would soon cease to be. I couldn't encompass it. Other people's mothers died, they died all the time. But not ours, not mine. How could it be?

Yet she'd made me promise, so many times over the years, that when the suitable time came I would ease her out of this world. She believed in euthanasia, she claimed. And so did I, when I promised.

'The time has come,' she'd said, only a few years before, when she'd felt herself becoming confused, before she'd gone into the Home. She'd said it when I was down on a weekend visit, alone with her in the house when Sal and her lot were away on a trip.

Now on the train, travelling down for her death, I went

over again and again in my mind that morning, that afternoon, that evening, that crucial night when, having agreed to aid her departure, I offered her the lethal cocktail, a clouded-amber mix of neat whisky and sleeping tablets.

'Put it on the side,' she said slyly, excited, animated at the thought of the journey ahead. 'Open the champagne now, and let's have a bit of a laugh before I go. Don't expect there'll be much of a drink on arrival, best to get some in now.'

'Depends where you arrive,' I twinkled back, my heart breaking.

I had spoken to my doctor about this. Though not belonging to EXIT, he did believe in euthanasia. He said my mother had had a good innings, but at eighty, especially with her mental record, her encroaching senility and incontinence were inevitable facts and she had the right not to go on if she had me to help her out with dignity. Hadn't I always promised her faithfully that I would do this?

I opened the champagne and between us we finished the bottle. The fatal cocktail remained untouched on the bedside table. We embarked on a 'do you remember when' session. We tracked back over every family incident as far as we could go. My mother was laughing so much she almost fell out of bed. She wondered cheerfully who would be there, at the pearly gates, to welcome her first.

'That's my Moll,' she said, hanging on to me. 'I only ever wanted to end on a laugh.'

She looked lovely. I sponged her down by the gas fire in her front room and put the bed by the window to give her a good last view of the sea and the sands of Barr Island. I washed carefully the white, wizened body that gave birth to me over fifty years ago. I soaped the shrunken breasts that had fed me, long since empty of milk. I towelled dry the hanging flanks and the concave belly and the sparse grey hairs on the ancient pudenda.

lifted the skinny arms and separated the bunioned feet, talcum-powdering beneath and between. I slithered a soft nightgown over the curved spine and stooped shoulders, and fastened the buttons up to the scragged neck. Then I placed her in a chair by the gas fire and painted her toe and fingernails. And while they were drying I plucked her straggling eyebrows, and smoothed creams and lotions into her wrinkled cheeks and forehead, before painting her eyelids and lips.

She wanted mascara, but my hand was not steady enough. I was going through the motions, completing the rituals, consenting to her every wish, while a voice was clamouring in my brain.

'You are murdering your own mother.'

We finished the champagne and started in on the bottle of scotch.

In the morning I woke to the appalling realization of what I must have done. But when I opened my eyes and saw the lethal cocktail now congealed into a glutinous mass beside my own bed, I burst into tears of relief. I was so crucified with a hangover that I could barely move, but I crawled into her room, my heart hammering. Please God, let her be alive. The breathing was shallow. I had to place a mirror to her nostrils to make sure breath was there, to prove that she was not dead. She slept, without waking, through to the afternoon. It gave me plenty of time to think.

'I'm not God,' I said to her when she came round. 'I can't go through that again. You must die like the rest of us, in His time not yours.'

'Whatever you say, Moll.'

I gazed at her and managed a smile. I would never be as close to another human being as I had been to my mother in the past twenty-four hours, with her life forced into my hands. I had never had to take care of anybody else, even my babies, as I had to care for her.

Sal met me at Cardiff. I saw by her face that our mother had almost gone. We drove in silence to Penarth, to her bedside. I held her frail bones as she lay dying in my arms, just two years after our aborted attempt at death together, and whispered, 'This is better, just let go now.' It was God's time and she was ready. The other was just a rehearsal and was never meant to be the real thing.

But her death left me stranded, with nowhere to run to any more. When I returned to London after the funeral, I gathered up my things from Deptford and moved, in the middle of the night, to Cadogan Gardens in Belgravia, into an apartment belonging to Fred, Sophie's wealthy boyfriend. My life was nothing if not one of contrasts.

After my mother's death I went on the stage, my final career. It was 1984, and I had run out of every other career, was incapable of concentrating on novels, and unsure if I'd be sober enough to appear on TV again (having just been banned for drunken behaviour on 'Pebble Mill'). I could still make people laugh though, I could still entertain in the bar. So I turned professional and did it on stage instead.

It came about when I was approached by the poet Mike Horovitz to take part in a poetry festival he'd organized at the Young Vic. I refused; the very thought of it absolutely terrified me. Mike had been a friend for many years, and he reminded me that if I agreed it wouldn't be the first time that I had appeared before an audience. I'd stood up and reeled off a rude poem for him, in front of a bunch of professional poets above a pub in Hampstead, a year or so before.

'But I was pissed then, I didn't know what I was doing Mike.'

'They liked you though. You have a way with an

audience. You can read from your book of poems, you don't have to memorize.'

The book he was referring to was *Molly Parkin's Purple Passages*, a volume of my own raunchy doggerel which had been published a few years before, with illustrations by the cartoonist Frank Dickens. Hardly suitable for a highbrow poetry festival, I thought. And who were the other poets anyway?

When he mentioned the name John Cooper Clarke, I pricked up my ears. I admired John's work very much. Now I was being given the chance of appearing on the same bill. It would surely be churlish to refuse.

I was fraught with trepidation; my bowels were playing me up all through the event until it was my turn to go on, just before the final act, which was John. This was something I'd never get used to, the petrifying effect of fear on the internal workings of my body. There's no doubt that I was already suffering the chronic symptoms of alcoholic dysentery, but the stage career certainly speeded up the process.

And yet when I stood on that vast stage for the first time and read my poems to an expectant and seemingly appreciative, warm audience, I had the feeling that this was exactly where I belonged. It was as easy as reciting my Bible verses as a child in the chapel. Lapped in loving applause, I took my bows and teetered off-stage in the direction of the bar. Now I really deserved to get plastered, didn't I, surrounded by new fans and old friends patting me on the back. The stage was the answer, I'd found my *métier*.

Jeremy Sandford, whom I hadn't seen for some years, was in the audience that night. He approached me, asking if he could interview me for the *Guardian*. The stage impresario, Stuart Lyon, who was organizing the International Poetry Festival at the Albert Hall, was there too and asked if I would take part. He said he thought I'd go down very well with my poems and perhaps some of the steamy anecdotes he'd heard me relate at parties, at Ronnie Scott's on Sunday Nights. What about next week? Jeremy overheard this and said he'd like to attend and then interview me afterwards about this new-found career. It was as simple as that – launched into theatrical orbit, despite myself.

The show at Ronnie's was a hit! *Time Out*'s Maria Lexton reviewed it:

Molly Parkin has style. Her one-woman show based mainly on sex, men, women, and more sex, is not so much porno-graphic as pure, self-confessed 'comic erotica' and is definitely not for the prudish. She relates a series of stories, anecdotes and poems centred on her experiences with an earthiness and wit that defies the laws of morality. She's a hell of a woman with a nice line in self-deprecating humour and some lovely indiscretions, and provides a highly entertaining show. Film stars, alcohol, crabs, dieting, odd sexual adventures all come under her piercing scrutiny, and after seeing her recently on a late-night TV programme I think she should be given her own chat show – X-rated, of course. Who needs Joan Rivers?

The gigs mounted up. I returned for another 'Sunday Night at Ronnie Scott's', 'due to public demand!' the poster said. I did the Drill Hall, and the Shaw Theatre and an appalling evening at the Cambridge Union, where half the petrified audience of upper-class, eighteen-year-old virgins walked out after the first poem.

This poem divided the men from the boys, as it were. It was a tester. I always opened with it and warned the audience before I started that the first poem set the scene, the tone of the show – which would go downhill from there on in.

'This poem,' I'd start, 'is based on a twelfth-century aphorism which I read recently. The aphorism goes like this. "A ring is a hole with a rim around it." Here is my poem:

'"A ring is a hole with a rim round it.
    Bloody good job that all the rims fit.
    If the one round my bum had not been the right one,
    all my clothes would be covered in shit!"'

I did a stint at the Edinburgh Festival, in the Lyceum Studio. *The Times* devoted an entire half-page to me, thus ensuring a packed audience for the run. I returned to London and Stuart Lyon engaged me to share a conversation with my dear old pal Quentin Crisp at Ronnie's. The tickets sold like wildfire, there was not even standing room available before we opened. Quentin was over from New York where he now lives permanently. We talked of life there and touched on many things, sitting on stage, he sipping his whisky and me my lager. We threw the evening open to questions from the audience. We enjoyed ourselves, and so did everybody else. He returned to his beloved America the next day.

Bookings were mounting up now. My show was 'in demand' and I started travelling all over the country. I signed with a manager, Steve Mather, who saw to my friends the Liverpool poets, Adrian Henri, Roger McGough and Brian Patten.

Steve thought that I needed a director to oversee the lighting, the timing and the content of my show. He suggested Nica Burns, who was currently directing Fascinating Aida to great acclaim. I had a sense of things moving far faster than I'd anticipated. Now my show was in danger of becoming 'professional'.

Pals warned me of this. I bumped into Barry Humphries, whom Johnny Timbers had brought to the show in its very earliest days at the Latchmere in Battersea. He told me to keep it personal, keep it spontaneous, always with the freedom to make things up at the last moment.

Quentin and Billy Connolly had also warned me about this. None of them would dream of having a director. But I was caught in a kind of trap and, in any case, I liked and admired Nica Burns. So I had another drink instead of voicing my inner doubts and I learned my material as if it were a script, with no departure, ever, from performance to performance.

But I did go my own way when it came to costumes. I fought fiercely for the right to wear what I wanted. I asked Mark Erskine-Pullen, one of the most brilliantly original of the young theatrical designers, to design and make me something extravagant, with the appropriate headgear. He produced two costumes which were the stuff of fantasy. One in a sunset range of reds and oranges, which included an item of exotic millinery with a feather that stretched almost the width of the stage. The other, a witty, transparent blue-plastic variation on a chandelier, with a horizontally elongated, heavily jewelled violet wig. Both outfits belonged in the Victoria and Albert Museum, and produced involuntary applause from every audience when I appeared in them. But neither Nica nor Steve approved of them. They claimed that the costumes detracted attention from my material. Their sane approach reminded me of every editor I'd ever crossed, every schoolteacher who had cautioned me on excess. I turned stubborn when it came to the crunch and was asked to choose by Nica, who said it was her or the costumes. I chose the costumes. I was without a director now, but it made no difference. The show was a set-piece and although nobody knew it then, its life was limited. I was swiftly approaching the stage of alcoholic burn-out.

I was launched in Edinburgh for the second year running. This time with the largest poster, at the largest venue in the Assembly Rooms, to the largest audience at the peak of the season. Mark, my designer, was forced to travel with me since I couldn't get into his costumes on my own. They needed as much care and attention every evening as me, the performer. But I couldn't imagine being on stage without them. What else would I have had to hide beneath and behind; they were my protection, the only shield between me and the audience.

My attitude had altered now towards my public. If it were not for them I could have razzled around Edinburgh all day, drinking to my heart's content. The previous year at the Festival, my show had been in the morning which meant that by midday I was free to pub-crawl. Nothing closed in Edinburgh, unlike London where afternoon drinking was still forced to take place in clubs. Here there were no restrictions. Wonderful! By the end of the day I fell, sozzled, into my bed and though I performed through a hangover, I was able to encompass all. This second year I had to devise a cunning drinking plan in order to get by.

At the beginning, it went something like this: I would go out on an all-night toot with Mark and his mate Matthew Hawkins. Matthew was a lead dancer with Michael Clarke, and when Michael had finished his show they'd all come and collect us from the Assembly Rooms. We'd invariably start off at a gay disco called Fire Island on Princes Street, then we'd dance and drink at wherever was open. Once, at three in the morning, we summoned a cab to drive us to Glasgow, where somebody knew of an open dive, so desperate were we to continue the party.

By the end of the fortnight the procedure had deteriorated along with my health. I was eating practically nothing now. I was terrified that my bowels would evacuate themselves on stage, as they had done, walking back from an attempted lunch one afternoon. I told my audience the next night. They seemed to find it hilarious enough, but it was no joke for me. I went to a chemist to explain that I couldn't keep down any solids. I didn't tell him about my liquid intake. He prescribed a potion that he brewed up in the back room, which he assured me would keep me bunged up for a further fortnight. But there were other symptoms: a tendency to hallucinate, to forget what I'd just said. One night on-stage I embarked on an anecdote which I'd apparently just told. A fan in the front row enlightened me in strict measure, and it brought me up with a jolt. I think now what was happening was what I'd always dreaded. I was experiencing alcoholic blackout, drifting in and out of full consciousness while still appearing to be in full control. Nothing to do with the medicine, everything to do with the drinking.

I was finding it increasingly difficult to get back to my hotel. Most nights now I spent out in bars. I soon found them in dingy back streets. By the morning when any companions were spent enough to call it a night, I would make my way to whatever daytime bar had opened. There I would remain until the time for my show came closer and closer. Mark would have no idea where I was. Nobody could keep up with my prodigious energy.

One evening I arrived back at eight, which gave me just a few hours' sleep before the midnight show. The next night it was nine. I was heading for collapse. I couldn't say where I'd been. I have memories of servicing an entire Welsh rugby team, who were staying in my hotel, on the same floor, along the corridor – I did it to make up for having turned down the Real Madrid footballers in Paris – I think. But who can say? I was too drunk to tell one from another.

I collapsed finally, finished, on stage in Dublin. Half the audience demanded their money back. They don't fork out at the Dublin Festival to see people pissed on stage when they can get it for free in the pubs. My manager, Steve, read about it on the cover of the *Stage*: 'Molly banned from Dublin for unprofessional conduct on stage'. I have achieved many things in my life but I have yet to meet another person who has been banned from Dublin for drinking.

Another career had bitten the dust. I didn't dare to go on stage alone ever again. The public was still there, more than ever, if anything. Human beings are drawn to the gruesome spectacle of another person at the end of their tether. It makes for fine viewing. But I had lost my cool, my confidence had gone.

The Dublin catastrophe was my nadir but it was still quite a while before I turned the corner. Now I was on my own. There was nobody. My mother was dead. Both marriages were over. My drunken behaviour had so humiliated and embarrassed my daughters that we had become distanced from each other: actual physical distance with Sophie who was in Australia; but with Sarah it was the agony of polite indifference. They must have been as sick of me as I was of myself. My debts were mounting, I had no money and little prospect of earning any. I seemed to have used up all my God-given talents. I wanted desperately to stop drinking but I couldn't let go of what I regarded as my best friend, although in its effects it was my worst enemy. I became a dry drunk. It was the worst eighteen months of my life.

I was trying to write a novel, but I couldn't concentrate. It was impossible. Some days I looked at what I had written and to my horror it was the same sentence with small variations – 'and' changed to 'but' and back again.

I was living on an overdraft. The Midland Bank was behind me and believed me when I said my new novel, a blockbuster, was nearly finished and would earn as much in royalties as the other ten. I had a good track record at the Midland. In fact, everybody believed me: my literary agent, Irene Josephy, that sweet and stalwart comforter who had supported me through the decades; Johnny Timbers; darling Sylvia, my surrogate mother, my oldest chum of all; my sister, Sal, who would do anything for me, anything; Barbara Hulanicki and Fitz; Andrew Logan; Jill Bennett; Wendy and David, and Ivy in Pontycymmer;

and all those other friends so dear to my heart. None of them knew. They all believed that everything was OK.

Why couldn't I tell them what trouble I was in? Why couldn't I explain the inexplicable, that I had stopped drinking now for almost eighteen months; but the drink dominated my life more than it ever did when I was drinking. Every morning, emerging from nightmare, I thought about drink and not having a drink, and how to avoid any situation which was to do with drink. Bleakness swept through me like a howling gale and never stopped now that alcohol was no longer there to numb my feelings. It was as if the anaesthetic had been withdrawn in the middle of an operation and the pain was unendurable. When I wasn't writing the same sentence over and over again, I was at the cinema seeing as many as four films a day to blot out the horror of my waking hours.

And now, with the emptiness inside threatening to devour me until I could stand it no more, I had taken to buying a ticket every morning at West Kensington underground station to throw myself under an oncoming train.

But I couldn't do it.

Shortly after this I bumped into Anita Pallenberg on the King's Road. She was unrecognizable from our Mudd Club nights.

'I'm clean and sober, Moll,' she said. She was radiant, the very opposite of how I felt. I wanted to be like her too. I wanted what she'd got. And if she could do it, so could I!

I started attending the College of Psychic Studies in South Kensington on Monday evenings. It was here that I met Ben, a clairvoyant who confessed to me that he'd had trouble with alcohol many years before. It was Ben who eventually took me to attend my first self-help group in Lambeth. He expressed surprise when I told him I had a problem with drink. He's not much of a clairvoyant, I thought to myself, but then he hadn't seen me drinking.

I now understand that it was God that was taking care of me and that meeting Anita and Ben when I did was no coincidence – 'When the pupil is ready, the teacher appears' I had been taught at the College. The very discipline of having to be there every Monday evening, clean and sober, was very difficult for me – not to say almost impossible. The paranoic fear of travelling by public transport would overcome me so acutely that sometimes I had to get off the tube and up to street level for the trembling, sweating and near-retching to stop. I was suffering from alcoholic dysentery still, although I was no longer drinking. I could never be sure after I had eaten the smallest amount of food how long it would be before I would suffer violent diarrhoea.

But my spiritual perception sharpened. I took weekend workshops there too, to develop my psychic potential. In effect, what I was doing was seeking some kind of spiritual meaning to my life, a familiar path for alcoholics when they have reached rock bottom. And, although I was chronically unwell, it was clear from my classes that I possessed gifts as a healer. Healer, heal thyself!

I began to be so encouraged by the results from my 'laying on of hands', that when people started suggesting I should take clients on in a professional capacity, for a moment I seriously considered this as another career.

I had given up trying to write my blockbuster by this time, but various TV companies would still half-heartedly approach me to write sit-com scripts for them. I asked a pal of mine, as heavy a drinker as me, if he was interested in combining our talents.

We started work. At the end of the first week of writing he suggested what I had been longing to hear him say.

'Well, that was a good week's work. What about a little drinkie?'

We started at the Chelsea Arts Club at 7 p.m. I had a lager. I looked at the amber liquid, at the creamed froth on the top. I felt my pulse racing, the dry constriction of my throat. I knew that when this nectar slid under my skin, the world and all my worries would disappear.

My final binge lasted a week.

When the lager hit the spot I experienced the most appalling panic attack about where the drink would come from when the Chelsea Arts Club shut at midnight. I began planning, with an alcoholic's ingenuity, to make certain that, for the next night and day at least, I would never be further than a few inches from my source. So I went back to the old routine: first to Ronnie Scott's and then on to the Greek place in Earl's Court. As dawn was breaking I found myself in Smithfield, in the pub with the meat porters. At eleven in the morning I was first on the doorstep of the Coach and Horses in Soho, even before Jeff Bernard. When this pub closed I trekked on up to the Colony, to join Ian and Francis Bacon. In the evening I was at the French with the usual gang. Then back to Ronnie Scott's, for the night haul, and so it went on. No sleep. No sanity. Just floating in limbo, buoyed up by sex with strangers to punctuate the intervals, in the back of taxis or up against brick walls. Who cared where; I just got on with it.

At one point I found myself in an underground garage at the Elephant and Castle in the pitch black, rubbing my genitals dry on cold concrete after sex with an Arab, whose Rolls-Royce I'd flagged down in Sloane Square. I discovered an unexpected clutch of ten-pound notes in my handbag, which he'd thrown at me after tipping me out of his front seat. He'd obviously thought I was on the game, not understanding that at a certain point of lubricity I would step in front of any old Rolls-Royce, never mind who was driving it. It was just one of my endearing ways of getting from A to B at greatest speed. I'd never yet had one drive straight over me.

I fell asleep over my final drink. It was seven in the

morning. I simply couldn't stay awake. I was with my pal, the writer. We were both asked to leave the Smithfield pub. I was so drunk that my legs couldn't carry me from the door over the pavement to where a taxi was waiting at the kerb. It drove off. I crawled on all fours, to the disgust of passers-by dressed in smart city clothes on their way to work. I managed to stand while my pal hailed another cab. I collapsed in the back seat. My drinking career was over. I'd had enough. I knew I'd come to the end.

PART SIX

✥

On Top of the Mountain

'Alcoholism is a disease, a fatal disease from which there is no recovery. The alcoholic rarely, if ever, remains sober on his or her own. It is the only disease of denial, which tells you that you haven't got it.'

It is the twenty-third of March 1987 at 7.30 in the evening when I hear these words at my first self-help group for alcoholics. I know I am in the right place. I have surrendered. I have put up my hands and admitted I need help. There is nowhere else to go.

I had reached my alcoholic rock-bottom a few days before. My last binge has finally convinced me that my drinking is not, has never been, and can never be *normal*. This is truly the first time that I have admitted it to myself.

'It's the first drink that does the damage,' they say at the meeting. How amazing! I'd always thought it was the seventh or the eighth!

I am still suffering withdrawals from my final bout, shivering in the grip of paralysing fear and prone to panic attacks which leave me drenched in sweat. They have given me a half-full cup of tea, recognizing that as a newcomer I am trembling so much that I'll spill it over myself anyway. I dare not even attempt to lift it to my lips. My nerveless grasp simply cannot be relied upon. I can't concentrate on what is being said but I can still identify with the speaker, who says he's an alcoholic just like the rest of us.

How does he know about me? Is this what my trouble has been all along? Am I an alcoholic? I have come to find out. But I know deep inside that the answer is *yes*. The glorious relief of finally facing the truth is overwhelming. Now I can do something about my life!

If I can stay off the drink will I look like these others, shiny-eyed and smiling, with such a light around them that they look like the illustrations in a child's Bible, each one with a halo? They have what I want. I suppose it's called sobriety. I'll do anything they tell me to stop this agony I'm in, anything at all, because I'm desperate.

'We admitted we were powerless over alcohol and that our lives had become unmanageable.'

'We came to believe that a Power greater than ourselves could restore us to sanity.'

'We made a decision to turn our will and our lives over to the care of God as we understood Him.'

I ponder these first three steps of the Twelve-Step Programme for Recovering Alcoholics. I just about grasp what they tell me at the meeting, that there is no such thing as a recovered alcoholic, that I only have a daily reprieve from this disease, and that however long I remain sober the illness is progressing. If I were to take a drink after ten years, or twenty, or thirty, it would still be there. Sober members believing themselves cured have taken a drink and ended up in worse trouble than ever. They reported back that the horror is unimaginable: the remorse, the shakes, the self-loathing, the total sense of isolation, the withering of the soul. The wandering, abandoned, in the valley of the shadow of death.

I stand, supported by strong hands, to join in the prayer at the end of the meeting. I don't know this prayer, we didn't have it in my Welsh chapel, but my eyes fill with tears at the simple beauty of the words, at the message of hope. I can see light, for the first time, at the end of my dark tunnel. They give me literature to take home with me, to acquaint me with my disease. They give me lists of other meetings in the London area, and they give me a copy of the prayer.

'God Grant Me the Serenity to Accept the Things I Cannot Change, Courage to Change the Things I Can, and Wisdom to Know the Difference.'

When my mother was dying I had gone to the top of my Pontycymmer mountain and prayed to God. I had opened my arms wide and asked Him either to take me, to end my life – or to show me how to live it in dignity and grace.

The response was immediate, although I hadn't spoken to Him this intimately for years, had barely acknowledged Him, the truth be told. But all at once the heavens had opened their floodgates. A crack of thunder heralded the lightning, and the rain poured down. Summer storms were not unknown on the mountain top, it's true. But I took it as a personal response to my plea and stood, arms outstretched, face to heaven for an infinity, it seemed, until finally cleansed and healed by the waters, I descended. The child in me, who had always been so at ease on that mountain and in the force of the elements, understood that I was within His embrace again.

That first meeting was over six years ago and I haven't had a drink since. I take it a day at a time. If someone had said to me that I could never again, for the rest of my life, touch alcohol, perhaps I would never have kept going back to the meetings. But they didn't say that; they said 'just for today'. They also gave me the initials HALT to memorize and help me:

H for Hungry: Never get hungry, because that's when you'll be vulnerable to the first drink. I think of the years spent on diets, starving all day not to put on weight, when I was a fashion editor, just surviving on white wine, because that's the least fattening drink, or vodka, which doesn't smell.

A for Angry: Never get angry, because that's when

you'll say, 'Sod this for a lark – give me a drink please so that I can get that bastard off my mind!' Etc, etc . . .

L for Lonely: Loneliness means self pity in large doses and large measures. Crying into pink gins. Taking comfort home in the shape of a bottle.

T for Tired: Feeling too exhausted to do anything except sink a large scotch on the rocks or a stiff martini to wake you up again.

Within four months of my first meeting, my Painting Muse returned as swiftly as it had departed. It whispered to me one evening in Hyde Park, as I was walking back from a women's self-help group for alcoholics, it told me to make a sketch of the trees on the back of an envelope. I got so absorbed that I forgot the time, and when I looked up it was already dark. I was locked in the park and had to climb the railings into Kensington High Street. The next day I bought a small box of water-colours and a tiny sketch-pad. A far cry from the vast canvases and oils of earlier years. I had lost confidence and moved slowly, but that month I accepted a travel-writing and painting assignment for the *Sunday Telegraph*.

I sailed to the Arctic on a luxury liner. There were six bars aboard and I avoided them all. Instead I stood painting and drawing on deck. The next trip was to Tahiti, the land of Gauguin's inspiration. I painted that for the *American Express Magazine*. Egypt followed, then Greece, and each time on my return I held an exhibition at the Stephen Barclay Gallery in Chelsea. All were sell-outs.

It took me some time to get back to canvas and oils. But I went down to St Ives and painted a series of portraits in Roy Ray's School of Painting, just doors away from the studio where I had written my novels in with Patrick. Terry Wogan showed these and other Cornish landscapes when he interviewed me about my exhibition at England and Co., my new gallery.

The BBC flew me to France and filmed me painting in Monet's garden at Giverny. The ghost of the great man stalked between the herbaceous borders and stared over my shoulder. The young art student would have been too petrified to paint, but I had faced more terrible ordeals than this. This garden was sumptuous, just like my grandfather's back garden, spilling with colour and love, but on the lavish scale of a magician. More people seem to have seen this programme than any other that I have made for television. It was an experience which still burns in my brain.

After a few years in recovery I decided to have a face-lift. I was getting tired of people expressing concern over how exhausted or depressed I looked, when all the time I was radiant and exuberant inside. I now wanted my exterior to match up with my innards.

I went to Dev Basra in Harley Street. He had been recommended and introduced to me by mutual friends as being one of the finest cosmetic surgeons in the country.

He gave me his book to read first so I would be fully acquainted with everything that cosmetic surgery could achieve, as well as what it couldn't hope to achieve. I took little convincing; my mind was made up.

I wrote about the whole experience for the *Sunday Telegraph* magazine. They put my face on the cover and turned it into a lead story. There is an overwhelming interest in any operation of this nature, but few are prepared to admit to surgery, let alone write about it. It seemed obvious to me to do so. I had nothing to hide, nothing to be ashamed of. Perhaps my experience would help somebody else to take the plunge – or decide to remain as they are!

I had the whole hog done, the full works. Eyes first; removing the loose and ageing skin on the upper lid, and the bags beneath. Then the full face-lift under anaesthetic, and lipo-suction to remove the unsightly double chin. There was no pain whatsoever, only slight discomfort at having to sleep with bandages on the first night. The stitches were removed in a matter of days. The heavy bruising lasted barely a fortnight. I was up and about within two days. And I felt *wonderful*!

Three weeks later I was on the tube standing next to a seated youth. The notice above his seat told him to give up that space to the elderly and infirm. I glowered at him. I was used to being given this seat. He glowered back. I could have kissed him.

I asked Dev Basra, when I was writing my article, what his first impression of me had been as I entered his clinic.

'A prematurely aged woman in her fifties, whose lifestyle had dictated her appearance. A victim of all the ageing factors. Namely over-indulgence in alcohol, nicotine and drugs. Consistent lack of sleep. Stressful relationships, such as divorces. Stressful careers in the media. And overweening ambition and workaholism.' Interesting!

With renewed confidence in my appearance I approached Jacqui Evans, an agent recommended to me by Jack King, the producer at BBC Wales who had impressed me the most (by training me in the art of running my own radio show. *Six* pilots!). Jacqui had already made a household name out of another pal of mine, a fellow Aquarian, the astrologer Russell Grant. I went to see her and she claimed she could do the same for me in two and a half years. But first I had to prove my reliability.

I had no television work at this time, nor had I for some years. On the first chat show I did, in the Midlands, the producer gave me a warm welcome. 'I've always wanted you on one of my shows but I didn't dare risk it until Jacqui assured me that you'd turn up sober.'

'What do you mean?' I was affronted.

'Well,' he said genially. 'You know how people gossip. Other producers, people in the business, they always said that you were great on a chat show as long as you hadn't had a drink.'

'I think that's rather rude,' I said, haughtily.

He chuckled and took my arm. 'Don't give it another thought. It's working the other way for you now. The word's got around that you're off the sauce for good – expect plenty of work from now on.'

I couldn't have done it without Jacqui and her support. She became more than an agent, she was a true friend, just as Irene Josephy had been when I was writing my novels and doing all my journalism. I remain deeply indebted to both these remarkable women.

And so the radio and television work rolled in, just the right amount, just what I could cope with at the time. I accepted anything and everything that was offered. Now I pick and choose, but then I had to re-establish myself as a professional and reliable performer.

It was in 1991 and I had been several years sober when I met the philosopher who would introduce me to the concept of the Universe, of asking the Universe for guidance and help and whatever my heart desired. This was Shaun de Warren, the spiritual help-mate and inspiration of many. He was born in India of a military family, became a Cavalry officer, and qualified as a barrister, before concentrating his formidable mind and creativity on the spiritual enlightenment of others.

I was taken over to a spiritual workshop which Shaun was holding at his home in Battersea. I didn't much care for the proceedings, in fact I wanted to leave almost as soon as I got there. My clothes suddenly felt too tight. I had difficulty in breathing. People were sharing in a particularly truthful and self-revealing way what was happening in their lives and whether there had been any progress since the previous session. The old defiance rose in me, coupled with fear, fear of change. I felt inexplicably angry. And isolated.

Shaun, an expansive genius with twinkling eyes and the smile of a pixie, turned to me. He seemed to possess a benign power which I was definitely choosing to resist.

'I understand,' I said, arrogantly, 'how people benefit from these sessions, but my own life is wonderful. I can't see that it needs to get any better.'

I was living at the time in a hovel in Bethnal Green, which I had moved into the previous year because I couldn't afford to live in my West Kensington flat any longer. I had rented it out and was hoping to sell it. I was riddled with fear of financial insecurity, and had personal debts of £26,000. I was still estranged from one daughter, although the situation was a million miles better than it had been. But it was perfectly true that I had found happiness in freedom from alcohol. My life, it seemed to me, was now on an even keel. That's what I was prepared to settle for, then.

'How much more wonderful can you take it?' Shaun twinkled.

'Well if the sky's the limit, I'll go the whole hog!' Anything for a challenge.

Shaun was an art collector so we arranged that I would pay for private sessions with my paintings. I went to him on a one-to-one basis, for a two-hour session, once a week for six months. For the first three months he would silently hand me the box of tissues on arrival. I had nowhere else to go to cry.

We covered my childhood, my mother, my father, their drinking, my drinking, our behaviour with each other, my relationship with my own two children, and both my ex-husbands.

Then, one day, I stopped crying. I handed the box of tissues back to him, untried, all dry. It was as if there were no more tears left. Now we could embark on the real journey, having offloaded all the emotional baggage.

'I can't think what to talk to you about today,' I said.

'How about telling me about where you'd like to go but have never been?'

'I've never been to India.'

'So when are you going?'

'Sure,' I answered sarcastically. 'With my debts?'

'I didn't ask about your debts. I asked when you were going.'

'Well, I can't go until after Christmas because I have a weekly show with the BBC in Wales to do until then.' This was a live radio show, lasting one and a half hours, with an audience of six hundred or more, that I still co-present with Frank Hennessy from St David's Hall in Cardiff. Though it hadn't begun to improve my financial position in any significant sense, it restored my professional respect. More importantly, it took me back to Wales, and reunited me with my roots.

'We'll tell the Universe that you are free to go to India after Christmas, then.' Shaun smiled his enigmatic smile.

'Is that it then?'

'Why not? What shall we talk about now?'

'Well, is that it?' I said sceptically. 'Won't I need to think about my tickets and where to stay and various other arrangements?'

'The Universe is in charge of everything.'

'Will I hear soon?'

'I expect so.' There was no ruffling Shaun.

Three days later, I was idly chatting to the producer of the 'Home Show', a series which I had recently presented with Roddy Llewellyn for Thames TV.

'What happens to you now?' I said. 'Do you have to start thinking about a new series right away, or are you given whatever project the powers-that-be decide?'

'I was meaning to ask – would you be interested in going to India just after Christmas? I thought it would be interesting to take you there with a view to doing a series on you travelling and painting all over India.'

'What do you think of that, Shaun! Isn't it amazing! Within three days!'

'The only thing that surprises me is your surprise,' Shaun answered evenly. 'Oh, ye of little faith.'

I spent two months in India, painting mainly around Rajasthan. On my return, I found myself peering through the shutters of my house in Bethnal Green one night, watching a gang fighting with broken bottles in the street outside. There were two strip joints at the end of the road, which emptied at two o'clock in the morning, and those fighting lads were as drunk as I used to be, behaving in the same fashion, looking for bother. I understood them, but I no longer needed to live like this; as a voyeur, in vicarious excitement. It was unhealthy. The peace that I had grown accustomed to in India had given me serenity. I had to move. I deserved a new home now.

I went out into my tiny backyard and looked up at the square of stars high above my old building. This backyard had been transformed by me in the past two years. When I first came it was full of rusty bedsteads and rotting mattresses, and piles of dusty bricks, and a row of stray cats sat on the end wall, hissing at me whenever I approached. The earth in the empty flower bed was tainted with their shit and the walls stank with their urine.

I had changed all that. There were hanging baskets on every surface, full of fuchsia and busy lizzie, and daffodils and hyacinths in the window boxes. The flower bed had fresh earth and was abundant with spring flowers. The wall was covered with vines and Virginia creepers. There was a scent of honeysuckle in the air.

The hostile cats had disappeared, replaced by two adorable tabby kittens who came when I called and put milk out for them on my step. They rubbed themselves around my legs and purred with pleasure when I stroked them. The backyard had been turned into a haven of love.

I put my arms up to the Universe as Shaun had shown me to do and I asked for a new home. I left it to God to decide where this should be, though I said I had always felt comfortable and familiar in Chelsea. I asked for the means to finance this move. Then I gave a prayer of gratitude for everything I already had.

That was on Monday. I moved back to Chelsea five days later.

The morning after my request my friend David told me that he had found a flat in Chelsea above Tulley's opposite the cinema on the Fulham Road. This was one of my favourite corners of London, there at the bottom of Drayton Gardens, where I was living on my own when I first met Michael. Home territory for me. There was another flat available. Mine!

My agent, Jacqui Evans, rang me to say that the Agony Aunt job on *TV Quick* Magazine which we'd been hoping to hear about for some months was now full steam ahead. It started immediately, that week. I had the funds to finance my move.

Shaun didn't turn a hair when I told him. We were having lunch, and I was bemoaning the fact that my flat in West Kensington was causing me awful aggravation again. I'd had a series of dreadful tenants after I'd moved to Bethnal Green. They'd either run off without paying the rent, or they'd stolen duvets and chairs. I couldn't sell the wretched place, but no agent would touch the block with a barge pole because of the litigation going on between the Tenants Association and the management.

'Why should anybody nice want to live in a place which is so reviled?' Shaun asked gently. 'Go over and bless it, turn the atmosphere around. Then put it on the market again if you don't want to live there. You have your new flat in Chelsea now, so why go back? You're moving forward. It'll sell if you do as I say.'

I was on my way to spend the weekend in Wales, compèring a fashion show at Carmarthen Art School. I stopped off at the flat on my way to the station after my lunch with Shaun.

I kissed the carpet and all the walls, the lavatory seat and the microwave oven. I kissed everything in each room and blew kisses all around, then I opened the windows wide and shouted out above the roar of the North End Road traffic, I shouted to the Universe.

'I'm ready now to move from this flat. I've loved it and had great times in it when I was first here but now it's ready for its new owner and I welcome them whoever they might be.'

I listed the amenities, how it was near the swimming pool, the underground station, the post office, the library, and that the shop below stayed open until midnight. I said that it was possible to do whatever you liked there, that nobody interfered at all with your freedom.

I blew kisses out of the windows, locked them up, blew kisses around every room, locked the flat and pressed the keys on the unwilling estate agent opposite. I thought about the flat once on the sands of Llanstefan, knowing that I had no need to worry any more, the Universe had the matter in hand. I rang the estate agent on the Monday morning at half past nine, when I got back.

'That was the swiftest sale I've ever done,' he said. 'Three hours, that's how long the flat was on the market.'

'You didn't do it,' I corrected him.

'I negotiated the deal, with a property investor.'

'It was a Universe job.' I enlightened him.

334

'Does that mean if I ask the Universe I could shift all these properties that have been on my books for all these years?'

'If everyone followed Shaun's words of wisdom regarding the Universe, he could turn the economy of this country around single-handedly.'

The agent, his mother, and his managing director began going to Shaun that very week!

The Universe is an abundant place; there is plenty for everybody, but we humans block off our own successes, that's what I believe now. Negativity breeds negativity, but the reverse is also true.

My own fear of financial insecurity has dissolved completely. My poverty thinking has been replaced by prosperity thinking. I have run evenings in conjunction with Shaun propounding the theory that we can turn our lives around as soon as we learn to go with the flow, and allow the Universe, God, to run things for us. Whatever happens to me is a learning experience. There is no such thing as a bad experience. Everything happens to tell me something. That's what the journey is about.

Writing this book has helped me in more ways than I could have envisaged. It has laid troubling ghosts for me, and kept me from harbouring corrosive and lingering resentments. It has enabled me to come to terms with my past, my self-destructive behaviour, without wishing to close the door on any of it. I understand the nature of forgiveness, and know that until I forgave myself I could not begin to forgive others.

My recovery has been slow and steady and altogether miraculous. My sobriety has given me gifts that I could never have dreamed of. My plans and hopes and aspirations always fall short of the good fortune heaped upon my plate.

I have three grandchildren, all younger than my sobriety. Sarah is a theatrical producer now and has a little girl called Jessie with her partner, Sandy. Sophie and her children Paris and Carson live with me at the moment, since her separation from their father, Alastair. She paints and is currently writing an autobiographical account of surviving an alcoholic childhood. I have rented an exquisite house with a garden near Paris's school in The Boltons. I am reminded of the wedding between his grandfather, Michael, and myself, which took place in there all those years ago. Life catches up with itself in ever-decreasing circles.

The mending time with these beloved daughters of mine has been gentle and slow. I would have preferred at the start to thaw everything out right away. I would have liked to kiss them and say, 'Hey, kids, I'm sorry for the past thirty years – please forgive me!' But it hasn't been like that. Sometimes, even now, when the mutual love flows so strongly that words cannot suffice, there are moments with either child of mine when the old uneasiness rises between us and I am aware of the damage I've caused.

But I know what to do now. I simply fold them within my embrace. We stand there, not speaking, arms around each other. And it's enough. Hasn't it always been so between mothers and daughters? Wasn't it thus with my own?

I think of my mother with such compassion, and of my father with a tolerance and understanding that I never had when he was alive. How different both their lives might have been if they had found what I have found, a way to live with their wretched condition. This disease that the three of us shared.

I understand the unhealthiness between my father and myself. I loved him very much. I accept the fact where I couldn't before. His frailties were revealed to me at an earlier age than I would have wished. My mother was helpless, suffering sorely from difficulties which were only emphasized, not relieved, by the prescription drugs to which she had become addicted.

I don't choose to live any longer blaming others for what I became. I am fortunate to have a loving sister, Sally, with whom I can talk about all these things.

I look into the shining eyes of my three grandchildren, and I see the eyes of my own children. But these three will never know their grandmother as a drunken spectre. Their mothers had to live that nightmare instead of them.

When I came out of that first self-help meeting I dumped four packets of cigarettes in the dustbin. I'd been on eighty to a hundred Consulates a day. The compulsion to smoke was lifted from that moment, just like the compulsion to drink. I don't swear any more, simply because I don't want to. Swearing, the use of violent words, no longer reflects how I feel. It would feel like a misuse of the gift of imaginative language.

I chose to be celibate for the first four and half years of my recovery, then I went to Greece with a bunch of pals and changed my mind.

I was swimming in the Aegean with a beautiful Texan girl. She was wearing a skin-skimming, electric-blue swimsuit with shoulder pads, which she'd bought at Harrods. Shoulder pads, of all things – real Dynasty-style! The chat got on to sex. I told her I'd been celibate for four years.

'I can top that, honey,' she drawled. 'Chalk me up for seven years!'

I looked at this vision of loveliness, at the brilliant blue skies behind her head, at the sumptuous shape in her snazzy suit, and I said to myself, 'This is ludicrous! This beautiful creature is denying a whole passionate side of her nature! Why?'

A small voice echoed inside me, 'So are you!'

At Athens Airport on the return journey, my friend suddenly stood up and shouted, 'I herewith announce to the Universe that I dump my sexual inhibitions and bodily shame in the dustbin.'

I joined her, with another friend. We all did the same.

'I'd like a lover.' Each of us put our arms up to the Universe. People were staring. Athens has been used to rituals for some centuries, but not of this nature.

I listed my specifications as Shaun had always suggested I do in rituals, saying exactly what I wanted. I met him, a handsome Greek, on the homebound plane within an hour. That very night I was enjoying five-star sex in the five-star Hyde Park Hotel. It was glorious!

I no longer regret my behaviour past and present. I will always care for Michael and Patrick, and am happy that they are contentedly married to other women.

I am reunited with Judy, though we had lost touch over the years. She has married a second time now, into the aristocracy. A successful painter and writer, she has three children from her first marriage and is a grandmother, too. We regularly take tea at Fortnum's, chuckling over old photos and present times. Naughty girls together, as ever.

Darling Sylvia is over ninety now. She has published two beautifully written books since her eighty-fourth birthday. *Fire Under the Carpet*, her political memoirs of the thirties, describes co-founding the National Council for Civil Liberties, with her lover Ronald Kidd. The other, an autobiography, *Finding My Way*, tells of our first memorable meeting at Silverthorn School at Elephant and Castle. I was twenty-two and she was thirty years older. First day of term. First day of teaching for us both.

And now just in time for assembly, stilettoes snapping up the stairs, a vivid newcomer lit up the scene; in her silky-shine scarlet mac. Molly Thomas with her black hair, green eyes

338

and colourless skin had something of a little Elizabeth Taylor face, but mobile, laughing, half-mocking, and a blithe self-confident air of accepting little in the way of rules, making her own as she went along. Mediterranean, I thought, maybe French or Spanish. In the staff room she was exotic. Yet everybody else seemed to take her for granted – the new art mistress. Molly, I was to find, had no contact with the Mediterranean. She was Welsh, from a mining village in the Garw Valley, over the hills from the Rhondda.

When I read Sylvia's account of me from all those years ago, before the alcohol tightened its grip and became the rapacious creditor, I marvel at how so exactly she has captured the essence of what is me today. I no longer regret the past, nor would I ever wish to forget it.

I think of delicious, divine, daft, Jill Bennett, who is no longer with us, and how we drifted apart, she and I, when I embarked on my recovery. 'But you haven't a problem with alcohol, darling! For Christ's sake if you're an alcoholic, so am I! Have a champagne this instant and stop this nonsense, you're just a fucking old drama queen, that's what you are!'

I regret that Jill isn't here to chortle over John Osborne's bitter diatribe against her in the latest volume of his autobiography. She'd have had a few larks over that. 'Obviously still besotted with me, the impotent darling – never could forgive me having it off in the afternoons with Albert Finney.'

I rejoice in the memory of Barbara and her bright, bubbling bravery. I see the sophisticated glamour of her bedroom today as vividly as I saw it then, against the unlikely backdrop of the bleak colliery and the black hill behind it. She died from a chest condition that callous winter of 1969. She'd tried to kill her smoking habit, but the Sobranies were with her to the end. She left, mourned by her devoted husband and two adopted daughters, a legion of friends, and a family for whom she represented everything we would have wanted to be ourselves.

Last summer I was invited to paint in a vast studio in Craig-y-Nos Castle in Brecon. The very castle that had sat on so many of our mantelpieces during my childhood. The same castle that my granny had lived in as a girl, the loss of which my mother had lamented all her life.

The ghost of my granny came to me one day by the lake, when I was painting there in the rain. She scolded me for not wearing warm enough clothes. I smiled, filled suddenly with the spirit of one who understood me so well.

'So, my child,' she said softly, 'was I right about everything, the drinking, the dancing, the men – did it make you happy?'

'It didn't, Granny. You were right. None of it made me happy.'

'And are you happy now?'

'I am, Granny. This is now the happiest that I have ever been.'

'That's all I came to ask. That's all I need to know, that the journey has been worth it after all.'

INDEX

345

Also available from Victor Gollancz

Mick Jagger
Primitive Cool

CHRISTOPHER SANDFORD

A full, revealing portrait of the rock legend, still going strong at fifty.

In March 1963, a thin, shy Economics student began a weekly singing engagement in a Richmond hotel. Over thirty years later Mick Jagger is still in Richmond: in a two-million-pound house overlooking the same hotel. In the interim Jagger has seen and lived more worlds than any entertainer this century. He remains, to this day, the only rock star to straddle contrary lifestyles – musician, sex symbol, actor, father, husband, boulevardier, rebel – and retain credibility in each.

Containing a wealth of previously unpublished material and illustrated with a dramatic range of photographs, *Mick Jagger: Primitive Cool* gives a unique – and always entertaining – insight into the perpetually adolescent figure who in July 1993 celebrated his fiftieth birthday.

'Hugely enjoyable' – *Oxford Times*

'Shows a light and often comic touch' – Julie Burchill, *The Spectator*

ISBN 0 575 05749 1   £5.99 paperback

Maggie Smith
A Bright Particular Star

MICHAEL COVENEY

Brilliant, mercurial and elusive, Maggie Smith is one of the few performers to have achieved stardom on both stage and screen. This much-acclaimed biography charts the progress of her glittering career: from the Oxford Playhouse, through the heady days at the Old Vic and the National with Olivier, to film stardom and recent West End triumphs. Inevitably, public and private lives overlap; and Michael Coveney chronicles both her turbulent first marriage to Robert Stephens and her enduring second marriage to her first love, Beverley Cross.

Coveney draws on the reminiscences of Michael Caine, Alan Bennett, John Gielgud, Michael Palin and Judi Dench among other friends and colleagues and, with the co-operation of Maggie Smith and Beverley Cross, has created a revealing, often hilarious portrait of one of the great actresses of our time.

'Brilliantly evocative' – Jack Tinker, *Daily Mail*

'A witty, detailed, perceptive study of a marvellous actress' Michael Billington, – *Guardian*

'Coveney's book is worthy of Dame Maggie, and I cannot speak more highly than that' – B. A. Young, *Financial Times*

ISBN 0 575 05626 6   £5.99 paperback